The Witness

The
Witness

UNFOLDING THE ANATOMY OF A KILLER

WANDA DRAPER, Ph.D.
WITH COLLIN A. STUTZ, MFA

New York

The Witness
UNFOLDING THE ANATOMY OF A KILLER

Published in New York, New York, by Morgan James Publishing. Morgan James and The Entrepreneurial Publisher are trademarks of Morgan James, LLC. www.MorganJamesPublishing.com

The Morgan James Speakers Group can bring authors to your live event. For more information or to book an event visit The Morgan James Speakers Group at www.TheMorganJamesSpeakersGroup.com.

Qualifier: This is a work of creative non-fiction based on true stories as the author remembers them. The names, characters, and the settings have been changed to protect the dignity and integrity of actual persons, living or dead.

ISBN 978-1-63047-901-5 paperback
ISBN 978-1-63047-902-2 eBook
ISBN 978-1-63047-903-9 hardcover
Library of Congress Control Number:
2015920149

Consulting Editor:
Sarah Nicole Partin
cover credit to Doug Pennington

Cover Design by:
Chris Treccani
www.3dogdesign.net

Interior Design by:
Bonnie Bushman
The Whole Caboodle Graphic Design

Shelfie

A **free** eBook edition is available
with the purchase of this print book.

CLEARLY PRINT YOUR NAME ABOVE IN UPPER CASE

Instructions to claim your free eBook edition:
1. Download the Shelfie app for Android or iOS
2. Write your name in **UPPER CASE** above
3. Use the Shelfie app to submit a photo
4. Download your eBook to any device

In an effort to support local communities and raise awareness and funds, Morgan James Publishing donates a percentage of all book sales for the life of each book to Habitat for Humanity Peninsula and Greater Williamsburg.

Get involved today, visit
www.MorganJamesBuilds.com

Habitat
for Humanity®
Peninsula and
Greater Williamsburg
Building Partner

In memory of my sister, Catherine

Table of Contents

Foreword   *ix*

Acknowledgments   *xiii*

Prologue   *xv*

Part One   **1**

   Chapter 1   3

   Chapter 2   16

   Chapter 3   26

   Chapter 4   43

   Chapter 5   54

   Chapter 6   57

Part Two   **63**

   Chapter 7   65

   Chapter 8   69

   Chapter 9   79

   Chapter 10   89

Chapter 11   100
Chapter 12   105

Part Three   **119**
Chapter 13   121

Part Four   **137**
Chapter 14   139
Chapter 15   161
Chapter 16   168
Chapter 17   180
Chapter 18   186

Part Five   **201**
Chapter 19   203

Epilogue   *220*
About the Authors   *226*

Foreword

All capital murder cases are decided based upon the emotional reaction of jurors to evidence presented to them. Jurors then search the evidence for facts, which support their emotional decision. In the battle for the hearts and minds of jurors, the prosecution begins with a distinct advantage: the prosecutor bats first. Jurors are subjected to horrible images of the deceased victim or victims and are taken on a visual tour of the often-gruesome crime scene. Autopsy photographs are displayed side by side with pictures of the victim alive—the grimness of death made more stark by the vivacity of life. The prosecutor then weaves the events of the homicide into a compelling narrative.

To counter the emotional story presented by the prosecution, the defense must present a counter narrative that will have a strong, poignant appeal of its own. The formula is easy to articulate but requires an enormous effort to bring to fruition. The defense looks for facts in the defendant's background over which he had little or no control. These details sculpted his life, adversely impacting his development. The threads woven by childhood intertwine into a compelling story, hopefully entreating at least one juror to vote for life.

It is axiomatic that every human being, no matter what despicable crime he or she may have committed, has a human story. While some stories are more sympathetic and contain more mitigating circumstances than others, each is a complex entanglement of trauma, hurt, and broken connections. The defense team must ferret out the trail of frayed threads. Wanda Draper, PhD, describes the incredible amount of work required by the defense team to uncover the mitigating history. She illustrates the inner workings of the defense team. In the initial stages, brainstorming takes center stage. As each new fact about the defendant comes to light, all ideas for presenting the mitigating facts are explored. Team members are encouraged to express their ideas and opinions, no matter how fanciful or bizarre they might be. Each case is different because each defendant is different. It is the responsibility of the defense team to learn everything there is to know about a defendant.

As the trial date approaches, the human story is formed. The defendant is cast in a new, revealing light. The story changes as new facts are learned. Ultimately, the lead attorney has the responsibility for creating and presenting the mitigation case. Interesting facts that do not move the mitigation story forward are jettisoned. A delicate balance must be struck between the absolute imperative that expert witnesses remain scrupulously objective in their investigations and presentations of mitigating evidence and the lawyer-advocate's goal of presenting the defendant in the best possible mitigation light. Capital trial lawyers and experienced expert witnesses understand the natural tension between these two viewpoints. There is rarely a problem.

Expert witnesses must be prepared for all of the prosecution's case, both in the guilt/innocence phase and the aggravation/mitigation phase. Prosecutors will routinely ask questions that begin with the phrase, "Were you aware?" They routinely end with the phrase, "Would that have altered your opinion in any way?" It cannot be emphasized enough that the facts upon which the mitigation story is based must be provable. If the jury believes that the defense is sacrificing the truth to present a good story, the entire defense against the death penalty collapses.

Wanda Draper is a master at ferreting out the facts of each defendant's life story. She has never been satisfied with half-truths or partial explanations. The more sources of information, the better. As a human developmentalist, she is able to make sense of seemingly meaningless data contained in countless records. Ideally, each fact would be triangulated, that is, referred to by three different sources, each source coming at the fact from a different angle.

Expert witnesses for the defense come in a wide variety, covering many areas of expertise. Psychiatrists are in a position to analyze the facts and the results of psychological tests. They hold a medical license, which allows them to prescribe drugs that may help control the condition which led to the murder. Because they are trained as physicians, psychiatrists are often viewed as credible witnesses, particularly when they testify concerning organic brain damage. Psychologists and neuropsychologists rely heavily on testing. Psychological testing can provide valuable insights into the defendant's mental condition at the time of the homicide. If a defendant who commits a homicide is suffering from paranoid schizophrenia or a bipolar disorder, he may not be insane, but his view of reality is severely distorted—a major mitigating circumstance. Similarly, pharmacologists, sociologists, and other experts can provide valuable insights into the conditions which led up to a homicide.

Wanda Draper, as an expert in human development, embraces all these fields and more. She is not dependent on any one approach to explain the mitigating circumstances surrounding a homicide. I once asked her the same question that is often asked rhetorically by prosecutors in front of the jury: "Why did the defendant commit this horrible crime while so many other children raised in poverty and horrific circumstances grow up and never commit a violent crime?" Her response was both illuminating and thought provoking: "If a child raised in poverty and subjected to all manner of deprivation and abuse has in his or her life one steady adult figure to whom the child is attached, receiving unconditional love, that child stands a good chance of growing up without committing a violent crime." It's when children's attachments are disrupted that problems occur.

Dr. Draper, in addition to her academic training and study, with years of actual experience working on over a hundred capital murder cases and testifying in most of these, has the instincts of a master detective who not only examines the evidence but also looks for the circumstances that are not obvious, those buried and hidden beneath family turmoil. All capital defense counsel reading these accounts of actual cases will know Dr. Draper's descriptions ring true.

In 2002, I received the Lord Erskine Award from the Oklahoma Criminal Defense Lawyer's Association for a career of defending capital murder cases throughout the seventy-seven counties of Oklahoma. Dr. Draper testified in many of these cases. Although we were not always successful in persuading a jury that death was not a just result, the overwhelming majority of the cases were successful. Time and time again, after the trial, jurors would remark, "I still support the death penalty, but not in this case—not after hearing Dr. Draper's testimony."

> James T. Rowan
> Capital Trial Lawyer
> Assistant Public Defender, Oklahoma County

Acknowledgments

Sarah-Nicole Partin, forensic epidemiologist and consulting editor, has participated in the development of this project with commitment and enthusiasm. I am especially grateful for her expertise in computer technology and for her personal dedication of time and energy in researching the details in each case while helping to move the manuscript to completion.

To Terry Whalin, my acquisitions editor at Morgan James, I am especially grateful for his wisdom, support and counsel in the development of this creative nonfiction, and for his continuing encouragement. I am fortunate to be one of many hundreds of people Terry has helped to pursue the dream of putting between two covers several decades of life experiences.

My loving appreciation goes to my two cousins, Don and John Kachtik, who encouraged me to write about my work and the endeavors I had to reflect upon in order to accomplish this awesome task. Their never-ending interest and enthusiasm for my work has given me the strength and determination to complete this project.

I give special thanks to my colleague, Jim Rowan, attorney at law, for reading the manuscript and giving his expert opinion as I transmitted first hand experience into manuscript form. Having the privilege of working with Jim on capital cases for over twenty years provided a wealth of experience without which this book would never be possible.

I am deeply indebted to Connie Pressler for her interest in this project and for her hours of dedication in helping to get this project underway. I wish to thank Connie for introducing me to Collin Stutz, a master editor and writing enthusiast.

Joy in writing this book is shared with my niece, Diedra Matthews Liepelt and her daughter, Tatjana Liepelt, for their excitement about the stories revealed in this book and for the role that Diedra's mother, Catherine, played in helping me work these cases. I especially appreciate the critique and suggestions that Diedra and Tatjana made as they poured through the draft manuscript.

I am especially grateful to Doug Pennington for sharing his talents in developing the cover design. His astute interpretation of the manuscript was particularly poignant in bringing forth a visual representation of the overall idea of this book.

Prologue

"Another stabbing! This is getting insane. That's the third this week!"

"Yeah . . . This time it's a kid who attacked his high school classmate. He's a sophomore."

"Wow! He's really just a kid . . . . What's happening to our nation?"

"I wish I knew 'cause it's happening too often. It's scary being a parent."

"Here, help me roll up this tape. The forensics boys just left."

"You heard about that forum over at the children's hospital? It's on Saturday morning."

"I hear the speaker's a woman who's been on the front line in several states, dealing with defendants up for the death penalty. Maybe it's time to go hear what she says about kids and killing . . . You wanna go?"

"Why not? We need any help we can get to help shed light on what's happening . . . and why."

"We are very pleased to have Dr. Wanda Draper as our special guest for this annual forum. I am your forum host, Julius Ladero."

Applause politely filled the amphitheater that seated no less than five hundred participants. The soft, rolling thunder of clapping diminished to a quieter muffling like lapping waves as the tall, stately woman glided gracefully across the stage. She wore her favorite hunter green and ebony herringbone wool suit, complemented by a tailored, ivory silk blouse. Her outfit was adorned at the neck with a simple strand of petite freshwater pearls, sparingly alternated with small jade beads. The simplicity of her apparel supported the *joie-de-vive* exuberance of her dignified features. High-heeled black patent leather pumps added even more height to her five foot, nine inch frame. Moderately cropped blonde hair, slightly waved and elegantly coiffed, framed her high cheekbones and compassionate, intelligent hazel eyes. Her attire conveyed respect and appreciation for the invitation to speak at one of the nation's top children's hospitals.

Wanda clasped the welcoming hand of Dr. Ladero, shaking it sincerely. She took a seat in a straight-back but comfortable Charles Eames chair across from the host and scanned the gallery that rose before her. No table or podium in front of or between them restricted their exposure to the audience. Wanda always insisted on seeing all members of an audience, whether in a packed lecture hall or in an intimate group. She always preferred eye-to-eye juxtaposition.

She was pleased to see such a varied audience. This particular forum's attendees were a composite of medical professionals, legal representatives, law enforcement officers, various members of health and human services, as well as child development personnel, and a few local and state politicians. Each group clustered to their fellow colleagues, resembling a patchwork quilt.

Ladero gave a brief but poignant introduction and immediately began with two questions: "How did you, a developmentalist, a professor of human development in a college of medicine, become an expert witness in capital murder cases? And why, after working on over one hundred death penalty cases and testifying in the majority of them, do you remain steadfast in your belief that every person has the potential to succeed?"

"America is blessed with smart children," Wanda Draper stated to the assembly, whose members eagerly anticipated the answer to be that she sought a position that would enable her to attack the epidemic of crime that plagues society—murderers, rapists, thieves, and gangs. This crowd was further stratified by parents and grandparents who were secretly motivated to attend in order to ensure that their children and grandchildren did not meet the criteria of a future offender. They were curious to learn what an expert in human development, who has interviewed and studied defendants and their families, had observed throughout her forty years of work with children and adults. They were impressed with her twenty-plus years of spending hours and hours in jails and prisons and in seeking out families in the remote and dangerous inner city and countryside habitats that most professionals would choose to avoid.

"Children are not dumb. They are not slow. And they are not lazy. Some lack opportunity, but they rarely lack potential. I would argue that there is no shortage of intelligence—only shortage in actualizing it." Her opening won a popping of applause by a large contingency of the listeners. If the audience was polled regarding the method of treating the social epidemic, a tie would occur between the proponents of creating more educational programs for children and those in favor of expanding jails.

"Children are smarter than we think!" Wanda emphasized. She could see smiles across the audience as they acknowledged the statement, like one would agree that kittens are cute. Anticipating this response, she elaborated, "They process and react to their world based on how they feel and how they perceive others' treatment of them. They often base their relationships on how they get along with their environmental modulators." Blank glances and confused silence swelled and surged before her. Again, she anticipated this. She had prepared her comments for that effect. In order to break through longtime societal beliefs, she needed to tear down preconceived notions about children as immature adults by describing an unfamiliar, albeit accurate, picture of children as astonishingly unique from adults. She wanted to convey the idea that just because they turn sixteen doesn't mean they suddenly think and behave like responsible adults.

Ladero interjected two more questions: "How are you convinced that every person has the potential to succeed? What makes a successful person?"

Wanda paused momentarily, considering these questions. She changed the direction of the discussion in order to respond: "In July of 1975, history was made when two nations, worlds apart and the bitterest of enemies, united to accomplish a cosmic endeavor. The Apollo-Soyuz Test Project was the first meeting in Space between American Astronauts and Soviet Cosmonauts that ended the international Space Race. It involved the docking of an American *Apollo* spacecraft with the then-Soviet *Soyuz* spacecraft." She paused as she scanned the gallery.

"Their differences in cultures, politics, ideologies, and languages were transcended. These astronauts and cosmonauts were successful in accomplishing this feat of human aspirations. They had to do two things: *one*, they had to build trust in one another, and *two*, they had to form personal attachments to one another. In my studies of successful people, I decided to explore the lives of these space travelers because the world agreed they were successful.

Fortunately, I became acquainted with General Tom Stafford, the pilot of the *Apollo*. After interviewing him, he became interested in my study, and I was invited to the International Conference for Space Travelers in Washington, DC, in the 1980s. I was able to personally interview General Alexi Leonov, the Russian pilot of the *Soyuz*. I learned that both men, prior to this historic mission, traveled back and forth for two years between the United States and Russia to learn each other's language and to build a friendship that, incidentally, has continued. My interviews of American astronauts and Russian, Romanian, and Czech cosmonauts confirmed my notion that to be successful, one must master five qualities: self-confidence, getting along with others, a broader view of the world and a sense of wonder, the ability to focus until the task is complete, and self-evaluation—how am I doing?" Wanda ticked these off on her fingers. The audience nodded in comprehension.

"But what about those people who never become world-renowned?" Ladero challenged her. "How can the common man inculcate those five characteristics of success?"

"Let me share a story with you of just such a person," Wanda announced with a glint in her eyes. "This man's name was John Carlyle." Wanda's arms gestured in story-telling fashion.

Wanda explained how one day while she was teaching human development in seminars for doctors in their third and fourth year residencies and fifth year psychiatry fellowships at the College of Medicine at the University of Oklahoma, she received a letter from a John Carlyle in McAlister, Oklahoma.

"I thought, as I was opening the letter, it was a request to do some consulting for the parent-child program affiliated with the guidance center there. However, upon opening it, a most intriguing and surprising first line greeted me: 'People, people who need people are the luckiest people in the world. This isn't true.' Of course, I was astonished that a consulting request would open with a lyric from the popular Barbra Streisand song. I read on, soon realizing this letter was not from some professional or a lawyer, but from John Carlyle, an inmate in the state's largest high-security prison. One cannot get more common than this.

"Carlyle ventured on to write that he was contacting me as a last resort. He had written to reporters, attorneys, and finally the governor. But, nobody had replied to his call for help. He didn't tell me why he was incarcerated or where he was from. Neither did his one-page request say how he procured my name to make a contact nor why he thought I could help him. I noted the neatly penned, well-written letter with perfect grammar, only to let it fall from my hands as I leaned back in my chair. I have to say, my curiosity mounted as I regarded the letter. I didn't know if it was from a friend or foe. After a few moments more, my own sense of wonder stimulated me to decide on a course of action. I carried the letter down the hall to show and ask the opinion of several of my colleagues. Each one *emphatically* advised me to throw it in the trash and ignore it. But, I remained curious. I kept it on my desk.

"One morning—a few days later—I decided to send Mr. Carlyle a note. I simply acknowledged his letter and stated that I was impressed with his writing style. That was it. No questions about who he was or why he was in prison. I asked only one question: 'Are you a writer by profession?' I assumed this would end any further correspondence.

"However, about a week later, I was graced with another letter from John Carlyle. He expressed appreciation for my response. Carlyle stated that previously he had written a couple of stories for a magazine, but they hadn't been accepted. He had enclosed both in this letter.

"Two weeks later, I responded by further complimenting his writing ability. Still, I asked no personal questions.

"Several days later, Carlyle wrote back. This letter explained that he was from Alabama. His parents were both killed in a car crash, and he was subsequently raised by his loving grandparents. Then, he expressed interest in writing and said he thought he might try writing a book. I decided to call a friend who was the governor's chief of staff and ask for a favor. 'Can you check this man out?' I asked. He said to give him a couple of days.

"After checking on Mr. Carlyle, the chief of staff called me, 'Wanda, John Carlyle is serving time for a serious, violent offense.' He advised me to drop him.

"Another letter arrived from John Carlyle about a week later. He was emboldened to reveal more about himself because of my response to his previous letter, encouraging him to keep writing. John Carlyle described that he was black and was in trouble because he wanted a computer system in order to start his business. Having been broke and impatient, he admitted to doing a stupid thing.

He robbed a convenience store. He was apprehended and sentenced to thirty years because he was armed. Carlyle then explained that he had read a newspaper article that featured an interview with me about relationships and decided to write to me because of one statement that caught his attention: *'That people with self-confidence and a very positive self-image make the best partners in a relationship.'* He said this impacted him so profoundly that he was motivated to contact me. He was trying to find someone to listen to his personal story. His hope was that someone might find reason to help him work for an early release by writing to the parole board or other influential people.

"I responded by thanking him for sharing his personal information, and again, I encouraged him to keep writing. I never mentioned helping him get an early release date. A few weeks later, a packet arrived containing a hundred pages of hand-printed manuscript, all on the back of scrap paper.

"'What a writer!' I wrote to him in my next letter. I commended him for good work and encouraged him to continue. As before, I made no offer to intercede for an early release date.

"A couple of months later, I was consulting in the eastern part of the state, and on the way home, I passed a sign advising drivers not to pick up hitchhikers. I was near the big prison where John Carlyle was an inmate. After a brief spark of thought, I found myself driving along a barbed wire fence encircling a tall, thick brick wall. I pulled up to the gate of *'Big Mac,'* as the prison is nicknamed. The facility towered before me, and while it appeared bland and old, the years had only increased its awe-inspiring effect." Wanda paused briefly in recollection.

"Naively, I parked, went inside of the visitor lobby, and told the guard I would like to see inmate John Carlyle. After a few minutes of checking, the guard stated that he had been transferred to a less-secure prison in Hominy, Oklahoma."

Wanda, in an aside to the audience, reflected, "Little did I know that years later I would be going to *Big Mac* to interview defendants on death row. This was years before any of my court work."

She then continued her story. "Eventually, another letter arrived from Carlyle. More manuscript was included. My response, again, was one of encouragement to continue his writing.

"In a few months, I discovered I was scheduled for a trip to Hominy to consult with a Head Start program. I decided to drive to the prison and attempt to see John Carlyle.

"The Hominy Correctional Center was a relatively new prison. However, the buildings looked cold and austere. The fences and guard towers were menacing as they towered above me. The barbed wire that encircled the facility sparkled threateningly as the sun descended in the western sky. Again, naively, I approached the window and spoke to a receptionist guard, asking for a visit with John Carlyle.

"He removed a folder and returned to tell me, 'Ma'am, John Carlyle . . . he was just recently moved.'

"'When?' I inquired.

"'Two weeks ago,' he said. 'To a less secure prison at Stringtown, Oklahoma.'"

I returned to my office to find an additional two hundred pages of hand-printed manuscript from John Carlyle. As with my previous letters, I thanked him and encouraged him to continue writing. And like before, I made no comment about my attempted visits or his earlier request for help to get an early release.

"Some weeks later, while on another consulting trip, a bright green sign announcing Stringtown Corrections Center alerted me that here was Carlyle's new home. I decided that this time I would finally get to meet John Carlyle. I followed the lonely drive through another menacing, barbed-wire-fenced entrance. A red-bricked, minimalistic institution loomed in front of me. While this prison didn't seem as imposing as the others, it nonetheless appeared to be inhospitable.

"I stepped up to the receiving window and said, 'I'm here to see one of your inmates, John Carlyle.'

"'Just a moment, please.' The guard walked to a file cabinet across the little office to check the files. He returned to the window and said, 'Ma'am, John Carlyle was released a week and a half ago, for good behavior.'"

Wanda, after a moment, reflected, "I was surprised, but very happy for John."

The audience was captivated. Polite applause followed, this time appreciating the ending to Carlyle's story. However, Wanda recognized that a significant section of the attendees understood the picture of the inmate that she described. She also realized that they were wary about him being released. Their experience had shown them that such happy endings as Carlyle's occur only in a fraction of cases.

"What a great portrayal of John Carlyle," Ladero offered. "Would you review how you determine his success?"

"John Carlyle is a successful person because he exemplifies the five characteristics. He had self-confidence." Wanda gestured, signifying the first with her finger. "It took confidence in himself to work towards his goal of regaining his life and sharing his history." She held up the next finger. "He got along with others. He was able to negotiate with other inmates and law enforcement in positive ways." She gestured with the third finger. "He had a broader view of the world and a sense of wonder. He wanted to rejoin the world and write his story by using his own creative spirit." As she raised her fourth finger, she explained, "John was able to focus until the task was complete—both in writing the manuscript and in achieving his goal of early release." She held up the last finger. "Self-evaluation. He exhibited this when he accepted and took responsibility for his actions. He didn't blame anyone else for his incarceration—only himself. He realized and admitted that he made the choice and would work to correct his path." She paused, panning the audience's faces, letting her words sink in.

"While we don't know much about Carlyle's childhood, we know that he did face sad circumstances and serious life challenges. But, he was able to overcome these obstacles and achieve success."

Ladero eagerly asked, "Did you ever hear from John Carlyle after his release?"

"No. Perhaps there was an unexpressed sense of mutuality between us that didn't require continuing the contact. But in my thoughts, I wish him well and great success in whatever he does."

Ladero spoke again. "How do you connect the dots between your focus on child development and adult criminal behavior?"

"You said the key words: 'connect the dots.' In all my years working with children and families before getting involved with criminal cases, I studied and researched the importance of the first few years of life and how children's development impacts their adult behavior. Since we've been talking about characteristics of successful people, let me give a couple of examples of how important these years are.

"If parents want their children to succeed in academics, all they have to do is enjoy playing and interacting with them during the first three years of life. They don't have to teach them their numbers or letters. They don't have to use learning tools. All they have to do is develop a close and meaningful relationship by spending quality time together. We call this bonding. We also call it attachment or the parent-child connection. The kind of connections that children make with their parents will determine how their character develops over the years until adulthood. A secure attachment that builds trust and mutuality will lead to success because the child will feel self-confident. There's no worry about 'Who cares about me?' or 'Am I okay?' The child is free to learn, explore, and enjoy life. Of course, if parents want to use learning games as a way to interact, that's great. But, play is the child's pathway to learning.

"It is absolutely paramount that children have love and commitment from their parents during the first few years of life. In over a hundred capital murder cases I've worked on, about 97 percent had very poor attachments with their parents or parent figures. Most of them changed parents more than once. Many were moved numerous times and shifted from relatives to foster homes. They became confused and traumatized by fears of abandonment, rejection, and humiliation. They felt betrayed by the people they loved. They grew up without self-confidence. They never learned to get along with others because they never had good role models. They had no sense of wonder because they were stuck in their own survival traps. They could only focus on what was happening to them at the moment; many were abused or neglected. How could they focus on schoolwork when they didn't know where their parents were or what they would do when they returned? They didn't learn to get along with others because they so often saw their parents fighting with each other."

"Dr. Draper, I want to go back to my first question. Why did you choose to become an expert witness in capital murder cases?"

"I didn't choose this direction for my work. It may have been by chance or maybe by some divine alignment. Yet, from the first capital murder case I testified in, I began to connect the dots between early childhood development and adult criminal behavior."

Ladero then asked, "I understand you're writing a book about your experience as an expert witness. Can you share your reason for putting pen to paper?"

"Several friends and relatives continued to badger me to write until I finally decided to give it consideration. What happened was that my own sense of wonder prodded me to do it. It's been a wonderful experience because not only did I have to relive all the cases I chose to write about, but it has also given me a deeper introspection into my own life. It has been a sobering task that has brought the realization that how our lives unfold is not merely a matter of chance but of choice, choice based on the synchronicity between ourselves and elements or events in the world we live in—and those we live with."

"What do you mean by *synchronicity*?" Ladero queried for the benefit of some in the audience who might not be familiar with the term.

"Carl Jung, the great psychologist, first used this term in his work with his patients. It means the coming together of events or circumstances that seem related but are not obviously caused by one another. We might think of it as the relationship between things that are happening or working together at the same time without being aware of it at the time—like sound and image in a movie that matches up with action.

"My greatest interest in working with these criminal cases is studying the defendant as a whole person, not just someone caught in one slice of time. I want to learn about this person's childhood and family and community life and about the influences that coalesce to have an impact—for good or for evil. I want to connect the dots."

PART ONE

Chapter 1

The north wind was blistering cold in late January. James Fields had been on the road for two days, without sleep, from Minneapolis to Oklahoma City, having hitchhiked several rides. When he entered the Oklahoma City area, the driver let him out in an area of highway construction, where traffic was slowed.

James was freezing, wearing only a light jacket, and had less than five dollars in his pocket. At about five o'clock, just before the sun was setting, a middle-aged man named Bostwick pulled alongside James, who eagerly accepted his offer of a ride. When Bostwick asked where he was headed, James told him he wasn't sure, but he readily welcomed Bostwick's invitation to be his guest at a local hamburger joint.

With a full stomach from a giant cheeseburger, salty fries, and a chocolate malt and with tired limbs and sore feet, James accepted Bostwick's offer of a bed at his place. They reached an apartment complex on the near north side of Oklahoma City and entered a modest, clean, two-bedroom apartment with a jack-and-jill bath, a living room, and a kitchen. As they walked through the kitchen, Bostwick offered James a beer, but he declined, opting for a soda instead.

After several days of hitchhiking, James was eager to have a shower and wash his hair. Bostwick showed James where the bathroom was and offered toiletries. He pulled a towel from the cabinet and set it on a bench near the wash basin. Then he led the way to the bedroom and showed James where he could sleep.

Feeling much better after a shower but still exhausted, James padded into the living room to relax on the sofa and watch TV, but he kept dozing off. Bostwick soon approached James and tried to come on to him. When James told him he didn't do that, Bostwick didn't put up a fight. He simply backed off. He soon excused himself and exited to the bedroom where he fell into a deep sleep.

The next morning, after James washed his face and combed his hair, he entered the living room, only to find Bostwick on the floor, apparently dead.

James kneeled and bent over to listen for a heartbeat. Nothing. A knock at the door suddenly sent him backpedaling on the floor, using his feet and hands until the wall prevented him from moving any farther. The wall didn't prevent him from shaking, however. After the initial shaking subsided, he remained still for several minutes until the knocking ceased. James panicked and didn't know what to do, so he dragged the dead Bostwick into the bedroom and stuffed him in the closet, piling some quilts on top of him.

With no more than a phone call and a letter of introduction from the defense attorney for her new case, middle-aged Wanda Draper walked the short distance from the parking lot across the street to the jail, a white, six-story, impressive edifice. The ample windows, neatly spaced in horizontal bands, contained panes resembling water shimmering in the sunlight. Even though she had driven by this building many times, she had never taken close notice of the architectural features, like those above the fourth story. Windows with stone rosettes encircled the building like a flapper's headband. The building presented a modest display of art deco design. Built in the 1930s as part of Oklahoma City's Civic Center, this structure had received the short end of the stick and ultimately became the home of the courtrooms with the penthouse floor serving as the county jail. However, the building remained standing, hanging on to its last shred of dignity.

Wanda exited the elevator and entered the top floor. The scent of male testosterone descended upon her with the force of a tsunami. It hung in the air and seemed to be imbedded in the old, peeling paint. She tried to ignore the decrepit staleness that assailed her nostrils and eyes as she approached the jail clerk. Wanda introduced herself to the salt-and-pepper-haired officer, asking to see James Fields. She needed a contact visit and presented her identification as she smiled at the middle-aged employee.

The guard responded skeptically, "Ma'am, this guy's a murderer, and you really wanna sit in the same room with him?" He adjusted his wire-rimmed glasses, trying to determine if his eyes were playing tricks on him. Wanda was dressed in a tailored blue suit. Her unclasped jacket displayed a cream, silk crepe button-down blouse. From her neatly styled blond hair to her patent leather black heels, she looked like she was about to enter into a high-profile meeting—not an interview with an alleged killer housed in a small, dingy jail cell.

"I have to have a private contact visit," she insisted.

"Sorry. We can't expose you to this danger," the officer responded, matter-of-factly leaning back to add emphasis.

Wanda, undeterred, calmly handed him a letter and respectfully pointed out, "As you can see, I'll be working with the defense team on his case."

"Well," he retorted, surprised by Wanda's polite insistence, "only way you're gettin' that visit is if we chain him to a bench out here in the hall."

She glanced behind to see an old church pew just opposite the guard station. "No, I have to have a private room," she said with determination. "You can watch through the window, but I must have confidentiality and the ability to speak candidly with the defendant." The guard, with a slight sigh of resignation, directed her to take a seat on the pew to wait.

Forty-five minutes later, Wanda still sat completely erect, trying to compact herself as much as possible so as to minimize exposure to whatever film thoroughly coated the pew. She watched the guard go about his duties and the other jail staff and employees move in and about the halls and the little office. *So this is our tax dollars at work,* she thought, more than once as she glanced at her watch. As she shook her head and wondered, *How do I get myself in these fixes?,* she also remembered the first time she was called as an expert witness.

"Dr. Draper, I understand you're experienced in child development?" inquired a rather young male voice with a hint of a Wisconsin accent. After a brief pause, he hastily added, "Name's Harrison Johns, by the way. I'm an investigator."

Wanda confirmed his query as she jotted down his name on a note pad on her office desk.

"Have you ever testified in court? Capital penalty cases?" Harrison continued briskly.

"No, I haven't done any testifying." Wanda, intrigued by this individual and his line of questioning, patiently waited for the punchline.

The long pause of hesitation continued on the other end of the line. Wanda was certain Harrison was wrestling with trying to figure out the best place to pick up on a story with someone who just walked in three-quarters of the way through. "I'm on a case . . . a murder case."

"Yes?" Wanda said in a nonjudgmental tone.

"It's being tried, now. Two children, ages four and six, watched their father shoot and kill their mother." Harrison drew a sharp breath before continuing, "We're looking for a behavioral specialist to testify as an expert in the penalty stage—that would be next week. Can you help us?" A tinge of desperation broke the hardened investigator façade his voice had projected earlier.

Wanda was surprised. She had never before considered such work. "What would you want me to discuss exactly?" she asked cautiously, interested as she started fidgeting with the pencil in her hand and doodling on the note pad.

"What, if any, impact this act will have on the children if their father gets the death penalty. You came highly recommended." Harrison poured on a little honey.

Seeing their father kill their mother? How could they not be affected? reeled through her mind. However, she was unsure how to respond. While her knowledge of court proceedings extended only to fiction and news clips, she understood the gravity and implications of such a request.

Harrison, afraid of losing his best lead, added, "Dr. Draper, we're desperate." To Wanda, his sincerity seemed genuine.

"Let me call you back tomorrow," Wanda said politely. After clearing her throat she admitted, "I need to give this some thought." Harrison thanked her for her time and left his contact information.

The receiver rested in its cradle for only a few seconds before she snatched it up again and dialed a lawyer colleague she greatly respected. He warned Wanda of her vulnerability and pointed out her inexperience with the judicial system. In between her daily duties and responsibilities, she contacted several other colleagues to obtain their opinions of the situation. The responses from the psychologists and psychiatrists were in concurrence with her friend: *Stay. Away. From. The. Courtroom.*

The next morning, Wanda was preparing her day's agenda. Top of the list was to call Harrison Johns with her response. She reached into her purse where she had previously tucked his number. Her hand instead pulled out a card featuring a pitiful child.

The only semblance of childlike joy and exuberance was in the blue-colorized ribbon that adorned the little girl's hair in the otherwise black-and-white photograph. Her body was small and frail, uncharacteristic of an eight-year-old. Her eyes had no brilliancy, not a spark of childlike mischief or fun. Her lips did not try to restrain a smile, laughing at some private joke between her and this wonderful world. Her body lacked the vitality, the ever-readiness to dash into a sprint, turn a cartwheel, or dance a special jig. Instead, the malnourished limbs were etched with lines of misplaced anger and scarred in hues of black and blue from being unloved. No, this was not a little girl who stood at attention, waiting for the next frivolity. This child cowered next to the severely ornamented chair from the Victorian era, bracing for impact. The vacant, fearful eyes of this ghost of a young girl seemed to echo, "What will become of me?"

Wanda flipped the card over:

The black and white photograph captures the image of little Mary Ellen Wilson, an orphan who was sent to be raised by foster parents in 1874's New York, in the harshest conditions of Hell's Kitchen. This little forlorn girl unfortunately became the first child in the United States to be rescued from her abusive living conditions. It is unfortunate because prior to 1874, there were no laws definitively protecting children and no organizations established to watch over children. Mary Ellen's rescue was facilitated by a missionary worker, Etta Agnell Wheeler, who after numerous pleas to legal counselors was turned away because there were no laws protecting children. Wheeler, desperately determined for a means to litigate the case in order to rescue this little girl, turned to an animal cruelty organization.

A sad thing that children were worth no more than animals. We together must protect our most precious resources. Join us as we take this month to remember all the children who, like little Mary Ellen Wilson, are waiting for rescue. Join our Blue Ribbon Campaign to prevent child abuse.

Wanda's resolution was strengthened at that moment. When Harrison answered, she replied without hesitation, "Mr. Johns, I will testify." As she ended the call, she contemplated, *Early childhood experiences . . . they* do *impact one's life in the present and in the future.*

In between surreptitious glances at her timepiece and observing the jail comings and goings from the corner of her eye, Wanda wondered what this man, or really kid, named James would be like. She reflected, *He's so young to be charged with such a crime! Only twenty years old! Will he even talk with me? Can I trust what he says?* She had no preliminary information on him. She hadn't even been given a sheet of paper describing his physical features. Her mind turned to the courtroom. As she was thinking what would eventually happen with James's case after this interview, she couldn't help but remember her first courtroom appearance several months before.

She entered that huge Oklahoma courthouse in early 1989, knowing slightly more about the judiciary proceedings than she had previously but still knowing nothing about testifying in court. She did learn that the judicial process was divided into two stages: first stage, or guilt/innocence, and second stage, or penalty/sentencing. As Harrison had informed her, she would be called on behalf of the defense to offer testimony in second stage about how the children of the killer would be affected. She would offer her expert opinion in child development to afford the jury consideration of this man standing trial for having killed his wife in the presence of their children.

The judge's bench was at the west end, flanked by the witness box to the judge's right and the jury box to the judge's left. The court reporter's desk was near the witness box. Two large mahogany tables in front of the judge's bench were placed parallel to the twenty-some-odd rows of wooden pews of the audience gallery. A prominent wooden lectern stood directly facing the judge's bench. A twenty-eight-inch mahogany partition separated the spectators from the court. Several 1950s art nouveau lamps, made of pressed metal squares with relief design, hung from the ceiling. Wanda reflected on how the pews, facing the judge's platform, and the partition that separated the laymen from the judicial representatives reminded her of a temple. The thought struck her more than once: *No wonder so many judges come to consider themselves as gods. All that's missing is a place to offer sacrifices.*

After being sworn in and asked the initial questions about her credentials and experience with children and families, Wanda was certified as an expert witness.

The defense attorney, whom she had met only hours before, cut to the heart of the matter, "Would you please comment on how the children will be affected if their father is sentenced to death?"

"The children, having witnessed this atrocious act and losing their mother in this manner, will require long-term therapy and a lot of emotional support from family, friends, church, and others. If the father is put to death, the children will have no way to resolve this issue with him or within their own minds and hearts," Wanda succinctly answered the question.

"Objection!" cried out the prosecuting attorney as he jumped to his feet. The face of Tom Roberts, known as "Cowboy Tom" for not only roping calves in the fields but for also roping defendants in the court, was blood red. He looked every bit the cowboy lawman, from his crisp, white shirt crowned with his trademark western bolo tie down to his polished-to-a-shiny-black leather boots. He was a man who believed in the law of the land. And this cowboy had just been brought to the beginning stages of apoplexy by outrage. Mr. Roberts did not want the jury to hear what Wanda had to say.

Wanda, in turn, was completely overwhelmed by such a violent display of anger. She did not know what was happening. She had never seen anything like this. This was not the civilized and decorous behavior she expected of the American legal profession. Thoughts of having somehow made a mistake or overstepped some unknown boundaries raced through her mind. Yet, her face was expressionless.

The judge cleared the jury from the courtroom. "Cowboy Tom" believed that something in Wanda's testimony was inadmissible and therefore not relevant for the jury. What was so grievous to "Cowboy Tom" was not clearly apparent to the defense nor the judge. However, this was the man who believed in putting to death anyone who, in his opinion, threatened the greater good; he saw it as a necessary sacrifice. After Wanda was questioned further, there was a brief recess. The jury then returned, and her testimony resumed. Though her knees were shaking, relief washed over her when she finally stepped down from the witness stand.

The next day, the attorney called to thank Wanda for her testimony. Still recovering from the jarring experience, she was still somewhat mystified about the previous day's proceedings. The attorney assured her she did an excellent job and provided compelling testimony. However, Wanda wasn't pleased with her testimony. In her mind, it was weak for one principle reason. She had neither interviewed the defendant nor the children. While she was able to comment and opine how children, generally, are affected developmentally after such traumatic events, she did not like to deal in generalities. As she replaced the phone's receiver, she thought, *Development is so much more dynamic and influential. It sculpts perspectives and relationships, defining life's possibility as a success or a tragedy.*

Wanda was finally ushered into a small room with a glass window that provided a view from the hallway so the guards could keep watch. James was already waiting in the contact room. She extended her hand to him and introduced herself. James stood up from his seat, grasping Wanda's hand in a firm handshake.

"I'm so glad you're here. I need your help," James greeted her. His brown eyes reflected his need, while his bright smile conveyed his sincerity and relief at meeting with a member of his defense team. Only twenty years old, James had been waiting in jail for eighteen months to begin preparing for his trial.

Wanda's intuition reassured her that he was friendly. She responded by conveying her commitment to helping him. As they sat down across the table from each other, she clarified her role on the defense team and then said, "James, if you should be found guilty—"

"I'm innocent," he hastily interrupted.

Wanda had read enough bestselling mysteries to expect all defendants to declare this. She smiled and gestured as if she believed him but didn't say so. Instead, she continued, "My purpose is to prepare in case the jury or judge does not rule that way." James's shoulders slumped slightly as he studied the floor. "Hopefully, my testimony will not be needed," she added. James jerked his eyes up and smiled. Wanda began, "James, I need to get to know you. I'll be working with you, preparing for your case. So, let me start by asking some simple but important questions."

"James, where were you born? What is your birth date?" Wanda was interested in details about his development. Even though she could get this information from the files, she wanted to begin this meeting with non-threatening questions. She not only wanted but also needed to know about the situation he was born into and the subsequent environment in which he was raised. She needed to distinguish the epigenetic factors, all of which influenced him and left their mark. Wanda's task was to identify the significant events and circumstances and follow their trail in his life's path, so she began at the beginning. She took out a new yellow pad and a freshly sharpened pencil from her document folder.

"I was born in Rhode Island. March 20, 1969."

"Tell me about your parents," Wanda requested.

"My mom's name was Lisa. My father . . . his name was Bruce."

"Their last name?"

"Balzo." James noticed Wanda look hesitatingly at the yellow pad. He smilingly spelled the name for her. "Now, some of this really early stuff I learned later on from my older brother and my stepparents," James truthfully cautioned, "but . . . my father . . . he . . . he had become a drug addict while in Vietnam. Guess he could never really shake the addiction. Mom, I guess, wasn't, uh, strong enough to live with an addict. So, they, uh, divorced when I was two, I think."

"Do you know where he is now?" Wanda inquired.

"Still in rehab somewhere. Mom then married Albert Fields, and we moved to Lakeside, Virginia."

"You said you have an older brother? Is that correct?"

"Yes, Luke. He's two years older than me."

"Is he your only sibling?"

"Yes. There's just the two of us."

"James, tell me about your mother, Lisa."

James's eyes sparkled. The warmth on his face radiated through the room. "I clearly remember she was rather frail and never seemed happy. I'd often climb in her lap and hug her and tell her I loved her. She always loved me and Luke. But, Luke was older and had made friends at school. I was often at home alone with Mom. She was my entire world, as they say."

Wanda, throughout their conversation, hurriedly scribbled details and tidbits of information that James shared. She tried to focus on looking at James and not the yellow pad in her lap. She focused on making sure nothing interfered or inhibited the human connection and the communication channels. Consequently, her notes consisted of unique combinations of abbreviated words and pictorial symbols—she had developed her own personal shorthand. However, she took an extra moment at times to copy James's words verbatim.

"What about Albert?" she asked, moving on.

Like someone had blown out a candle, James's warmth and the light emanating from his eyes suddenly vanished. "He didn't like me. Never did.

Always got on with Luke, though. I think . . . I think I reminded him too much of my mother. If Mom . . . if she was unhappy, I was unhappy."

"What else do you remember about that time?"

"One morning . . . after Luke left for school and Albert left for work . . . I . . . I went to find Mom." Wanda noticed a change in James's demeanor. He was suddenly void of any words for several seconds. His eyes seemed to focus somewhere else. He was stone still. Then he spoke as if in a trance, "She was in her big easy chair where she often sat alone. She always enjoyed me climbing up in her lap for a while before I'd hurry off to play alone. That morning . . . I remember it was bright and sunny . . . I climbed in Mom's lap. She said nothing. She felt . . . felt cold when I tried to hug her. I tried to wake her. I thought she was asleep. I didn't know what to do so I just curled up in her lap and stayed there until Albert came home. Mom . . . she. . ." James paused, swallowing hard. "She . . . had died with a brain aneurysm." He looked away, blinking back tears.

"I'm so sorry, James," Wanda said, giving him a sympathetic smile. "I can't even imagine how traumatic that had to be."

"Pretty tough," he softly lamented. A dark cloud seemed to descend upon him, causing his shoulders to sink under its load. For a moment, his eyes fixed on some indiscriminate speck that only he could see in the contact room's window. He murmured, "The truth will set me free," like a child reciting a comforting verse.

After taking a few moments in an attempt to ascertain James's thoughts, she innocently asked him, "What do you remember happening next?"

"A few weeks . . . I don't know . . . might've been a few months," James stammered, turning his mind from depressing thoughts to the task at hand. "Soon after Mom's funeral, Albert married this woman, Amanda."

James continued, "They offered to take me and Luke."

"So, now you and Luke had two stepparents?"

"Yeah. Luke . . . he adjusted to Amanda and Albert really quickly. I didn't. I was a big problem for them."

Wanda could see the beginning of James's development and how it took a different course all together from Luke's. She mentally delineated the difference between Luke and James: *Where Luke was able to make a secure attachment with his mother and father before Bruce went to war, James's was an uneasy attachment, created by Lisa's depression and inability to cope with her husband when he returned. Luke benefited from the firm foundation that he had for a couple of years without the dynamics of a drug-addicted father, a depressed mother, and a new stepfather. Luke's selfhood and his autonomy were well on the way to development, but James's was shattered.* Wanda further reflected: *James was like a starved seedling, struggling to reach the sun.*

She wanted to learn more about the dynamics in James's early years when she asked, "And how was life with Albert and Amanda?"

He paused a moment, gazing down towards his left, before admitting in a dark tone, "Albert liked to grab me and bang my head against the wooden arm of our living room sofa. I never knew why Albert didn't like me." James looked up at Wanda, the bewilderment etched in his face. "I really didn't." He looked to her as if she might know the answer. But then he said, "Luke was the good example, and Amanda and Albert often told me I should be more like Luke." As Wanda jotted down the details of his accounts on her yellow pad, she perceived, *The more they held Luke up to him as the model child, the further James's self-esteem fell.* Yet, Wanda stoically continued her notes and interview, keeping her thoughts to herself, remaining expressionless.

Wanda sensed that the present line of inquiry she and James were traversing could lead to his withdrawing if he became overwhelmed with dispiriting memories. So, she switched tracks. "What about school?"

"What about it? I don't know what to say," James faltered. He scrunched his forehead, grasping for a characterization. "I didn't like it. Used to overhear Amanda and Albert saying I had 'serious behavior problems,'" James made the quotation sign with both his hands. "I began to run away from home—"

"Where would you go?" Wanda interrupted.

"Not far. They'd find me curled up somewhere in an alley or hiding by a dumpster. I was labeled a 'runaway.'" Again, James gesticulated the quote.

"Was there a particular reason you started running away?" Wanda prompted. She was intrigued to learn why he felt the urge to run. She leaned forward, listening. Her pencil was ready. His answer would be yet another brush stroke to his developmental portrait.

"I just wanted to be free." James sighed as he turned his head away toward the window. "Free," he mumbled to himself. He paused, his attention again captured by some invisible object in the hallway. "And when I go to court," his voice gained momentum, "the truth will set me free." He sat there quietly agitated, his eyes refusing to move from the object. *He's either hallucinating, or he's had some psychotic break,* Wanda speculated.

She cleared her throat, then asked, "James, what really made you want to run away?"

James fixed his gaze on Wanda and confided, "I always felt like I lived in a cage with Amanda and Albert. They corrected me constantly." His shoulders slumped dejectedly. "I could never be still enough to suit them," he admitted as he slowly deflated in his chair. "I was always in trouble in their eyes." With each word spoken, the life seemed to trickle out from his body. Wanda had never seen so many shifts in body language within a matter of seconds. "I guess I just stopped caring." There was then complete and utter silence until James straightened up and said, "Once, after school, I climbed through a window and took cups of ice cream from the cafeteria freezer so I could give them to my friends who waited outside beneath the window."

"Did you receive a punishment?"

James held up an invisible rod, making a striking motion with his hand. "I received a whipping from Albert, and the school reprimanded me." James's hand dropped into his lap. "That certainly wouldn't be the last time I got into trouble," he stated wryly, trying to add some levity.

Wanda collected her thoughts, then asked, "James, what's the worst memory of your growing-up years?"

"When my stepparents had me admitted to a psychiatric hospital, I guess they thought . . . I'm sure they thought I was crazy. But, I never had to stay long. I, uh, got along good with the nurses and doctors. They were . . . really nice. I always got better, and they'd send me home. Then in a few months, or sometimes weeks, I had to go back. I used to think my parents just . . . well, they didn't want to deal with me."

James seemed eager to talk. He openly answered Wanda's questions and explained his perspective about his own life up to this point. The time flew by. Wanda's hand scribbled quickly, and the yellow pad became full. After about three hours, their first meeting came to a conclusion. As Wanda collected her pencils and closed her yellow pad, she noticed that James had withdrawn. He leaned back in his chair and stared out the window into the hall. The sun had continued its daily trek and was now in a position to send rays of warm, bright light down the hall through the only window. While James stared, Wanda mentally noted, *He doesn't seem quite himself. He seems just outside the realm of reality.* James then murmured once again, "The truth will set me free."

As Wanda shifted in her chair, she wondered: *Is this because he has been living in a musty, eight-by-ten cell for eighteen months with no visitors other than an occasional investigator or lawyer? Or is it because he has perhaps been falsely accused? Or is it because he has a personality disorder?*

James and Wanda extended handshakes in a gesture of parting. As he took her hand warmly and firmly, he thanked her again for helping and expressed pleasure in meeting her. "I look forward to the next time," Wanda sincerely returned the polite expression of departure. She felt that in the first minutes of their meeting she was able to establish a connection with James, and the subsequent hours only reinforced the feeling.

As she walked past the guard, waving her appreciation for his assistance, she contemplated this strange conundrum she had just encountered. James was an accused killer. However, while she distinctly noted developmental issues, he was nevertheless a nice, polite, affable young man. James was like a distorted origami paper crane, one that somehow in the process of the many folds and refolds became twisted. Wanda was intent on unfolding the jumbled mess of James's life.

The clock striking the hour from a distant church signaled her to hurry on her way. Now, she had to return to the children's center, for which she was the founder and executive director. Soon, the psychiatry residents would be coming to observe the children. Yet, she couldn't get James totally out her mind.

Chapter 2

Spring matured into a blazing summer, and life continued. James waited in jail for his day in court. Wanda continued administering, teaching, and consulting. As she moved across the University of Oklahoma campus to her office, the hot breeze encouraged her to walk more quickly. She had awakened at five in the morning to ensure she would be at the child development center by six to support the teachers and greet the children and their parents. She also needed to brief the psychiatry residents before they began their work with the children by midmorning. This was one of her main reasons for desiring such a center—a place for medical students and residents to learn about development by interacting *on the floor* with children. She would then return to campus to prepare for resident seminars and to follow up with consults in the diagnostic clinic. She thought little of the trek back to the center at the end of her day in the Psychiatry Department since she enjoyed reviewing with the teachers, debriefing the students, preparing for the next day, and meeting with concerned parents. Following her daily commitments and duties, she didn't return home until well after six, and it was then that she worked on James's case. She would fall into bed close to midnight, only to rise again at five the next morning to get ready for another full day. Wanda's life was a complex pattern of projects and deadlines, interwoven with time constraints and obligations and tenuously held together by priorities and her joy of working.

As she stepped into the elevator, she rummaged in her purse for her lipstick. Her hand instead once again found the black-and-white photograph of the little girl with the careworn face. Wanda saw in the photo a little girl who looked older than her years, with a face that had witnessed much sadness and trauma.

Wanda tucked the card back into her purse as she made her way to her office. The card had been handed to her by a young collegiate a few months before. The most shocking revelation upon which she reflected as she boarded and pushed the elevator button for the third floor was that an animal abuse organization was the child's liberator. *What sort of reflection is this on man?* Her gloomy thoughts were interrupted by shrills of children laughing as the elevator door opened.

Gazing down the hallway through the big window, she saw the source. Children were playing in the diagnostic room. This area, which looked more like a playroom, was an attractive setting for several young children of varying ages and stages of development who were there for evaluation. Romping right along with the children on the floor were a couple of residents. Wanda ambled by and waved, greeting the children and residents.

"Dr. Draper, I, uh, I . . ."

Wanda turned to find one of her new child psychiatry residents. "Hello, Dr. Barrington, walk with me."

"Dr. Draper, I, uh, well, I . . ." Dr. Barrington struggled to get the words out. It was clear to her he had a question but was embarrassed to ask. "I don't . . . don't know how to play with these children in order to study their possible diagnosis. I mean . . . I have children of my own and love to play with them, but I'm . . . well, I'm just not sure what to do with other children—especially those who've been brought here because they're thought to be . . . troubled."

Recognizing his apprehension, she was quick to reassure him. "Dr. Barrington, you don't need to worry. The child will guide the play. First, take off your white coat and tie. I'll hang them up here in my office. Just go sit on the floor, pick up a toy, stack blocks, or open a book. Soon, you'll have children wanting to join you." She smiled encouragingly at him as she took his coat and tie.

After hanging up Dr. Barrington's coat, Wanda's next task was to conduct a telephone interview with James's stepfather, Albert. She picked up the phone and dialed the number that Harrison gave her. As it rang, she could hear the children's squeals of joy across the hall, accompanied by adult laughter from the child development clinic. There were a few more rings, and a male voice answered.

After Wanda introduced herself and her reason for calling, she said pleasantly, "Thank you for agreeing to talk to me."

"Always a pleasure to talk to a woman," he said in a voice that made her skin crawl.

She let that one pass. "May I ask a few questions about James's childhood?" After he agreed, she followed up with, "First, can you tell me about your marriage to Lisa?"

"At first, it was okay. But soon she just became so down and depressed. I had certain expectations of her as a wife and a housekeeper. Trust me when I tell you, she never met my expectations. I, um, lost interest in her, basically." Albert lowered his voice, conceding the truth. Wanda made no response, though her eyebrows twitched.

"And when did you meet your next wife, Amanda? Was it during your marriage to Lisa or after her death?"

"While I was married to Lisa. Amanda was—wow—drop-dead gorgeous! Oh, she was so attractive. She was able to meet my expectations." As Wanda listened to him, her eyebrows twitched again.

"Did Lisa know about your affair with Amanda?" she asked, faltering mentally at mentioning "Amanda" and "affair" in the same sentence.

"Yeah, she knew. She wasn't happy I was spending so much time with Amanda and not with Luke and James."

"Did you consider divorcing Lisa?" she queried, keeping her voice completely professional.

"I was planning to, but I felt a commitment to hold the family together." Wanda swallowed soundlessly.

"After Lisa's death, did anyone notify Luke and James's father, Bruce Balzo?"

"Yeah, but he was still off-and-on in drug rehab and couldn't care for them. So, I kept them, and when Amanda and I got married, we became their parents."

"How was your relationship with Luke and James?" she asked, eager to hear his response.

"Luke was . . . he is . . . a good boy. Always has been. Very few problems with him. James . . . I don't know. I tried to be a good father to him. He was only interested in being with Lisa. Then, when he was with me and Amanda, he could never sit or stand still . . . always misbehaving and causing problems. I had to punish him a lot."

"What kind of punishment?" she asked conversationally.

"Whippings. Lots of whippings. That's all." Albert added disparagingly, "Not that it did any good." Wanda's eyebrow arched, noting the discrepancy between James's description of the punishment and Albert's.

Albert then concluded the interview by saying he had to leave for work. She thanked him for his time and ended the call. As she returned the phone to its cradle, numerous thoughts struck her in succession about Mr. Albert Fields as she reviewed her notes. *He was certainly blunt enough,* thought Wanda. *And, such a wonderful male role model to carry on an affair for the sake of the family!* Wanda reflected about how Mr. Fields's "whippings" consisted of banging James's head against the wooden arm of the couch. She reasoned that Albert's glossed-over omission was more for protecting himself in the eyes of others than anything else. *Oh, but such a great father!* she mentally expressed the sarcastic remark towards Albert.

Wanda was intellectually agitated by Albert and his parenting of James. With a deep sigh, she turned and stared out the window at the blue sky. Realizing the thought train she was about to board, she reproached herself: *Now, Wanda, it's not your place to judge. It's your job to focus on now and help present James as a whole person.* It had been a short interview, and he was definitely circumspect about certain things, but Albert had still helped crystallize a few aspects of James's troubled beginning. Yet, she still hadn't acquired all the pieces of the puzzle. There were more questions than answers. She picked up the phone and called the investigator.

———

At the initial team meeting for James's case, Wanda surprisingly found herself working with Harrison Johns once again. This athletically built man of average height had deep brown hair with natural, rusty gold streaks and brown eyes. He walked with confidence, ever ready to laugh. Harrison warmly greeted Wanda, sincerely shaking her hand like an old friend. "How're you doing, Dr. Draper?" Then, in a teasing voice, he said, "We gotta stop meeting like this!"

Wanda laughed, replying, "I know! People will begin to talk." The mirth bubbled over into laughter. Both discovered they had a shared joy in spending time outdoors, doing what one called gardening and the other called landscaping.

Wanda felt the two would work well together. After Wanda discussed the information she needed, Harrison committed to secure it. She reminded him that she needed James's records as soon as possible.

He asked, "Which ones?"

"Anything and everything. I need to know as much as I can about his life."

"Okay, then. I'm on it."

———

After about three months, Wanda opened the door of her home to a courier delivering several boxes. A note came with the boxes: *Merry Christmas! –Harrison*

Wanda eagerly plowed into the mounds of mental health and school records that had been delivered. *This is like Christmas,* she reflected as she opened box after box. *It's just not the kind of gifts that would make a person smile.*

While James's IQ scores placed him in a high range of intelligence, his behavior was documented as incorrigible. By the time he was a pre-teen, he had been through several psychological evaluations. In the early 1980s, James spent months at a time in psychiatric hospitals for teenagers. He always seemed to improve rather quickly and was released—only to get into trouble a few weeks after being at home and at school. Wanda couldn't help but notice and lament, *Only a decade later, these same hospitals are now keeping children only a few days. All in the name of the financial bottom line!*

Wanda surveyed the mounds of information before her. Suddenly, a feeling of being overwhelmed struck her as she stared at the monumental task laid at her feet. *This is a job for a small army,* she mentally stated, exasperated. Aloud she said, "I'm going to need her help."

———

"James does not fall into either classification: psychopathy or sociopathy," Wanda was bringing the blond-headed woman, sitting across from her in the home office, up-to-date about the case. Wanda further explained, through summing up the work of Jack Pemment, a neurobiology researcher of criminal behavior and aggression, and psychopathy and sociopathy experts, Robert D. Hare and industrial psychologist Paul Babiek, "Their study of psychopaths characterizes the individual as one who has no empathy or sense of morality— among a number of other antisocial traits. Sociopathy, on the other hand, was found to be indicative of having a sense of morality and a well-developed conscience, but behaving without integrity as to either right or wrong. James is neither a psychopath nor a sociopath. However, he appears to have some psychological behaviors that border on the bizarre." The woman nodded in understanding, with the same intent gaze Wanda often exhibited when focused on a task.

"What do you mean by bizarre?" she asked. Wanda stared at her glamorous younger sister—younger by five years. She could see why she had always been a head-turner: five feet and seven inches tall, perfect figure, broad smile, and beautiful teeth. Catherine was a natural beauty. She, like Wanda, inherited the Czech work ethic. While she would grace any high-society soiree, she could roll her sleeves up and work any man into the ground, be it administrating an office or managing a construction site.

Wanda told Catherine, "The last time I went to the jail for a visit, I had to wait over an hour to see James. While waiting, I asked one of the jailers about the moaning and shrill-like crying I kept hearing. He rolled his eyes and said, 'That's your guy. He seems to be going nuts.' I couldn't believe it. I never had any proof, but I wouldn't be surprised if the guards spent a considerable amount of time egging him on. Quite frankly, I expected James to be a walking zombie when he came in for the visit—if he would even show up."

Catherine eagerly asked, "Tell me . . . How was he?"

"I was thoroughly surprised. When he entered the contact room and saw me, his eyes lit up. It was like I was a mother figure. He was very courteous. He didn't seem at all like a screaming idiot but more like a child concerned about his mother. The visit lasted a good two hours. I was able to glean a lot of good information about James's more recent behavior prior to being arrested for the crime in question."

Catherine whistled as she leaned back in her chair. "What a mess!" Catherine exclaimed while she glanced around the piles and boxes of records neatly stored around the office. "Where to start?" Catherine looked around her. "How about here?" She matter-of-factly picked up the notepad laying on the desk. "Which visit is this one?" Catherine began reading Wanda's notes.

Wanda smiled to herself. She was thrilled that Catherine was so eager to help her. Although Catherine never completed her fourth year of a degree beyond high school, Wanda never thought that hurt her or was any reflection on her intelligence. In fact, Wanda would often remark about how much smarter Catherine was than she. Catherine's confident and fearless enthusiasm fueled her intellect, and in Wanda's estimation, her experiences were better than many post-graduate students anywhere.

"This interview with James . . . I wanted to learn more about his behaviors that got him in the most trouble." Wanda set the stage for the interview. "James was actually eager to talk." Wanda paused a moment. "I think it's hard for him to be alone so much. Even though the home he came from was abusive, it was still a far cry from living in a dingy cell in this place." Wanda continued recounting her visit with James, going back in her mind.

After a few minutes of pleasantries, she had started the interview with James by stating she wanted to talk about his running away. They had talked briefly about it in a previous interview, but she needed to know more.

"Haven't I told you about the time I really ran away from home?" he asked, but before she could respond, he continued, "This time for good."

His pattern of running away continues, she mentally noted.

"No, you haven't. I'm eager to hear," she encouraged him.

"I was seventeen. Amanda and Albert had just told me I'd never amount to anything. They were through trying to help me. So, I turned to hitchhiking."

"Did you meet a lot of interesting people on the road?" Wanda queried.

"I did. I liked visiting with strangers. They had no agenda and no expectations of me—unlike my parents and teachers. After leaving Lakeside, I made my way through Tennessee and Kentucky to Kansas, then New Mexico. I stayed along the major interstates, including I-10—"

"Why along the major interstates?" she cut in.

"It provided the best rides with truck drivers in fast-moving eighteen-wheelers," he clarified.

She followed up with, "How did you feel during this time, being alone and far from home?"

"I felt free," he replied. "I enjoyed meeting people who cared about helping me."

Wanda paused before asking the next question, "James, how did you get the money to travel?"

"Most times truckers gave me money for food and coffee, and I usually slept while riding. Sometimes, I'd sleep in a truck stop behind a building or even under a bridge if the weather permitted."

"Were you ever afraid during your travels?" she was anxious to know.

"Never. I was never afraid," he said adamantly. "I just felt free."

She took a brief moment to glance down at her notes. When she looked back up, he was smiling at her. And, when James smiled, he was as good-looking as a young movie star. This certainly wasn't a crazy lunatic smile like a psychopath in the movies flashes at another character. This was a genuine smile. Wanda smiled back. She could tell he enjoyed talking with her, and the feeling was mutual.

She carried on with her questioning. "Did you ever reach a state where you thought you might want to settle down?"

"California. I thought it was time to find some work. I thought California was a good place since it was at the opposite end of the country from Lakeside."

"Were you able to find a job?"

"At a music store but without a high school education they let me go."

"What did you do then?"

"I took off again . . . traveling. This time across the mountain range and through the upper northwest. By the time I reached Minneapolis, I was pretty tired of running from no place to some place. I asked my trucker friend to leave me at a bus station in the downtown area. He gave me a five dollar bill. That's when I wandered into the bus station's cafeteria. I purchased enough food to keep me going until the next day."

Wanda took a sip of water, pausing in her description of the meeting.

"And what happened next?" Catherine interrupted. Engrossed in the personal history, she couldn't bare even the slightest intermission.

"That's what I asked him." Wanda smiled. She was thrilled that her sister was so interested in this case. She continued relating James's narration.

"While I was sitting there alone, a pretty girl . . . she had a slight limp . . . she kept glancing at me across the aisle," James said a little sheepishly. "I smiled back. I noticed she had a guitar case in the chair next to her. I asked her if she played. She said only for pleasure but not as a professional. We struck up a conversation and ended the evening at a nearby park where she played and sang ballads. Some I recognized. Some were improvised to fit the occasion."

"How did the evening end?" Wanda asked, interested.

"I never made an advance or even an innuendo toward approaching Molly. That's her name . . . Molly. But I was attracted to her."

"Was the feeling mutual?" Wanda smiled.

"I think so," he smiled back. "She invited me to spend the night at her parents' home."

Wanda was wondering, *Where's this going?* But she chuckled and said, "I'm sure it was nice to get a real bath."

"You bet it was. Think I used an entire bar of soap that night. I'm sure Molly and her parents must have been wondering if I was ever going to come out of that shower. That night in the guest room, I had my first full night of sleep in I don't know how long. I awoke to freshly brewed coffee. It was a really robust aroma.

"Then, Molly's father entered the room carrying a big mug of coffee for me. He was so nice. He said, 'Say, son, where do you come from? My wife took the liberty to wash your clothes. They're about ready to come out of the dryer.' He handed me one of his robes and invited me to breakfast in their kitchen. The sun was shining through the windows. Molly and her mother were already dressed. I did wonder something at the time."

"What was that?"

"I wondered why Molly had been at a bus station with her guitar when she lived in such a nice house with such nice parents. But I thought better of asking such personal questions."

Their two-hour contact visit came to an end, but Wanda knew she would be talking with James again.

Wanda concluded James's story to Catherine. A thoughtful silence enveloped the two women as Wanda contemplated where and how he traveled: *I need to develop some way to illustrate his "running" pattern—and the major events and circumstances that impacted his behavior.*

"He appears to have a running pattern," Catherine said after a moment of processing this story and the other information Wanda had shared with her. Wanda looked up at her sister, quietly flabbergasted.

"He just keeps searching for something," Catherine continued, looking down and shaking her head for the sorrow of such a life. Wanda beamed at her sister with satisfaction. She was confident in her choice of a recruit for this case.

Catherine started moving about the office, her own yellow pad in hand. She started to scout the lay of the land in preparation for a plan of attack. Wanda turned toward her desk, stacks of yellow pads and official documents lounged about, waiting for some purpose and organization. Wanda let the air out of her lungs, sighing. "I'm going to have to start processing these interview notes and combining them with the records."

Catherine looked up from reviewing James's childhood information and Wanda's notes from the most recent contact visits. "Then what? How in the world are you going to show all of this in court?" she asked pointedly.

"I don't know."

Chapter 3

Like a pesky fly, James's plight continually buzzed in the back of Wanda's mind. *How do I help James? There is just so much information. How can I tell the jury about his life? How can I help them understand how a person's development shapes the flow of his life?* These questions haunted her. She needed a way to illustrate all of James's traveling back and forth across the country when he was running away from his family and from his own trauma.

The answers did not become more apparent, despite the stacks and stacks of records flooding in from Harrison and the attorneys, compounded with hours of interviews. It was during this time that Wanda was especially thankful for Catherine's help. And now that Wanda had shifted from writing textbooks to court work as part of her contribution to the Psychiatry Department, she needed her sister's help more than ever.

Wanda reviewed and re-reviewed all of the documents, including Catherine's excellent notes, often late at night, organizing and reorganizing. Still, nothing seemed to express the fluidity of development in James's complex life.

"It's not something that's stagnant," Wanda expressed to Catherine one evening while the two worked in her garden. Both had inherited their mother's love of gardening. As Catherine fertilized flowers, Wanda deadheaded roses. "It's like the butterfly effect," Wanda motioned with her flower shears. "The slightest flutter from a butterfly, which may seem trivial now, could have a major effect several years down the road. It all depends—"

"But, we're still no closer to an answer on how to depict that," interrupted Catherine while mixing fertilizer in a barrel of rainwater. "I tell you what. No one . . . let alone a jury . . . wants to listen to an essay on development and butterflies."

Catherine's practicality, while a wonderful attribute that Wanda often admired and appreciated, often brought levity to an otherwise austere situation. At the same time, Catherine neither acknowledged her sister's gazes of admiration nor could she fully accept her sister's statements of appreciation.

"I just have to keep hoping for some divine inspiration," Wanda sighed as she reached up and took her hat off, only to replace it as she pondered her next move.

On the sixth floor of the county courthouse, Wanda, with rolled-up, heavy paper nestled under her arm, strode out of the elevator into the public defender's offices that occupied the entire floor. She headed to the conference room where Harrison was waiting for her. As usual, he had a big smile on his face and repeatedly ran his left hand through his hair. "So I'm finally getting to see this LifePath."

Wanda immediately unrolled the twelve-foot-long sheet on the law library conference table, and Harrison secured the ends with books for paperweights. "This is it," she said. "All the significant changes and critical events in his life are illustrated for each stage of his development. We've used different colors, broken lines, boxes with important information, and so on. Along the lower part of the chart, we've identified the Developmental Expectations and the Developmental Stressors during each stage of his life. The expectations are on the bottom left corner here. And the stressors are on the bottom right corner. The jury will be able to see James as a whole person, including the traumas and critical events."

"Like being in and out of the psychiatric hospitals and when his mother died?" Harrison broke in to clarify.

Wanda nodded as she pointed to his early adolescence on the chart. "The purpose is to educate the jury about how James's life circumstances and critical events influenced and impacted his behavior, both during childhood and as a young adult." After a pause, Wanda smiled, "They'll be able to see his life's path and consider mitigating factors."

Harrison smiled at Wanda. "What I really like is the visual display—and the colors. They help to move the eyes along."

Wanda continued, "This is helping me follow his travels as I get to know James and his family, especially between jail visits. I think using the PERT concept really makes it possible to track time and events." After gazing at the chart for a moment, she said in a breathless whisper, "I still have so many questions for him."

Harrison stared at her with one eyebrow hiked. "PERT? What?"

"Oh, program, evaluation, and review technique, or PERT," Wanda explained casually. "It was used by the military to complete the Polaris missile project two years earlier than originally scheduled."

"Hmm . . ." Harrison rocked back on his heels in an exaggerated manner. "Oh, that!"

Wanda quickly added, "It's basically an efficient method for working as a team to accomplish a certain goal. The entire team works together to plan, beginning with the end goal and working backward on a chart to the starting point or initial concept. A critical path of events and tasks is mapped out from beginning to end. Dates are assigned to complete each event or task. The team then identifies who will work on tasks to achieve these events. Every event depends on team members completing their work before the next event can be accomplished. If anyone falls down on the job, it delays progress for all the others and for the project. This approach will keep us on task for his case."

Harrison looked at her quizzically. "And this senior at the Oklahoma School of Science and Mathematics really put you on to the LifePath idea?" After Wanda nodded, he asked, "How so?"

"Ron was a student in the behavioral science class I taught there, and I was his mentor because he was interested in human development and forensics."

"I thought you taught at the medical school?"

"I do. When I learned about this high school for juniors and seniors who wished to pursue advanced studies in mathematics and the sciences, I approached the school's president and offered to teach behavioral science as a visiting professor."

Harrison shook his head in disbelief. "A senior in high school who's interested in forensics? When I was a senior in high school, that's the last thing I was interested in."

Wanda laughed briefly before continuing. "He worked with me on James's case and devised a way to display James's travels across the country—as well as a way to show how he went in and out of psychiatric hospitals."

"What a contribution!" exclaimed Harrison.

"I think maybe this time Ron was the mentor—"

"And you were the student," Harrison interrupted with an even bigger smile than usual.

Wanda's smile was equally as big. "Exactly. I was hoping James's trial would've occurred before Ron graduated, but time continues to pass us by. I must have repeated one hundred times to him how outstanding his idea was."

"Walk me through James's LifePath with what you have so far."

"Along the top, these horizontal lines represent the parent figures and changes in family: when James's parents Lisa and Bruce married, when his brother Luke was born, when James was born, when his parents divorced, Lisa's second marriage to Albert, her death, and Albert's marriage to Amanda. It's all shown with dates and places." Wanda glanced sideways at Harrison, who was busy taking everything in. She carried on, "By the time of James's fifth year, it's obvious his life was impacted by critical events over such a relatively short period of time. His attachment and bonding with his parents, especially with his mother, were all shattered. Before he was four years old, he was already suffering from fears of abandonment and rejection."

"And what about all those IQ tests, mental health service records, and psychiatric hospitalization evaluations I helped you track down during James's grade school and middle school years? Have they been helpful?"

"Those documents you provided, together with my interviews, are giving me what I must have to prepare for testimony in James's case. I've been able to identify patterns . . . recurring behaviors . . . that soon become predictable in James's unfolding development."

"What kinds of patterns?" Harrison asked curiously.

"Ones of intense feelings of loss and loneliness, of running away from his 'fake' parents, running to find a sense of freedom from his own despondency and creating an imaginary world that would allow that freedom to exist so he can search for a home and family." She paused before adding thoughtfully, "What James can't have in reality, he seeks in fantasy."

"Knowin' James came from a middle-class, Caucasian family with a comfortable home, clean sheets to sleep on, and healthy food on a table surrounded by family members with manners—"

She jumped in to finish his sentence. "Makes it easier to see why he's been exhibiting elements of prison psychosis. And even though he felt rejected by his stepparents and inferior to his older brother, he nevertheless had a home." Wanda took a deep breath, then continued, "This LifePath format . . . it's helping me stay on track while talking with James. He likes talking and easily carries on intelligent conversations, but he also gets easily distracted. I have to keep bringing him back to his own history."

Harrison remained silent for a few moments before asking, "While James is telling you 'bout his travels, are you ever thinking: 'Is this for real or did he create this story to keep his sanity while sitting in a hell hole of a cell at the county jail?'"

"I'll give you my take: He's not only articulate but very bright and certainly capable of imagining a world he would like to be in. James reflects a sense of sincerity—whether it's real or not. I have to keep my head on straight to keep from falling into a thinking-trap, wondering if this is just a fantasy or his wishful thinking. He may be psychotic, but it's obvious he's an intelligent and caring person."

Harrison scrunched his eyebrows. "That's a rather confusing statement."

"Actually," Wanda shook her head in disagreement, "psychosis is a break from reality. It has nothing to do with antisocial tendencies." As Harrison sighed, gesturing understanding with his head, Wanda returned her gaze to the LifePath. "I'll just have to keep working on it. I . . . I don't believe in making assumptions. James definitely has some problems. I can see how Attorney Frankfort is having trouble getting any help from him."

"Right now," Harrison heaved, "James is facing the death penalty, and our job as of now is to help get him LWOP."

"Life without parole. I agree."

As they wrapped up their meeting, both recognized the challenge now facing the two colleagues. All the gaps in information would need to be filled in. Every source of information would need to be checked and rechecked. This meant more interviews and cross-checking records—all in preparation to give

James his best day possible in court. Wanda pondered, *What must I do to help the jury see how the confluence of early childhood relationships and experiences influences the unfolding of one's development and how that development impacts adult behavior?*

"What happens if you get some info wrong, and it comes out as an error in court?" a concerned Catherine asked after her sister finished walking her through James's LifePath. The two colleagues were burning the midnight oil inside Wanda's home office.

"That's why I have to get it right," Wanda murmured pensively. "I don't want to get the LifePath thrown out because of an error. It'll make everything else I say questionable, and James won't have a chance at LWOP."

Catherine's voice and body language slowly changed as she approached her sister and asked, "Dr. Draper, is the LifePath your own creation?"

Wanda gave a quick laugh, then remarked, "Oh, so you already have me on the witness stand?"

"Please answer the question, Dr. Draper," she said firmly.

"Yes, it is."

"Did a lawyer help you construct the LifePath?"

Wanda snickered before replying, "You think I'm letting a lawyer help with this?"

"A yes or no, please, Dr. Draper." Catherine held her ground as she continued to play the game.

"No. A lawyer did not help me with this," Wanda responded seriously.

Catherine couldn't hold her stern expression any longer. She cracked up, and Wanda quickly followed suit.

"You would make such a good prosecutor!" Wanda wiped tears from her eyes.

Catherine squared her shoulders, feigning the posture of a gunslinger. "Just call me Cowgirl Cat," she said in a western drawl. The two burst out in a renewed fit of giggles.

A few days later, Wanda and Harrison were in touch again and met at their favorite coffee shop. They didn't even have to place their orders. Their usual waitress automatically brought a hot cup of coffee for Harrison and a hot cup of water with lemon for Wanda. Before Harrison could say anything, Wanda said excitedly to Harrison, "Congratulations on the Packers's win this weekend." Although he always dressed professionally for work, she could just picture him wearing a "Cheesehead" jersey with jeans and sockless loafers—all while having a beer at his favorite sports event.

"I'm glad you could meet," he said urgently. "Got some new info. We need a preliminary report on James. Looks like we'll have a hearing in a few weeks." He paused a moment before happily adding, "It was a great game, wasn't it?"

Wanda returned to the LifePath format and continued to study James's medical records. The more she searched, the more information she found that led her to think James was absolutely not competent to stand trial. While talking with James at their last interview, he gave a lot of history but never connected the murder in any way to his involvement.

Wanda called and asked Harrison if she could talk with James about the incident. She knew that some attorneys didn't want to know if their defendant was guilty or not. But her philosophy was to lay it all out on the table and deal with the facts. Harrison checked with Attorney Frankfort, who gave her the go ahead.

Her next visit to the jail was met with resistance by the jail officer. "We can't let you talk with him. He's out of his mind."

"Tell me what he's doing," Wanda persisted.

"He's talking to himself, urinating on his cell wall, threatening suicide, and screaming a lot."

"I have to see him," she insisted. "He's coming up for a hearing as soon as I can get a report to the attorney."

Wanda was finally led to a contact room where she found James seated at a table but chained to the wall by his right wrist. His hair was dirty, greasy, and longer than when she last saw him. While she had no good reason not to believe the officer's claims about James, he certainly never displayed any of this disruptive behavior in front of her. She didn't doubt that he behaved in that manner when he was by himself. But, when he was told that Wanda was there to see him, he settled down. They chatted a few minutes until she felt he was calm enough to handle some serious talk.

"Why did you leave your family again? You said you left Minneapolis because you wanted to make up with your family and try again to be part of the family."

"I did try. I got more and more excited as I got closer to Lakeside, but I also got scared. I was afraid they'd reject me again. And they did. I just felt it. They didn't want me to stay. So I left again."

Wanda asked James to tell her again about his hitchhiking to Oklahoma City after leaving Virginia. He recounted his story of Bostwick picking him up, taking him to eat at the burger joint, and then taking him to his apartment. Finally, James told about finding him dead the next morning.

"Wait," she said, looking puzzled. "Give me details. Give me something Harrison and I can go on that might clarify your story. Did anyone see you enter the apartment complex?"

As James shook his head from side to side, she thought, *This fits his auditory style.* He continued, "It was dark—'round seven or eight o'clock. We passed through the guard gate, but the security guard knew Bostwick and just waved. I don't think he even saw me. We parked in his place and walked to the apartment. No one saw us that I know of, but . . . but I was really tired. I didn't hear anything or see anyone."

"What did you talk about when you were on the sofa?" she wanted to know.

He shrugged his shoulders. "Not much."

"How'd you feel when he made a pass at you?"

"Like I told you before. Nothing. I just told him, 'I don't do that.' And he stopped. Then I went to the bedroom and fell asleep. He told me what bed to sleep in."

After pausing a moment, Wanda continued, "Tell me again about waking up. Do you know what awakened you or what time it was?"

"I heard sounds, voices, but I thought it was the TV. But, I was really, really sleepy. The only other thing I can remember is hearing two popping sounds."

"Like gunshots?"

"Like opening soda or beer cans. But I kept falling asleep, and finally I just fell back and put the pillow over my face and was gone."

"Tell me exactly what you did and what you saw when you got up in the morning."

"I got up and went to the bathroom. Then, I washed my face, combed my hair, and went into the living room."

"What did you do when you found the man on the floor?"

She sensed some unease with James answering this one.

"James, you know I'm not the investigator. That's Harrison's job. I do have permission, however, to talk with you about the incident. So, please . . . tell me exactly what happened."

James drew a long, deep breath before he replied, "He . . . he was lying on the floor with his knees bent, and his ankles . . . they were tied to the back of his neck. A rag or cup towel was around his neck and a cord was around it. This cord was tied to his ankles. He was wearing a plaid shirt and jeans."

"Were his clothes on? Partly off? Or, were his pants pulled down?"

"No, he was completely dressed. His shirt may have been a little rumpled around the waist. I was too scared. I didn't even want to look at him . . . laying there . . . all tied up."

"In your memory, go back to the night before. Look around the room. Describe anything different than the furniture you saw that night."

"There was a necktie hanging on the door knob in the hall. I didn't pay attention to anything. I was too tired."

She pressed on. "Let's go back to that morning. When you found the man on the floor, why'd you drag him and stuff him in the bedroom closet?"

"I was scared . . . scared they'd find him and think I killed him."

"When you put him in the closet, what did you see? Describe any boxes, shoes, or clothes you remember."

James looked at Wanda with a shy grin of embarrassment. "Yeah, there were, uh, some ladies' dresses hanging there. One had, um, dots in the design—a dark color, I think. And there was a pair of lady's shoes. Also men's shoes and clothes."

"Didn't you think it—"

"Oh, and there were some quilts, too," James added.

"Some quilts," Wanda acknowledged his answer. "Didn't you think it was unusual to see women's clothes in this man's closet?"

"At the time, I just wanted to get outta there. Later, I thought about the dresses and shoes and wondered if he had a lady friend who slept over sometimes. I also wondered . . ."

Wanda could tell he was growing uncomfortable and was anxious to change the subject when he asked, "How was your drive here today?"

She ignored him and tried to get him back on track. "James, what else did you wonder?"

After an excruciating pause, he answered slowly, "I wondered . . . wondered if maybe . . . maybe he dressed up in them."

"Why'd you think that?" she asked curiously.

"Because he tried to come on to me. I think, maybe, he was a . . . a homosexual."

Neither spoke for at least a minute as she tried to figure out how to proceed.

"My drive here today was very nice," she said genuinely.

He smiled that she answered his personal question from earlier.

"Okay, let's go back. What did you do after you put him in the closet?"

"I panicked. I was so scared. I didn't know what to do. I finally took his wallet and car keys and stole his car. I drove west on I-40 until I reached New Mexico. That's where I fell asleep at the wheel and ended up in the median ditch. I ran off and left the car with the keys in the ignition."

"Then what happened?"

"I decided to go west again to California. I hitchhiked all the way to the Santa Monica Pier. I had spent whatever money was in the wallet, so I dropped it in a trash barrel."

Although Wanda knew everything that James was telling her would end tragically, she still hoped for a "happy ending" to his story as she asked the next question. "How did you survive? Did you try to get your job back at the music store?"

"I went back there, but they didn't need anyone. I began to get desperate."

"So, what did you do?"

"I rolled several males in the back seats of cabs." This was exactly what he said he didn't do with Bostwick, whom he would soon be charged with killing. *That's exactly how scared, confused, and desperate he must have been,* Wanda mused.

"Did you stay in California for long?"

He shook his head. "I hitchhiked for three days to Minneapolis, wishing I was dead the entire time." *I can't even imagine,* she thought.

"Did you make your way to Molly's?" She smiled as she asked this question, knowing he had fond memories of Molly and her family.

This time he nodded his head. "And she took me in. I slept the entire day, then had a hot bath. They washed my clothes. Boy, they were sure filthy. I joined Molly for hot coffee, eggs, and bacon. She quizzed me about leaving like I did the last time."

"Did you tell Molly about what had happened to you?"

"My conscience was killing me. So, I told Molly about my ordeal in Oklahoma City, New Mexico, and Santa Monica. She begged me to go to the police, but I was afraid they'd think I killed Bostwick in his apartment. She looked at me optimistically and said, 'James, the truth, it'll set you free. I'll stand by you no matter what.'" He paused, staring at some invisible object. Wanda, recognizing the familiar behavior, tried to bring him back to reality.

"James, before I forget. Do you remember Molly's phone number? I need to talk with her."

He seemed pleased that Wanda would call her and recited the number.

"So, go ahead. I didn't mean to interrupt you."

"I told Molly I'd go to the local police and tell them what happened. But, on my way, I saw a phone booth. I called the police and without giving my name told them I knew where a dead man was in Oklahoma City. The police talked me into giving my name and where I was staying in the Twin Cities area. By the time I returned to Molly's, the police were at her door to take me in for questioning."

"What happened when you arrived at the station?"

"They cuffed me and told me I was a suspect for the Oklahoma City murder. They had contacted Oklahoma City authorities to verify the dead man in the apartment. I refused to make a statement, except to claim my innocence."

"Did they question and interrogate you immediately after being brought in?"

"Immediately—and for several hours. I finally agreed to tell them anything they wanted me to say if they'd bring Molly to be with me so I could hold her hand while I talked. They wouldn't agree to my request." His voice slowly trailed off.

"And what happened next?"

James drew a sharp breath before answering. "Finally, I couldn't take it anymore. I said I'd confess to anything if they'd let me see Molly. In a couple of hours, the detective brought her in. She sat holding my hand. They told me she could stay with me for a while after the questioning. They kept pushing me, and finally I said I did the killing. Molly was quickly escorted out of the police station, and I was placed in police custody for a long ride back to Oklahoma City."

Wanda's interview with James was interrupted at this point when a guard entered the contact room saying her time was up. Attorney Frankfort had arrived to talk with James.

She then called Harrison to report in about her contact visit. He told her that James's account matched what happened at the Minneapolis Police Station. But, after arriving in the Oklahoma City jail, James claimed and continued to maintain he was innocent and stated that the only reason he confessed was that he was desperate to see Molly and was exhausted from hours of interrogation. He said he had read enough in the newspapers to give an account to the police when questioned. He said they asked a lot of leading questions, and he just responded to suit them.

"What in the Sam Hill is 'rolled several males'?" Catherine blurted out as Wanda reviewed her last interview with James. "Had sex with them. Prostituted himself," she clarified matter-of-factly. *Like I am an expert on the subject!* Wanda thought.

A strange look crossed Catherine's face. "You really get around."

Wanda smiled at her sister's teasing remark, responding, "Remember, I've been teaching human development for years to doctors studying psychiatry. Our seminars cover lots of territory."

Suddenly, Catherine's expression changed to that of shock as a thought struck her. "Does James have a problem with his sexual identity? Is he gay?"

Wanda explained the situation to her ever-inquisitive sister. "James wasn't gay. He enjoyed relationships with girls. That behavior was for a few days in California when he was desperate to earn enough money to begin traveling again to Minneapolis to be with Molly and her gracious family. All my interviews with James and his various family members indicate he didn't have a sexual identity problem."

Her sister paused, her mind moving on to another thought. She made a tsking sound, shaking her head disapprovingly. "It's awful the way the police interrogated James."

"It upsets me greatly whenever I hear a defendant is interrogated for hours immediately upon being brought into the police station." Wanda agreed with her sister. "Even though James's case is different because it's been days since Oklahoma City, I still believe that questioning for hours immediately after they brought him in put a lot of stress on him and interfered with his ability to think clearly and talk rationally."

"How do you think police interrogation should be done?"

"In most cases, it's my firm belief that the police should wait twenty-four hours before questioning a suspect, but I don't think they ever do. A suspect's mind is filled with so many jumbled, chaotic thoughts upon being brought in for questioning that he is usually unable to respond in any coherent way. The mind needs to have the pressure released—not increased—if the rational brain is to recall and talk with accuracy."

"So we're actually further away from the truth than we think," Catherine surmised.

As the time approached for the hearing, Wanda realized that James was progressively deteriorating. She couldn't get over how pale and disheveled he looked. James appeared to have aged beyond his youthful years, with a gaunt face, eyes descending into dark, pit-like recesses, and hair hanging in stringy strands. However, Wanda was more alarmed by his mental state. He obsessed over two questions: "Why can't I see Molly? Why don't the authorities believe me?" Wanda watched him become more and more emotionally and psychologically unstable. She wondered seriously if he was, indeed, competent to stand trial.

A psychiatrist for the state had initially been called to evaluate James's competency. Her results indicated that he was competent to assist in his own defense. *Ha! I've heard that state psychiatrists always say they're competent!*

Wanda argued that James was rapidly deteriorating. "He needs rehabilitation before continuing, Mr. Frankfort," Wanda expressed her concern to James's attorney. This attorney, who was able to get along with the prosecutors, DA, the judges, as well as with his own colleagues in the public defender division, took Wanda's concern to the judge. The judge agreed to a competency hearing.

Wanda worked several hours preparing her recommendation, taking additional care to cite specific reasons. She wanted to be well-equipped with facts and documentation for her first experience to stand before a judge and declare the need for institutional treatment. Wanda was especially aware of the risk facing her by taking a stand for James's lack of competency.

As she stood before the judge, Wanda was prepared to state her rationale. She was eager to articulate the specific reasons for recommending that James be admitted to the state forensic hospital in order to regain competency. Upon being sworn in, the judge asked her to tell him about James.

"Your Honor, I have met with James Fields several times over the past eight months. After interviewing and observing him for no less than a total of twelve hours, in addition to studying records of both his jail behavior and his personal history prior to his arrest, I am confident that he needs professional observation and treatment. He is currently emotionally and psychologically unstable and will require psychiatric rehabilitation in order to restore his mental capacity to assist in his defense."

"Have you performed any standardized testing on Mr. Fields?" the judge inquired.

"No, Your Honor, I have not. My evaluation is developmental, based on his overall conduct and his perception of reality while waiting to stand trial. While James Fields presents himself in our interviews as a kind and genuine young adult, he is unable to understand the severity and the magnitude of being on trial for his alleged crime and for his life. His jail behavior manifests character flaws that prevent him from exercising self-control and emotional stability. For example, he cries, screams, wails, and makes such statements as, 'My parents will be here soon to take me home,' and 'I just want to go home.' He urinates on his cell wall while chanting unintelligible phrases. He is unable to cope with isolation and has exhibited intentions of suicide."

"But you say he is kind and genuine in your visits with him? Are you certain he is not malingering?" *The judge just asked the major question in this hearing.* Wanda pondered: *Is James malingering or not? Is he feigning mental illness to avoid going to trial?*

"I am certain. Each time I meet with him, it takes several minutes for him to settle and be calm enough to carry on meaningful conversations. There have been times when, in the midst of our visit, he appears to be hallucinating . . . focusing on an invisible object or person in the hallway beyond the viewing window of our contact room. But, he is able, gradually, to work with me and focus for short periods of time. I continually have to bring him back to the topic in order to continue. He has never complained about his situation, his health, or treatment by the jailers. I am confident he would be unable, at this time, to focus on court proceedings. Although he is an intelligent person, he is unable to grasp the concept of what it means to go to trial."

Silence dominated the courtroom for several moments before the judge finally spoke. "Let's take a short recess, and I'll return with my decision."

Attorney Frankfort and Wanda gave each other sidelong glances, wondering what the outcome of the hearing would hold for James.

The judge returned in ten minutes and took his place at the bench. He ordered James committed to the state forensic hospital until he could be declared competent to stand trial.

The hospital, located in a rural area of eastern Oklahoma, was an awesome-looking place. An old brick building that looked like a school but with barbed wire encircling it performed the role of the state forensic hospital. *Such a dreary place is supposed to restore mental capacities?* Wanda remarked to herself. She did not know what to expect on her first visit to a forensic hospital. Yet, the stark grounds and foreboding entrance still surprised her. When she walked in, the interiors weren't any better. In fact, they were worse. All of the walls were beige. There wasn't even a flower or plant to break up the monochromatic color scheme. It was an incarceration setting filled with nurses, psychiatrists, psychologists, and medical doctors.

James seemed glad to see Wanda, expressing appreciation for her coming to visit him. But, he believed he'd never get out, since the doctors there were too busy to spend much time with him. Wanda left there feeling somewhat sad. It was a five-hour drive home, so she had a lot of time to think about James, his family, and the confinement he faced.

A couple of weeks after visiting James, a call came in from Harrison. "We just had a call from the hospital in Vinita. James ran off."

"I'm not surprised. Unfortunately, I can't predict future behavior, which is why I didn't warn the staff and why I didn't warn James against doing something that would hurt his case."

Harrison replied in a sympathetic tone, "I understand."

"This just shows more of his running pattern," she observed. "Tell me about it."

"Well, he found some gardening gloves to protect his hands and put on two layers of clothes so he could climb over the barbed wire security fence. But, he didn't go far. They found him lying in a field of grain about twenty-five feet beyond the fence. When the security guards found him, he said, 'I just wanted to be free for a while. I'm ready to go back.'"

"So, was there a special punishment?" Wanda asked inquiringly.

"No," he noted. "They reported he had been behaving very strangely for several days."

"I had a letter from him last week. He said he was turning into a lizard and had been drinking his own urine. He scaled that fence to get out long enough to save his sanity. It'll happen again," she replied with certainty.

A few weeks later, after receiving a couple more letters, Wanda began to see a drastic change in James's verbiage and his handwriting. She asked Attorney Frankfort if he had any correspondence in James's file. He showed her two letters. She compared four letters of correspondence. Each was distinctly different. One read like cockney: "I din't even have a dime to use the tele." Another was more like gibberish. *Is this feigning, and if so, what is the reason?* But over time, his letters became more coherent, showing marked improvement. He was reading the Bible and began reflecting an interest in the spiritual dimension. Reports from the doctors were more favorable for James's competency to stand trial.

Frankfort told Wanda during one of their discussions that he thought James's improvement could be attributed to several factors. "I think one in particular is his grandmother, Matilda. Her religious convictions and the encouragement in her letters seem to give him hope. And your letter writing most likely helped him get back on the sanity track."

Wanda replied, "In the more recent letters, he's been able to focus on some of his activities and routine at the hospital. He's also answering each letter from Matilda and me in a coherent fashion and a timely way."

"His grandmother seems to be a key to his well-being."

"Yes, she is. I've talked with her by phone, and she's agreed to send me copies of James's letters."

After another six months, James was returned to the Oklahoma City jail to await trial. The jail system had him placed in solitary because he was going to stand trial for murder and was assumed to be dangerous to himself and others. Wanda could see that if he had to wait a long period of time he would revert to prison psychosis.

After much discussion with Harrison, Wanda requested a sodium amatol examination to get at the validity of James's story. Frankfort agreed, and the judge approved. Wanda called Dr. Ryan Hudson, a highly regarded psychiatrist at the VA hospital and a specialist in administering truth serum. Wanda developed a list of 120 questions for use during the examination.

After making the request for his help, Dr. Hudson agreed to work with them. "Let me know when everything's set up. I assume this'll take place at St. Anthony's Hospital?"

"Yes. And I really appreciate your helping us," Wanda thanked him profusely. "It'll be a pleasure working with you."

Harrison soon set up a video camera in the designated room at St. Anthony's. Dr. Hudson was on his way, and all was ready. Wanda was to arrive at the hospital for this event and be in the room when James arrived. After entering the hospital lobby, she heard her name being paged. Upon inquiring at the reception window, she was handed a desk phone. Harrison was on the line. "Guess it's all off. Six guards can't remove James from his isolation cell."

With urgency in her voice, Wanda said, "I'll be there in fifteen."

Chapter 4

On Wanda's way to the jail, a red traffic light stopped her progress along with the other job commuters. Standing on the side of the road was a tall, lean, disheveled man. He was the typical, just-need-a-helping-hand-to-get-on-my-feet veteran of a hard life. In dirty, oversized clothes, he gestured with his tobacco-stained fingers to his HOMELESS—PLEASE HELP cardboard sign.

As Wanda observed the man, a distant voice from her past echoed in her mind. She was suddenly five years old again and waiting with her mother in their truck while her father was in the store. Wanda stood on the seat to peer out the window and observe people ambling by. She saw an old beggar—now called a homeless person—on the sidewalk and began to cry meekly with tears streaming down her face. Her mother, concerned that she was ill, asked in her Slavic-accented English, "Why are you crying? What's wrong? Are you sick?"

"No. Look at that old beggar," replied a heartbroken Wanda. "It's so sad." The little girl wiped her wet face with her sleeve and continued, "I—"

"Stop," ordered her mother gently but firmly. "You can't take on another person's burdens. We don't know his situation and what led to it. When you feel sorry for someone, you rob him of his responsibility—you might make him weaker." She took a handkerchief that she had embroidered with tiny pink flowers out of her purse and wiped her daughter's tears away.

Wanda was abruptly brought back to the present by the green light. Her mother's lesson of taking on others' burdens taught her that to pity others strips their dignity and renders them helpless. *But there is a difference between taking on others' burdens and helping others to carry their burdens*, she told herself.

A crutch under each arm, Wanda hobbled her way down the somber passages of the old jail. She easily found her way to James's cell, past the cells of other inmates. Her nose never reacted to the unmitigated body odor as she walked the hallways of confined housing for those who had become wards of the state. Nor did her eyes turn away in embarrassment or disgust at the sight of depravity or the onslaught of foul language. She projected the apathetic expert.

Wanda arrived to find six guards standing by the door to James's cell. They glared at this woman on crutches and dressed in a skirted suit. One of the guards stepped forward, regarding her as a helpless woman who shouldn't be in a jail on crutches. "He'll never come out on his own. We tried to drag him out, but he went nuts."

Another guard, distracted, pointed at her crutches. "What happened to you?"

She raised one crutch slightly. "Broke my hip a few months ago."

"Where'd you do that?" another asked, clearly interested out of friendly concern.

"Over at the clinic on my way to make a presentation in the doctors' conference room. I stepped from a carpeted hallway into a room with a highly polished parquet wood floor. The rest is history." As the guards winced, she asked, "Now what about James? He's scheduled for a sodium amatol today over at St. Anthony's Hospital."

Before anyone could say anything, Wanda glanced in his cell to see that James had gone catatonic, curled up naked and covered by a blanket, on his cement bed that was imbedded in the wall. They had taken away his clothes several days earlier because they were concerned about suicide. She remained expressionless as she addressed the guards, "Step back, please. I'm going in." The guards at first tried to protest, but Wanda's determined advance towards the doorway convinced them to step aside.

Venturing into these dark places, darkened even more by perpetual callousness and lack of compassion, Wanda leaned on spiritual protection to sustain her.

While the silence of her confidence was often mistaken for detached authority, she was, in reality, the mindful—and sensitive—professional. The light bulb had been removed a couple of weeks earlier. It was part of the jail's inmate suicide risk policy. His toothbrush and toilet paper had been removed for his protection as well. As she approached the crumpled figure, this lady in the briar patch of society silently repeated to herself, *Let me do this with least effort, with grace, and in a sacred manner.* This personal mantra had sustained her spirit throughout many of her life's challenges.

She spoke to him as though he was a little boy: "James, it's me, Wanda. I've come to see you. I'm on my crutches with a broken hip, but I wanted to see you. If you want to talk with me, just stick your arm out from under the blanket and move one hand up and down. I'll tell them to get your jump suit. Then, you can come out, and we'll go where we can talk."

Soon enough, one hand started waving from beneath the blanket. She asked one of the guards to get his clothes. Then, as she was telling him, "I'll be just outside the door waiting for you," she thought, *Of course he'll come out. What a respite from this dungeon. But, he also knows he's not ready for any kind of examination. He's scared spiritless.*

James eventually emerged from his dreary, foul-smelling cell. They followed one of the six guards down the hall to a contact room where the two sat opposite each other, with an old yellow table between them. Wanda was shocked to see James's deterioration as he sat rocking back and forth, saying repeatedly, almost absently, "My parents are coming to get me. They're taking me home."

They talked for a while without saying much of anything important. During the small talk, Wanda wished she had snuck in a bottle of bleach to disinfect the contact room and quell the smell that not even daily mopping could eradicate. Then she told him, "We still want to do the sodium amatol examination. It's needed to help your case."

He was silent for a few minutes. Finally, he agreed, "Okay, but when?"

She informed him, "We'll wait 'til you feel better." Wanda wanted to bring James back to some semblance of reality from the ordeal he endured in his cell, so she asked, "Do you know why they took out your light bulb and took away your tooth brush and toilet paper?"

He continued to rock back and forth but only slightly. "I don't think they like me."

"Why do you think that?"

"Because they want to punish me."

"Are they concerned you might hurt yourself?"

James stopped rocking. "They said I, well, I needed to stop yelling. Then they told me that when I settled down, they'd give me the toilet paper."

She paused before asking calmly, "Why were you yelling?"

His expression was blank as he declared, "I just want to go home."

"Have you written to your grandmothers lately? Matilda or Nan?"

"No, I . . . I can't concentrate."

"James, you need to start writing again. I've told you before that you're an excellent writer. Both of your grandmothers really look forward to your letters, and they always answer back. That will help you begin to focus again. And start your exercises, too. You had been doing them, and you told me that exercising made you feel better. I'll come back to see you in a couple of days."

"I'm so sorry I've caused so much trouble."

"Stop the trouble and start on a new path. You can do better. I know you can."

———

Two weeks later, James was doing better. Arrangements with St. Anthony's Hospital were re-established, this time at eleven o'clock in the morning. Harrison once again set up the video camera in the designated room. Wanda arrived, this time carrying her briefcase, followed by Dr. Hudson, and then James was brought in. Still dressed in his bright orange jumpsuit—a clean one—he climbed into the bed like he was a little boy. Dr. Hudson, with a voice like a broadcast anchorman, spoke firmly, yet gently, telling James what to expect and reassuring him of his safety. He administered the 'truth' serum, and James was soon in a state of complete cooperation. Wanda drew the 120 questions she had prepared out of her briefcase. They covered his travels to California, Minneapolis, Virginia, Oklahoma City, and to Bostwick's apartment. Harrison worked the camera while Wanda asked the questions.

At one o'clock, they finished the interview. Dr. Hudson brought James out of the sedation. As he became alert, Wanda's heartstrings were pulled when James uttered, "Did I say any bad words or wet the bed?"

Dr. Hudson then smiled and said, "This was one of the best I've administered in over twenty years working in the VA!"

Wanda and Harrison expressed appreciation to Dr. Hudson as he hurried off to his daily routine at the VA. "Let me know how the case goes," he said as he quickly departed.

While eager to talk about the interview as soon as they left the hospital room, Harrison and Wanda maintained their silence. They agreed to meet at the public defender's office at four in the afternoon to discuss their findings and their next step.

Wanda was relieved to have a break. *I'm exhausted. It took a lot of energy to focus on all those questions. I just hope it pays off.* She walked towards the exit, her stomach reminding her that it was past time to refuel.

"So, what did you think of the amatol test?" Wanda was eager to review. She and Harrison were seated at one end of the huge table that dominated the conference room in the public defender's office.

"Impressed. Dr. Hudson knows his business. I think the test was certainly valid."

"James's story was consistent with the information previously gleaned from him over the months of interviews. He also gave more details about prostituting himself while in Santa Monica. I think the amatol will be very helpful for his case."

Harrison agreed, nodding his head. They decided to visit James the following week to again verify his story.

James was already in the contact room when Wanda and Harrison arrived.

Wanda spoke first. "How are you feeling now that the examination is over and you've had some time to think about it?"

Somewhat perplexed, James responded, "I don't remember what I said during the test."

Then, Harrison stated, "We know everything you said. It's recorded on video. Now we need to hear your account of what happened. That way, we'll be able to verify your memory of what happened with what you said during the examination."

Wanda began by asking questions in a random fashion. She skipped around both in time and circumstances, but her focus was mainly on what happened in

Bostwick's apartment and what happened on James's second trip to California. James's responses were clearly authentic. They matched what he said in the sodium amatol examination and what he told Wanda during their many hours of interviews. When the two professionals left the jail, they felt secure about being on the right track.

Wanda and Harrison were both eager to meet with Attorney Frankfort, confident they had documented the data they needed to prepare to go to trial. While Frankfort acknowledged the accuracy of the examination, he shocked Wanda and Harrison with his next comment. "I've decided not to use the evidence from the sodium amatol in court."

Astonished and disappointed, Wanda stated, "But we've corroborated the facts of the case. James is telling the truth."

Frankfort replied, "Yes. That's precisely why I won't use it." He saw the looks on the faces of both his investigator and expert. He continued, "James made reference to male prostitution behavior. That won't set well with a jury."

Although this was her first big case, Wanda couldn't remain silent. "Why don't we deal with what we have and take our chances? It may help rather than hurt when the jury sees this in relation to the whole scheme of things."

Frankfort, in a low-key but authoritative manner, stated his position, "We won't take it into court. You still have a strong case for mitigation."

Wanda ceased all protest. The lawyer took her silence for acquiescence. She still didn't agree with him, yet she understood that she had to respect his decision. She left the meeting eager to talk to Catherine.

"What?" Catherine nearly yelled into the phone. Wanda had to position the receiver farther from her ear. Wanda had called Catherine that very evening as soon as she got home from work. Catherine was living in what she referred to as her little bungalow only a few blocks from Wanda.

"That's what he said," Wanda reiterated. "He thought that information would turn the jury against James."

"But, it corroborates everything! It proves that he's not a killer." Catherine took a breath. Wanda got ready for the storm. "It proves that he's telling the truth. I would think that a jury would want to know that." Catherine continued to vehemently express her disapproval with the attorney's strategy. *It would have been interesting to have Catherine in on the meeting.* Wanda smiled at the thought of that scenario.

"That's what I argued," Wanda further agreed with her sister-colleague. "He wouldn't listen. He made his decision—end of discussion."

"Wow . . . I guess he put you in your place," Catherine said in a lower voice, her frustration spent at the moment. "I bet he didn't listen because you're not a lawyer."

Wanda could only agree, *Yes, I've just been put in my place. I clearly don't call the shots.*

James remained in the Oklahoma City jail, awaiting a trial date. He was still contained in a solitary cell with no light, no toilet paper, and no toothbrush. Just as Wanda expected, he lost his sanity again.

The judge agreed with her in another hearing that James needed to return to the forensics hospital in eastern Oklahoma. As she and Harrison left the courtroom, she turned to him and said, "I think because the judge is familiar with the archaic jail policies and the condition of the solitary cell, he took pity on James. So, back he goes. At least James knows the living situation at the hospital. He'll be safe there. Perhaps over time he'll get stronger."

Wanda was soon granted a month sabbatical from the Department of Psychiatry to travel to Hong Kong and Singapore to conduct seminars and workshops for graduate students and professionals. This was another opportunity to share her work in human development and what a powerful impact the first several years of life have on an individual's personality and behavior. She was thoroughly impressed with the enthusiasm of the participants in all the groups with which she worked.

On her first day back to work from her long trip, her office phone interrupted her while she was preparing for a morning seminar with her third year psychiatry residents.

"Harrison, good to hear from you. What's going on? You sound exasperated."

"James. He's escaped from the hospital at Vinita."

"What? How this time?" she asked, only mildly surprised.

"Strange, strange."

"Oh, I'm ready. What happened?" *And the James saga continues,* Wanda told herself.

"First, I need to tell you he's in the health sciences area. They think he's trying to find you. So, be on guard for calls from the authorities."

"How'd he get here—all the way across the state?" she was dying to know.

"He was being transported to University Hospital for dental surgery. They departed Vinita at four in the morning in order to get him to a nine o'clock appointment. When they slowed to round a corner, just about three blocks from your office, he jumped out of the van and vanished." *His history and pattern of running again,* Wanda noted to herself.

———

"But, how did he get free in that van?" Catherine asked, puzzled. Wanda had called Catherine to alert her to the new development as soon as she got off the phone with Harrison.

"That's a good question," Wanda replied. *I sure would like to know.* The sisters hung up, Wanda promising to keep Catherine posted on any new developments.

———

Later that afternoon, Harrison called Wanda again. "Around noon, James was spotted wearing a pair of civilian walking shorts and a t-shirt. He was walking down a sidewalk in the neighborhood where you live."

"That's just a few blocks from the health science center where I work."

"Yes. The city police were patrolling for an escapee, expecting him to be dressed in inmate clothes. They stopped James to ask if he had seen anyone who fit the description. He said he hadn't. Then they inquired about his identity and where he was headed. He said he was looking for his brother's house in the neighborhood."

"So, what happened then?"

"James was exhibiting nervous behavior that caused suspicion. The cops asked him to sit in the back seat of the patrol car so they could ask him a few more questions. He complied. By the time he sat down, several patrol cars surrounded the police vehicle. James immediately confessed to escaping from the van, although they didn't ask him how. And, he didn't volunteer to elaborate."

"Will they take him to jail here? Or back to Vinita?" *Questions, questions, questions,* Wanda remarked to herself.

"I'll let you know as soon as I learn what's happening." Harrison signed off.

Wanda returned the receiver to its cradle only to pick it up again. She dialed Catherine. It rang several times before a breathless Catherine answered the phone.

"You're out of breath. What were you doing?"

"I just got back from outside. Did you hear any more about James? Did they find him?"

"Yes, they just did. I'll go over it with you over dinner tonight." Wanda's curiosity perked and made her ask, "What were you doing outside running around at this time of day?"

Catherine paused briefly. "I was looking for James. I wanted to see him." Wanda shook her head at her sister. *She'll never cease to surprise me.*

When Wanda received word that James was on his way back to the institution, she called and asked his case worker to allow him to call her, which he did very quickly.

"James, how'd you manage to have on civilian clothes?" she hastily asked.

"I hid in the rafters of a building and waited and watched renovation workers leaving on their lunch break."

"In one of the health science buildings?"

"Right. I stripped off my inmate suit, dumped it in a construction trash barrel, and climbed back into the ceiling rafters," he divulged. "I had put on the civilian clothes before I left the hospital."

Wanda then queried as to how he escaped from the van.

"I unlocked the ankle manacles while we were en route. It was still dark. And the driver and attendant in the front couldn't see what I was doing."

"How were you able to unlock the manacles?" she persisted.

There was silence on the other end of the phone. Finally, he said, barely above a whisper, "Um, I can't tell you that. On the phone. I, uh . . . I might get people in trouble."

She didn't press it. "Why'd you try to escape? You knew you'd eventually get caught, right?"

"I just wanted to feel free for a while. I didn't mean any harm." *How familiar is that behavior?* Wanda asked herself. *James is still running, still trying to be free.*

During the week after James returned to the hospital at Vinita, Wanda called and asked to speak with him again. This wasn't customary, but they knew she had worked on his case.

She was still itching to know the answer to one question. "James, please tell me. How'd you get your ankle shackles off and jump out of that van?"

This time, he was more forthcoming. "The people here believe I'm not crazy. That I shouldn't be here. They gave me a key, told me to get loose, get out, keep going."

Wanda sighed and said resignedly, "Where did you think you'd go? What would you do?"

"I just wanted to be free. It was wrong. I knew it as soon as the cops picked me up. But, I shouldn't be here."

After a couple of months, Wanda visited James at the hospital. While there, she talked with his attending physician who assured her that James was showing marked improvement and would be ready to stand trial in a few more months.

During the next month, Wanda made a visit to Bryan, Texas, to visit James's maternal grandmother, Matilda. She told Wanda more details about the sudden death of James's mother, Lisa, and how she thought it made a serious and detrimental impact on James's development. *What a sense of loss for such a young child—broken bonding and fear of abandonment.* Matilda also shared the many letters James had written her. All of them, without exception, were filled with kind words and gratitude to her for standing by him. Matilda offered to send Wanda copies of all the letters as she received them from James.

James's paternal grandmother, Nan, the mother of James's biological father, Bruce Balzo, lived in Rhode Island just a short distance from her son. Wanda and Nan spoke from time to time by phone, and she provided additional family history as Wanda prepared for trial. Nan affirmed that Bruce was so damaged by drugs as a Vietnam Veteran that he would never be able to help James.

When Wanda spoke with Bruce by phone, he was able to confirm the collateral information that she had secured from James and Matilda. He expressed appreciation for her assistance and stated that he wished he were in better health so he could help.

Wanda also spoke with James's older brother, Luke. He said he was sorry he couldn't be more helpful, except to say that Albert and Amanda favored him over James because James was such a difficult child. He also said that James was never mean to him or other children. He loved animals. He never set any fires. He never told lies. Even though Luke spoke well of James, he felt that James had betrayed his family by running away after being released from the psychiatric hospital when he was a teenager. Luke said he had separated himself from James and so had his parents. Wanda thought after that phone conversation, *He's given me a lot more information than he realizes.*

She next talked by phone with James's stepmother, Amanda, who gave the impression of wanting James to "take his medicine" for his sins. Albert spoke only briefly with her. *Evidently our first telephone conversation had been enough for him,* Wanda thought.

"Will you come to James's trial?" Wanda asked, already knowing the answer.

"No," Amanda and Albert said simultaneously. Amanda then explained further, "It'd be too expensive. And, we can't be gone from work that long."

Albert added, "We won't testify on James's behalf. There's no hope for his future. Plus, he's not our biological son." As Albert was telling Wanda this, all she could think of was Albert grabbing James when he was a little boy and banging his head against the wooden arm of the living room sofa.

Wanda's impression was that they saw James as the one who contaminated their family name and reputation. The farther away he was, the better. Although they were religious and committed to their faith, she saw no element of forgiveness or compassion in their behavior toward him.

James, on the other hand, wrote several letters to Amanda and Albert, apologizing for the problems he caused them, never in any letter blaming them for his misfortune. James's stepmother was willing to send copies of his letters to Wanda; this would help to build her arsenal of information.

Wanda surmised that she didn't need a sodium amatol to tell her why James was in such deep trouble. As she worked to consolidate information from her phone interviews, her memory was struck by the Biblical phrase, "the sins of the fathers."

Chapter 5

After James was declared competent to stand trial, a date was set by the court. Wanda and Catherine sat at Wanda's dining room table, enjoying hot kolaches fresh out of the oven and coffee. The two were preparing for the upcoming trial by reviewing Oklahoma's requirements for death-deserving circumstances.

"I printed out my research results," Catherine explained as she took a stack of papers from a folder. "It says here that in Oklahoma, to be considered for capital punishment, the defendant has to be charged with at least two aggravating circumstances. So, what does that mean?"

"Those are actions that are especially heinous, atrocious, cruel, or torturous," Wanda clarified.

Catherine didn't take her eyes off the printed material as her voice rose in emphasis. "Says it can also be a situation in which a defendant commits a crime to prevent arrest or to conceal the commission of a crime. How do they even decide what is 'especially heinous, atrocious, cruel or torturous'? To be killed sounds like all of the above to me."

"These aren't limited to the event," explained Wanda. "An aggravated circumstance can also be a situation in which the defendant knowingly creates a great risk of death for one or more people in addition to the victim." Wanda added as an afterthought, "The prosecutors take all the events into consideration and then decide if the circumstances warrant seeking the death penalty."

Catherine nodded her understanding, then returned to her research. "Oh, listen to this. Every state has its own set of aggravators. Oklahoma currently has eleven, Missouri nineteen, Idaho twelve, and Texas ten. Guess Texas isn't always the biggest and the baddest, huh?"

Wanda laughed. The solemnity's hold was broken. "But, in this case, I don't mind."

———

James's Grandmother Matilda and her brother Roy arrived in Oklahoma City a couple of days before the trial opened. Wanda made arrangements to talk with them over dinner in a nearby restaurant to clarify a few facts of family history.

During their initial small talk, Roy asked, "Wanda, where're you originally from—before comin' to Oklahoma City?"

"A small town at the very tip of Texas. You've probably never heard of it," she shrugged. "Most people haven't."

"Try us," Matilda dared her.

"It was a town of about three hundred back then. It's a little more now, I think." Wanda told them the name of her hometown and explained briefly about the little community she and her family moved to when she was ten that was closer to the coast. She waited, expecting blank glances to confirm that they had never heard of her hometown and birthplace.

Matilda's eyes widened in astonishment. Roy spit the ice cube he was sucking on into his water glass. "You're kiddin' me! I'm . . . we're from there, too!" Matilda told her she was from the neighboring town.

Wanda's jaw dropped open. "Boy, this really is a small world. Hard to believe we lived so close and never met each other. Our hometowns weren't that big!"

Matilda chimed in, "Ain't that the truth!"

Roy added, "I married a girl from your community. Perhaps you know her."

"Who was . . . sorry . . . who is she?"

"Karen Strong," he announced.

At that moment, Wanda's hand slapped her forehead. She was flabbergasted. "Am. I. On. Candid. Camera? KAREN STRONG?"

"She and I've been married forty-five years," Roy explained.

"We . . . she . . . she and I used to go to choir practice together. Every Wednesday night. For, I don't know . . . four or five years."

"Unbelievable," Roy acknowledged.

"She'd pick me up in her old Ford Model T and after practice we'd go to the drive-ins where we knew the carhops. We'd have soft drinks or milk shakes before heading home where, you know, we lived in the same neighbor . . . Well, you wouldn't know that, would you?" Wanda remarked, talking a mile a minute with excitement.

He shook his head, smiling.

"Karen Strong," Wanda repeated in astonishment. "Our families went to the same church. As kids, we went to the same country school . . . And, well . . . how . . . how's her brother . . . How's Sandy?"

"He's great. Married to a really nice woman who—"

"Looks like Liz Taylor," Matilda finished his sentence.

Roy then offered, "They have three children, two sons and a daughter. The boys run the family farm along with Sandy—big operation, several thousand acres. And their daughter's a professor at the university there."

When Wanda, Matilda, and Roy finally ended their visit, they did so as long-lost friends. The unknown relationship between their families forged a meaningful connection. Wanda, still astonished by this unusual coincidence, could hardly fathom this twist in life. A part of her past was thrust into her present. *All these months working on this case, and I had no idea that we had this remote connection . . . Is this all some sort of strange synchronicity?*

Wanda carried her musings with her as she pulled out onto the highway. Her car was directed towards home, but her mind was returning to the past. Memories of her youth and teenage years came flooding back to her at the mention of Karen and Sandy.

Chapter 6

Living and working only about fifteen minutes from the courthouse, Wanda was on call to testify in James's case. She began to feel anticipatory anxiety even though only the first stage of the trial had begun that day. She was uncertain when she would be called. The attorney told her that it could be a few days or even a week later. It was contingent on how long it would take to select the jury and then after the guilt/innocence stage to reach a verdict. It all depended on the jury.

I need to speak not only to the minds but also to the hearts of the jurors, mused Wanda as she walked to the children's center. She chose to walk from a distant parking lot, hoping for a little exercise and a moment to enjoy the fresh air. Though the course of James's life was being decided only a few blocks away, life for everyone else, including Wanda, continued. Yet, she was keenly aware of her commitment and responsibility to James and his case. Wanda's concern was centered on forging a strong communication with the jury. Her experiences consulting and working with a variety of groups and individuals gave her the insight that people often make judgments based on arbitrary details and personal feelings. She believed juries were no different. She also recognized that while many aspects of James's life would be presented, a jury could convict him based on only one segment of the whole picture.

While Wanda waited to be called to the court, she couldn't help but reflect on her own thoughts—pre- and post-court work—about the death penalty. Before she started working on capital trial cases, Wanda had often turned on the television and heard a news story about an alleged killer and immediately thought that the accused was guilty, without really knowing anything about the case. But back then, the death penalty wasn't a concern of Wanda's.

Living in a democracy, her position had been that if the people of a state or nation wanted the death penalty as a form of punishment, she had no objection. That was the price of freedom. If that was what the majority wanted, she had to respect that. It wasn't something she really thought about other than when a discussion might come up in a social conversation. It certainly wasn't something she pursued as a special interest. However, things had changed. As someone now confronted with the complexities of the legal system, Wanda increasingly recognized the projection of guilt by society. Before a trial ever begins, the judgment is often already decided and waits only for execution.

Now she concentrated on presenting James as a whole person to the jury, connecting the dots between early childhood development and adult criminal behavior. She contemplated, *Hearing about James and seeing the path his life has taken will not be enough. In this life or death decision, these jurors will have to reach into their souls and into their deeper consciousness as they weigh the evidence that will either catapult James to the ultimate punishment of death or open a door to life within the prison walls, forever closed off from the outside world.* The ringing phone interrupted her thoughts. She answered it.

"No, not yet," Wanda answered her sister's questions about where they were in James's trial process. "I probably won't be called until later—after the jury reaches a decision. Of course, if they find him not guilty, my testimony won't be needed."

There was a brief silence on the phone. Then, Catherine responded with another question, "What are your perceptions of juries?"

Wanda took a moment to respond. "There are many ways to view the actions of a jury, and none are either right or wrong—I would never attempt to anticipate their decision." Wanda looked out her office window. She added, "My notion of what some jurors do during a death penalty case is to subconsciously reach deep within themselves and pull up all their own misdeeds. Then they thrust these inner feelings of guilt upon the accused and send him on to his death. He carries their load with him, and they are absolved of their own unexpressed feelings of shame." Catherine signified her understanding, adding that she would like to continue this conversation later and to keep her posted on the progress of the trial. With that, the sisters hung up.

When she arrived home from teaching doctors and working at the center, Wanda was contentedly exhausted in her role as professor and executive director. Now, like someone slipping into a pair of favorite shoes, she slipped into her role as lady of the house. She changed from her suit into her home attire and went into the kitchen to prepare dinner. She felt good about what she accomplished that day. As the rice simmered, filling the air with its grainy aroma, her mind returned to James. She hadn't heard anything from court. She didn't expect to until Attorney Frankfort could provide a better time frame for calling her to testify. She hoped, however, that she wouldn't be needed because James would be acquitted.

Wanda contemplated her own personal feelings that he was actually innocent of the crime. The task in this case is not to be an advocate, she chastised herself, but to be an objective message-bearer of the facts and circumstances as I discovered them. She then reminded and reassured herself, James's LifePath is the best tool or format in preparing to testify—without any preconceived notion or feeling about his guilt or innocence. Wanda had to be able to step away from that courtroom, knowing that she did everything she could to present a true and just picture of James while maintaining her integrity and respecting her role in the judicial process—presenting facts and circumstances for the jury's consideration as mitigating. Then, his fate would be up to the jury and out of her hands. Anything less on my part will be a burden on my deeper conscience, she pondered. Familiar with the next task, looming like a mountain before her, she asked the bubbling rice, "How did I get myself into this?"

As Wanda reached for the mayonnaise in the refrigerator to make a sauce for the asparagus, she was interrupted by Matilda's call; it was about six o'clock. Right away, she sensed Matilda's confusion and displeasure. "Have you, uh, have you talked with James's attorney, Mr. Frankfort?"

"No, I haven't…I—"

Matilda burst into tears. Wanda's first thought was, *Did James escape from the trial?*

"Matilda . . . Matilda, please tell me what's happened."

She settled enough to sputter, "Mr. Frankfort . . . he said it'd be better . . . better if I talked to you first. He, uh, he . . . thought if he called you, you . . . you'd be quite angry."

By this time, Wanda was in a total fog and trying to get Matilda to proceed with telling her what occurred that day.

She finally blurted out, "Before the jury entered the courtroom, Mr. Frankfort and James were talkin', at the lawyers' table. They were whisperin' for a long—"

Wanda heard talking in the background. It was Roy's voice. He was reminding Matilda of events to tell Wanda. She could hear Matilda tell him, "I know, I know. I won't forget anything."

She continued. "They were whisperin' for a long time. A really long time. When the jury . . . when they were coming in, James nodded to Mr. Frankfort—"

Wanda's olfactory senses suddenly alerted her to something. Oh, no . . . the salmon! "Matilda, hold on a sec. Something's burning."

Racing to the oven, Wanda put on her mitts and hastily removed the fish, then quickly turned off the oven. After turning the oven vent on high and opening the back door to let some fresh air into the room, she returned to the phone and Matilda.

"Matilda, so sorry. Please go on with what you were telling me. You were saying that James nodded to Frankfort—"

"Yes, James seemed really nervous. Mr. Frankfort . . . he approached the bench, and the prosecutor quickly met him there in front of the judge. Then I couldn't hear a thing. After . . . after several minutes of whisperin' with the judge, they returned to their tables. The judge spoke to the jury, asking them to return to the jury room."

"What happened next?" Wanda was eager to know.

Matilda said, seeming confused, "We watched James and Mr. Frankfort approach the judge's bench. James stood there looking lonely, like he might cry."

"And then?" Wanda was beginning to get nervous. *What's going on?* she asked herself.

Matilda replied in a shaky voice, "Frankfort told the judge James agreed to waive his right to a jury trial and take a . . . I think it's a . . . a blind plea . . . Does that sound right?"

"The terminology's right. Go on."

"A blind plea from the judge. The judge then asked James . . . asked him if this is what he wanted to do. James, oh, my God, I can't believe this, he, uh, he said that it was. The judge called for a short recess. When, um, he returned—"

At this point, Wanda's husband Edwin arrived home from work. Wanda placed her hand over the receiver, gave him a light kiss, and mouthed, "Dinner'll be ready soon." Edwin went through the kitchen and upstairs to his study. This was his routine—to relax a while before dinner. Wanda often heard his distinct snores reverberating all the way down to the kitchen.

Wanda apologized to Matilda for the interruption. She continued, "The judge returned from his chambers and asked James to stand. He then sentenced James to straight life and committed him to the forensics hospital at Vinita."

Wanda was completely speechless as Matilda started to cry again. Finally, she mustered the words to ask, "Matilda, are you all right? Will you be all right?"

Disillusioned, she said, "Yes, but I don't know what all this means."

"I'll talk to Frankfort and get back to you," she reassured her.

"Anything you can find out for us would be . . ." she refrained from finishing her sentence. "Roy and I are leavin' for Texas in the mornin'."

The next day, there was still no word from Frankfort or anyone else for that matter. Wanda called his office to schedule an appointment. He genially said to come in anytime. She was there in twenty minutes.

Before she sat down in his office, Frankfort said defensively, "Don't get upset. Let me explain." *I hope you have a good explanation*, Wanda thought.

Frankfort, a gentle man in his late fifties, presented himself in a quiet and unobtrusive manner. Unlike some attorneys that Wanda later worked with on death penalty cases, Frankfort, with a well-trimmed mustache and thinning hair, always had a kind expression on his clean-shaven face. His gentle and settled manner would make it difficult for most people to get angry with him, especially someone like James with his weak self-image and reticent style.

Frankfort summed up what had happened: "In getting ready for trial, it was obvious, obvious James would be unable to adequately assist in his defense. I believed the jury was going to give him the death penalty and the best defense would be for James to take a blind plea and hope for something less than LWOP or, at the worst, the death penalty. When the jury began to file in—"

"James was scared to death. He reluctantly agreed to your plan," Wanda filled in the blanks based on what Matilda had told her.

"Correct," he confirmed.

"I think James still has a lot of issues. But, he also told me many times he wanted his day in court to prove his innocence," she said in a dry and unperturbed tone.

Frankfort replied understandingly, "Reason the judge didn't send James to prison was he thought he'd never be able to get well enough to leave the forensics hospital."

As Wanda departed Frankfort's office, she began to let go of this case. There was nothing more for her to do. She filed away all of the documents, notes, and LifePath. She turned her attention to another case that had come her way in the course of working on James's. She called Matilda and encouraged her and Roy to write to James. "He will need your support in his new life of confinement."

PART TWO

Chapter 1

The old, stolen pickup rumbled down the farm road with Joseph aimlessly driving to nowhere. It was two in the morning, and he was high on drugs he had purchased at a truck stop about seventy-five miles back. When he crossed the state line, Joseph was numb to the world he left behind. The black night offered only the faraway specks of a few stars that danced in and out of his range of vision.

His drugged state then prompted his right hand to turn the truck down a lonely gravel road leading to a farmhouse, illuminated by a security light some fifty feet from the front door. As he turned the truck into the driveway, he reached for the twenty-gauge semi-automatic shotgun on the passenger seat. Fueled by anger and fear, mixed with drug delirium, he moved with the ease of a slithering snake into the bedroom of the old farmhouse.

As he stood in the depth of darkness, the moon suddenly illumined the room. He saw the peaceful family sleeping soundly. His confused mind returned to his own family that had rejected him. Without a rational thought, he pulled the trigger and blew away the life and future of the father and the mother. He then moved into the bedrooms of the son and daughter and ended their lives as well. But the eight-year-old daughter only pretended to be lifeless, as Joseph departed into the darkness from which he came.

The cell started vibrating in Wanda's coat pocket as she waited to board a connecting flight from Phoenix. "This is she," Wanda confirmed while striding toward a deserted gate.

An unfamiliar, business-like voice inquired about her working on a new case. Wanda had to ask the voice to repeat itself. The problem wasn't that her phone had bad reception, but the general airport cacophony made it difficult to hear everything this woman was saying. She understood only about every other word. Still, she was able to fill in the blanks.

"Tell me about it. I just completed one in Phoenix. We—" Her words were interrupted by an announcement for a failed connection. She then finished, "We won, by the way."

"You may be familiar . . . this one." The noise was still overpowering.

"Oh? Who is it?" Wanda's brows furrowed in concentration as she raked her memory bank for any recent major headlines.

"Joseph Allen . . . believe you . . . on his case. In Georgia."

She made out enough words to know what the woman was saying. "But I never had to testify. I was practically packing my bags when I received a call telling me he took the deal offered by the DA. He pled guilty. Took LWOP."

In front of Wanda, plenty of drama was unfolding. A little boy with blond hair and blue eyes ran away from his parents, only to have them catch and reprimand him. Within seconds, he ran away again. *Ah, ambivalent attachment at work,* Wanda thought.

The voice continued to explain the situation to Wanda. However, she recognized that now the technical difficulties were more than just ambient noise interrupting. It was a bad connection. *I'm learning to be a fan of modern technology, but this is too much,* Wanda told herself. "Hold a sec. I'm losing you. Let me try and get a better connection."

She trotted over to the window. Voilà! The connection was perfect. "I can hear you a lot better now. Mind repeating what you just said?"

"Sure. I was saying they want to give Joseph the death penalty again because, after killing that couple in Georgia, he crossed the state line and killed three more." Wanda sighed a deep moan. The woman continued, "Now, he'll stand trial in Florida. Since you've worked up lots of data on him, we'd like your help with this one."

"When do you anticipate going to trial?" she asked, flipping through her new 2008 pocket calendar.

"Not for several months. In fact, the trial's expected to last about six weeks. There'll be 'bout five, six attorneys for the defense. This is a big one."

"Wow! That's unusual for a public defender case." Her eyes widened as she shook her head. *How'd they ever get those kinds of funds?* she asked herself. She knew this was going to cost a small fortune and wondered where the money would come from to pay her on this case.

Wanda's mind quickly returned to the task at hand as she reasoned, *That's not my problem.* Her job involved defending the defendant—not the budget.

"Will you do it?" the woman's voice inquired.

A sober pause followed. "I think I can," Wanda said as her eyes fixed on a kiosk in the terminal loaded with southwestern resort wear, Native American trinkets, and southwest cookbooks, all meant to celebrate the Valley of the Sun. Thinking out loud, she continued, "I have a few other cases, but they don't go to trial for a while yet."

The silence on the phone crackled with expectancy.

"Okay, I'll commit. Send me everything you have. I need to begin putting this together. I take it you want a LifePath?"

"Absolutely. It's one reason why we want you on the case. I'll send you everything I have. Let me know what else you'll need after you receive the case file."

They clicked off. Joseph's life was a nightmare. No horror writer could have ever made up an environment more repulsive or more abominable. Every time she worked a new case, she thought it couldn't get any worse, but it always did. The attitude prevalent in many of the southern states, Florida being one of the most prominent examples, was that blood was the only atonement. Wanda knew that Joseph's case would clearly be a battle.

"Excuse me, Dr. Draper, but I have to interrupt you," Dr. Ladero stated. "You can't tell me James and Joseph are similar. How could you have defended a man who killed five people? It seems a foregone conclusion what should happen to him. He's a stone-cold killer."

Wanda smiled, understanding Ladero's perception. It was a familiar one to her. "It's astounding the impact that children's early development has on their adult behavior. Joseph is a prime example of a failed outcome. His life experiences directly influenced his present circumstances. His development could lead nowhere else. I'm not surprised Joseph's life spun into such tragedy. It was all a web of drug-infested violence. His family disintegration, led by his parents, Terrance and Jenny, could only lead to further complex trauma and egomania. Infant and early childhood bonding was never a part of Joseph's early years. He and James never had a secure attachment, a safe base from which to explore and learn. They shared the same trap."

Chapter 8

Did you find those reports from Dr. Sutter?" Wanda asked Catherine. "He was Jenny's doctor early on."

"Yes, I remember," responded Catherine. She and Wanda were standing amidst boxes and filing cabinets in a little storage shed on Wanda's Texas Hill Country property. The twelve-by-ten shed was surprisingly well lit, with its corrugated plastic roof and big window in the rear. However, it was still hot and stuffy in the Texas heat. The sisters found themselves once again in a familiar scene, up to their necks in paperwork. "I made a few notes that seem to be significant," she confirmed as she leafed through the open folder. She closed the folder and replaced it in the box. "It's a good thing you don't throw anything away," Catherine mused as she picked up the box, making her way to the door.

"Not with court work—I wouldn't dare. You never know when the case might get reopened as a result of an appeal or something." Wanda followed her sister with another box in hand. "I think that's it. Ready to go inside?" Catherine showed her agreement by heading towards the house.

"Can you enumerate your notes on Dr. Sutter's reports?" Wanda requested. The two sisters were cooling off, seated at the dining-room-table-turned-office, rehydrating with cold water. The boxes and document stacks were spread between them.

"Jenny was breastfeeding Kyle when she conceived her second child, Katie. Kyle was eleven months old. So, Jenny had two young children while pregnant with Joseph. Report states the two preschoolers were maturing toward language and speech skills, autonomy, toilet training, and socialization," Catherine summarized.

"If you took what you just said out of context, it would seem they started out with a pretty healthy beginning," Wanda observed.

"Thankfully, we have the context," Catherine added. "According to the doctor's report, one of the main stressors for Jenny and the children was that Terrance became preoccupied with drugs and began growing pot," Catherine explained. "So, Jenny had two young children; Joseph was a toddler; and the money for living expenses was minimal. This was all just too much for Jenny. Another factor reported in the social services records was their tenuous living quarters."

"Let's review Joseph's early health problems," Wanda switched tracks.

"When Joseph was two, he was admitted to the hospital with swollen legs and joints and a skin rash. He was diagnosed with a peanut butter allergy. But the main problem during Joseph's early years was the onset of both parents using drugs. Their makeshift housing and parental neglect, combined with poor nutrition, created a setting for disaster. They continued to have issues with social services. Even so, by the time the two older siblings were in school, they received free lunches and attention from their teachers. And Joseph was at home with a mother who became pregnant again and didn't feel up to giving him the attention that he needed. Later, when Joseph was five, his one-year-old brother, James Spencer, was hospitalized with spinal meningitis and almost died."

Wanda offered her developmental thoughts to Catherine. "It's easy to see Joseph, from day one, developing with a sense of fear and anxiety. By the time he started school, he had feelings of inferiority and emotional emptiness. Then, if I remember the records correctly, oh, where are they? I just had them here a second ago." She searched the dining room table covered in paperwork until she finally located them. "In third grade, he missed sixteen days, made Ds and Fs and was diagnosed with reading and spelling problems. He clearly hated school. Terrance wasn't concerned about this situation as he was focused on his drug habits."

Her sister chimed in. "He wasn't concerned at all—neither was Jenny. Some of these other records indicate Joseph started smoking pot by the time he was ten."

Wanda took a couple of sips of water before moving on to more school records. "Then Joseph had to repeat fourth grade, and there's a note here that he was running around with a fourteen-year-old buddy, stealing cars and shoplifting. He was still missing school, and you can see a pattern beginning to take shape."

Catherine stared down at the paperwork in front of her. "These records show he was using drugs, alcohol, and tobacco by the time he was twelve. And there was still no response by Terrance and Jenny when they were confronted by school or social services personnel."

Wanda skipped through a few school grade records. Then she pointed to one. "Look here. When he was thirteen, his sister Lydia was placed in the gifted and talented program, and he was placed in special ed, likely making the fear of failure even stronger. Plus, his substance abuse naturally interfered with his emotional stability."

Catherine grabbed another file and skimmed it with her finger until she found what she was looking for. "After neighbors reported Terrance and Jenny to the DFS—there, they call it the Department of Family Services—for neglect and substance abuse, the agency referred the Allen Family to Family Preservation Services," Catherine added. "That's a community agency that began in-home support of eighty-five hours per month."

"That was the time when Jenny said to Joseph, 'You're a total loser. I wish I never had you.'" She paused briefly before proceeding. "That bombshell of a statement just added to his pattern of substance abuse, fears of failure and rejection, school truancy, and ultimately, betrayal trauma—all by the time he was in his fourteenth year. We've got our work cut for us with this LifePath."

Catherine shook her head at all the paperwork in front of them. "That we do."

Wanda proceeded with her preliminary analysis. "Joseph's life story makes it perfectly clear that this child without parental support is going to feel the pain of neglect, the pain of failure and rejection, and the pain of betrayal trauma—not to mention the lack of love, trust, and mutuality. Any wonder he turned to substance abuse? Terrance and Jenny ignored Joseph's serious problems by neglecting and disregarding them—"

"And, by the time he was an adolescent, they were in the process of separating from one another," Catherine clarified.

"Ultimately, Joseph's behavior became a manifestation of disorganized attachment. He dropped out of school before he finished the eighth grade—"

Catherine broke in. "Then Terrance and Jenny were granted a divorce. And to make things worse, the court granted Jenny's request that Joseph be emancipated when he was only sixteen years old. Neither Terrance nor Jenny would take Joseph into their custody when they spilt the children up. It wasn't too long in this same year when Joseph overdosed by taking twenty pills."

"This was his call for help," Wanda mournfully observed, "help that never came." While these circumstances were a review, they nonetheless renewed her concern about so many other children with similar problems.

"How could any mother want to legally free herself from responsibility for one of her own children?" questioned an angry Catherine. "No wonder Joseph had such a tragic upbringing. No wonder he wanted to run away. He actually became depressed and alienated from society and from himself, using alcohol, weed, and speed. He had blackouts and was diagnosed with bipolar and psychotic features."

"Wasn't it then that he was admitted to Athens Psychiatric Hospital?" Wanda wanted to clarify.

Catherine nodded, grabbing the hospital records to verify the information. "He was only seventeen."

"And when he was discharged, Jenny . . . she . . . she abandoned him—" Wanda referenced her notes.

"Again!" flared Catherine. Her face was reddening with each terrible incident in Joseph's life.

Wanda remained the calm professional. She had learned many years ago in working with children and parents that, regardless of the situation, the professional could not afford to get emotional. Remaining calm and unbiased was the only way to work effectively with parents and the only way to avoid getting upset with children. Wanda believed that when one understands, one does not have a need to get angry because it's possible to see the situation from the other person's viewpoint—even while disagreeing.

"He was readmitted to the hospital and prescribed medication for manic depression and bipolar schizoaffective disorder," Wanda continued.

"Weren't there even more diagnoses about this time?" Catherine queried.

Wanda nodded. "The Blue Ridge Mountains Center diagnosed him with psychosis—also as dependent, obsessive, paranoid, and depressed. How could any seventeen-year-old pull himself together without parental support or support from someone else?" Wanda added after a moment of reflection, "There was no one else."

"How could Terrance and Jenny ignore the trauma that was overwhelming Joseph at this time?" Catherine asked rhetorically.

Wanda took a deep breath before proceeding with the tragic tale. "Two months after these diagnoses, Joseph's brother James Spencer was shot and killed in Terrance's house while playing with a gun that Terrance gave his sons to play with."

"I can certainly see how disorganized attachment became an underlying feature of Joseph's pattern," commented Catherine.

Wanda nodded. "This was a critical time in Joseph's life for developing a strong sense of self-identify. However, Joseph became the poster child for identity crisis. Both parents rejected him over and over again, and he lived in one place and then another, with acquaintances here and there. And then Jenny relinquished all support for all the boys and went to Florida."

Catherine took a moment to study her notes. "It appears the divorce decree gave sole custody to Terrance and required Jenny to pay child support and required parenting classes for both parents."

Wanda looked at Catherine and shook her head. "Again, this was a time when neither parent wanted to have Joseph living with them. He became caught in the confusion of family turmoil. His substance abuse continued as a way to numb the pain of rejection and betrayal trauma."

"And get this," Catherine eagerly exclaimed, excited about something in the file. "Joseph went to the ER when he was twenty years old, asking for help. He said, according to these notes, 'I haven't been myself for three months.'"

Wanda continued to offer her analysis. "Joseph was again calling for help through desperate acts. This agony of betrayal and loss of love from his family propelled him to steal and commit arson. Maybe he felt like his family had been stolen from him and now he was going to steal from others. This behavior got him sentenced to fourteen years."

Catherine picked up where Wanda left off. "And by the time he was twenty-two, he was released from prison and sent to a halfway house in the Atlanta area."

"And when he was twenty-three, still desperately hoping to reunite with his family, he walked away from that halfway house and hitchhiked over two hundred miles to Terrance's house. But again, he was rejected by Terrance after spending four days there. So, he stole some of Terrance's guns and left. This led to the killing of that couple in Georgia."

It was April 2008 and time for Wanda to prepare for a new round of interviews for Joseph's Florida trial. And that meant another trip to Georgia. Her first stop would be the Allen residence to interview Terrance and also Joseph's brothers, Leonard and Mike.

The investigator met Wanda at the Hartsfield-Jackson Atlanta International Airport. Tricia was an attractive brunette in her thirties. She had a perfect figure, big smile, and sparkling, dark brown eyes. Her hair was cut short, similar to a man's but still maintaining its feminine style. A conscientious fashionista, she dressed in the latest casual fashion—tight gray slacks and a gray and navy speckled turtleneck sweater with an expensive navy blazer. She was articulate and calculating, yet pleasant and well organized. She had worked for several years as a pharmaceutical representative. When she became disenchanted with her company's expectations, she decided to try her hand at working for a law firm. Tricia, highly motivated and driven by the challenge, worked diligently to succeed.

Tricia and Wanda drove up the gravel lane, through the still densely wooded areas, to reach the Allen residence. Mountain oak, hickory, and pine trees had given away to loblolly pines in this part of central Georgia. The fewer deciduous trees were bare. Winter had been rearing its ugly head for several months now. But, beneath the light blanket of pure white snow, the terrain was marred by debris. Old tires, metal throwaways, broken boxes, and even discarded clothes, among other junk, welcomed them at the end of the road where Joseph's two brothers and their father were currently living. The entire area was probably once a magnificent setting. The ramshackled, two-story house sat on a knoll overlooking a river where swimming in the summer must have been a respite from the crowded and deplorable living quarters.

Wanda recalled reading the social worker's report. This was the same home that the social worker had once noted as "isolated, with no phone and rutted roads; a project house in various stages of completion and remodeling; children all sleep in one room upstairs."

The temperature was in the thirties, but to Wanda it felt like the teens. The wind was howling. Snow was falling gently as they approached the entrance where there was just a broken screen door frame. The screened porch was no longer protected from the elements or vermin or any manner of four-legged trespassers since the screen had long since rotted and blown away. This was certainly the filthiest place Wanda had ever visited in all of her years working these murder cases. She wondered how anyone could actually live and sleep here. She felt fortunate to have worn a polyester, quilted, all-weather coat. But even so, without heat, it was icy cold. Yet, the low temperature was a blessing in disguise because the cold helped to lessen the stench that broke through to her freezing nostrils. She stepped carefully over all sorts of junk and male clothing that surely had not been washed in months. From underwear to bedding, the floor had not one foot of clear walking space.

Terrance wasn't at home, as he had moved in temporarily with a friend, but the two brothers, Leonard and Mike, were staying in this godforsaken place. *Staying*, she thought, *because this can't be called living.*

Wanda began with Leonard, who leaned against the kitchen counter, about ten feet across from her. He was lanky and disheveled, standing about six feet tall and wearing dirty jeans, a ragged, filthy T-shirt, and a plaid flannel shirt jacket, opened because there were no buttons. When Leonard talked, his teeth revealed the havoc caused by too much crack cocaine.

Wanda proceeded to question him about Joseph, his life, and the family. Leonard continued to smoke a cigarette while recalling the family history. Wanda was surprised and impressed to discover the family historian. She was pleased by all the useful information. As they talked, he reached across the kitchen counter, piled high with dirty dishes, to retrieve a can of what looked like potted meat. He pulled the tab, opened the can, and using two fingers, fed himself a bite of the unrecognizable contents. Then, casually and deliberately, he took the can and moseyed to the middle of the room where a raccoon in a wire cage was eagerly awaiting him. Leonard used his same two fingers to dip into the can and feed the wild friend, and then he dipped in again to feed himself the remaining portion.

Returning to the counter, he continued with the family history, leaning in the same place. *I think I've seen it all now!* Wanda thought. *This is the most awful eating situation I've ever witnessed. And, this kitchen and whole area looks like it breeds disease. I wonder if this raccoon will get sick from eating after Leonard.* Wanda calmly continued writing and gathering information. Her external reactions never betrayed her internal feelings.

When her interview with Leonard was finished, she asked that he call Mike from upstairs. When Mike came down, she realized how cold she was, having transcended the last hour's temperature by focusing attention on the two mesmerizing subjects of boy and raccoon. Wanda suggested to Mike, "Let's go sit in the car for our interview. Leonard then can be free to get on with his day." She made no mention of the fact that her toes and ears were numb or that she needed relief from a stench worse than a garbage heap.

"Sure. No problem." Mike was ready. *Thank goodness*, she sighed within.

Wanda waited for the rental car to warm up and defrost her hands so that she would be able to take notes on what Mike had to say.

She began by commenting on the property. "Seems like there are a lot of things you can do out here—when it's not so cold."

"Yeah, I like to swim down in the river in the summer and hunt during the fall and winter."

"What can you tell me about your parents?"

He shook his head. "Just that they've never gotten along—ever. At least not since I've been around. Dad must've called Mom a "whore" about ten thousand times." *Charming guy*, thought Wanda.

"I sense that doesn't make you feel very good," Wanda offered.

Mike lightly shrugged his shoulders as he gazed out onto the falling snow. "I'm used to it."

"After your parents split up and some of you went with—"

Wanda's question was interrupted by an enormous sneeze from Mike, who refrained from covering his mouth. As thousands of germ particles flooded the rented vehicle, Wanda wanted to roll down her window, but the thought of the freezing cold prevented her from taking that action. *If I wasn't going to get sick before,* she thought, *I sure am now.*

Wanda finished asking her question. "After some of you went with your mom and some of you went with your dad, what happened with Joseph?"

It took no time for him to answer. "They didn't want him."

"Do you know why?"

"I don't. All I know about Joseph is that whatever he does, he does a lot of. Never was here at the house a lot. Missed school a lot. Made bad grades a lot. Had trouble with the law a lot."

"Did you miss school a lot?"

Mike shrugged. "I went when I felt like it. Mom and Dad, they didn't care."

"What can you tell me about your siblings?" Wanda pressed on.

Mike reflected for a few moments before answering, "Only one of us who's doin' okay is Kyle."

"He's the oldest, correct?"

"Yeah, he got out before things got really bad between Mom and Dad."

She concluded the interview by asking Mike, "Tell me about life with your mother. And life with your father. How were things different?"

He offered, "Mom's living with a boyfriend in a nice house just over the state line. But, there's too many rules, too many expectations over there. So, I live with Dad." Mike told Wanda where his father was working, but said he didn't come home very often since he lived with a friend much of the time.

Armed with the name of Terrance's workplace, she now needed to speak with Tricia. She had to get to Terrance and interview him.

Tricia made telephone contact with Terrance to set a time for them to talk with him. They were to meet at a café near his place of work at four o'clock, just after he departed from work.

After an hour of waiting, Tricia said lamely, "Might as well mark him off the list. He's not gonna cooperate. Rumor has it he's cooperating with the state on Joseph's case."

Determined to talk with him, Wanda said, "Let's show up at his place of work tomorrow. Since he works in a factory, they have to give him a morning break. We'll be waiting for him. If he doesn't know we're coming, he won't know to avoid us."

So, they were waiting for him at ten o'clock the next morning. Sure enough, he came out the door to the parking lot and lit up a cigarette; they made their approach. Terrance was so thin. If the wind blew hard enough, he'd be unable to stand. After they introduced themselves, Wanda told him she was on the defense team for Joseph.

Terrance confessed, "I told my kids, wanna use drugs? Use 'em with me first." Terrance's attitude was pretty much live and let live. Affection for his children was either nonexistent or tucked so far back in his psyche that it would likely never surface. When asked about Joseph, Terrance simply shrugged and replied, "I can't be responsible for what he does. If he's guilty, he needsta be punished."

Terrance admitted, "Me and Jenny, we didn't want Joseph . . . didn't want him." Yes, this further confirmed Wanda's notion that Joseph never had a chance for a "normal" upbringing. *What must he think about himself and his parents that neither of them wanted him?* she asked herself. As much as she wanted to say something, she just continued the interview. It wouldn't be ethical to get into parenting philosophies with him, and it wouldn't undo a tragic life. Terrance then added, "Jenny's a crazy, party girl now. She doesn't want any home responsibility."

After standing in the parking lot for a half hour talking with Terrance, Tricia and Wanda drove across the state line to talk with Jenny. She confirmed much of what Wanda found in various social services records and from family interviews; she admitted that neither she nor Terrance wanted to be responsible for Joseph. As they drove away from the restaurant where they had met Jenny, Wanda said to Tricia, "And we wonder why Joseph has a case of identity crisis. His first ten years of life propelled him into adolescence with a guarantee to connect with drugs, truancy, and psychiatric services—but with no way to connect with his parents, the one thing he wanted most in life."

Chapter 9

The prison mess hall was empty except for a couple of vending machines and lonely looking tables with chairs stacked on top. Wanda glanced through the large glass window as she walked by to see one inmate mopping the floor. It was midafternoon, and Wanda was accompanied by a guard to the contact room where she was to wait for Joseph.

As he entered, she stood and extended her hand in greeting. She wanted to get a sense from his handshake. Generally speaking, a strong grip signaled sincerity, strength of character, and one who was going to take the contact seriously. However, it could also signal power and the need for control. On the other hand, a limp handshake usually signaled disinterest, fear, depressed feelings, a noncommittal attitude, or self-centeredness. Wanda had found that the first five minutes with the accused had proven to be a very valuable litmus test. If she could make an initial friendly connection, she knew that the interview would be good. If she couldn't connect within a very few minutes, something was wrong, very wrong.

When she first shook hands with Joseph a few years ago, the handshake was firm but not tight. It had seemed sincere to Wanda, and from that moment on, she was sure to have a good connection for the interview. But, Joseph's handshake during the Georgia case had been what Wanda described to Catherine as plain vanilla: nondescript and noncommittal. She wondered how he had changed over these past few years while waiting for his fate to be played out in court. His handshake quickly told her he was not the same.

She began the interview by letting Joseph know, "It's good to see you again." When they were both seated, she gave him a pad and a pencil with an eraser on it. "Joseph, I don't know if you remember, but I asked you to draw a tree during my visit with you for the Georgia case. I'd like for you to draw another one today. As before, this is not a test. There's no right or wrong way to draw the tree."

Joseph reached for the pencil and began drawing. He soon stopped, erased, and started again. Remembering that he had taken almost half an hour to draw the first tree, Wanda had a hunch that this might take some time. She glanced down at the floor, trying to hide her smile as she remembered Catherine's reaction to seeing tree drawings in her notes.

———————

"Why in the world would you have these alleged killers draw a tree?" Catherine had asked.

"It's an exercise. It gives both the defendant and myself time to get ready for the long interview, which often lasts three or four hours. The tree drawing is usually short . . . less than a minute for some. Most, though, take about five to ten minutes."

Catherine retorted, "All exercises have a purpose."

"You're right. This gives me time to make some observations. Is there a good attention span? Or is there reluctance to do this? What, if anything, does the defendant say? Most don't say anything. What's his facial expression during the drawing process? Most have a rather innocent or shy-like smile, perhaps embarrassment. Others seem to enjoy the task. Some comment on their earlier years like, 'I used to draw a lot when I was little.' It's a time for idle talk. It seems to loosen the tension. Maybe it's as much for me as for them; I have time to get comfortable."

Catherine shook her head incredulously at her sister. "Anyone ever refused to draw a tree for you?"

"Not so far."

Catherine, an artist in her own right, asked, "Do any of these inmates have artistic ability?"

"Some trees look like a child's art. Some are more advanced. Some are outstanding."

—————

The replaying of this conversation with Catherine in Wanda's mind was soon interrupted when Joseph pushed the notepad back to her. Wanda was very surprised. It had only taken him two minutes to draw this tree, compared to thirty minutes to draw the first one. His first tree in the Georgia case was perfectly drawn and reflected a great talent. Yet, when Wanda took a look at his new drawing, she could see why it was completed so quickly. This tree was night to the first tree's day. It was completely dead, whereas the previous tree had been alive and drawn with considerable detail.

Joseph's second tree drawing gave Wanda an insight into his current mindset. Unlike the first contact visit in Georgia, in which he seemed so much more alert, he now rarely looked her in the eyes. His eyes remained slightly downcast. This didn't surprise her. After all, he had been moved since his trial in Georgia, where he entered a plea for LWOP. Now, life had taken a different turn. He was obviously depressed.

Wanda needed to review his life, especially when he was young. "What are some of the things you remember about school?"

She could tell he was really thinking about this. It took him about a minute to answer. "One day, when I was, uh, in first grade, a teacher . . . she told me to come in from outside 'cuz I wasn't wearing a sweater, and it was cold outside. I left school instead. Walked the two miles home. My mother never contacted the school, never put a sweater on me, and never sent me back that day." *During first grade, Joseph was already experiencing life with a growing fear of failure and rejection,* Wanda thought. *It was the beginning of a potentially troubled life.*

"Tell me about when you and Lydia started sixth grade at the same time."

"Lydia was smart. They placed her in the gifted and talented program, but me in special ed. Lydia's teachers were real supportive of her. Mine always wanted to know why I wasn't more like her. So, I stuck to the streets. Got into quite a bit of trouble."

"Did you have to see a juvenile officer?" Wanda followed up.

"Yeah, but 'cuz I was younger, I was usually only 'slapped on the wrist.'"

"Tell me about your parents when you were growing up."

Joseph shook his head. "They never seemed to know where we were or why we were absent from school or home."

"In the records, I see that parent counseling was recommended when you went missing for several days and were discovered to be out past the city curfew."

Joseph chuckled sarcastically. "They didn't even realize I was missing."

That comment wasn't difficult for Wanda to believe. Jenny and Terrance had nine mouths to feed: Kyle, Katie, Joseph, Lydia, James Spencer, Leonard, Mike, and themselves.

"Also, in the records, I see you were mandated by family services to attend group counseling for pot problems."

"I went two times, then dropped out."

"When DFS began in-home support visits, was this really helpful, or do you think it gave your parents an out not to deal with you?"

"What do you think?" Joseph smirked.

"Joseph, were you upset with the lack of parental concern for your brothers?"

He nodded. "I was. I threatened to take 'em and raise 'em myself. But. I, well, I . . . I couldn't even deal with my own problems."

She approached the next question rather delicately. "Would you mind talking about James Spencer's death?"

She could tell this question, more than any other, was really painful. He took about two minutes before he answered. There was a lot of heavy breathing as she waited.

"When, uh, James Spencer, Mike, and Leonard were living with Dad, he gave one of my brothers a gun. The kids went upstairs, and Dad stayed downstairs, smoking pot. The boys began to wrestle, playing with the gun. The gun went off and shot and uh . . . well . . . it killed James Spencer."

"And he was thirteen years old, correct?"

Joseph nodded in anger.

"How did you feel at that time?"

"Angry. Upset."

Wanda wondered if Joseph ever learned that James Spencer's toxicology report showed lidocaine and marijuana in his system at the time of his death.

"At, uh, at, um, James Spencer's funeral, Dad handed out copies of a poem he had printed at a print shop. It was one that James Spencer had . . . had written about Mom. The words James Spencer had written were nasty to everyone except Dad."

Wanda gave Joseph a moment to collect himself. She gently asked, "Did your family ever talk about James Spencer's death?"

"Never. I wanted a headstone for his grave. Me, my brothers, Dad . . . we bought one with contributions, but we . . . we never talked about his death. Actually, I shouldn't say that. There was one mention of James Spencer. Dad lined us up . . . his sons . . . put guns in our hands . . . made us shoot. He said to us, 'Just 'cuz of what happened to your brother, you're not growin' up 'fraid of guns.' One of the guns . . . that was the one that killed James Spencer."

As much as Wanda's stomach was turning at that very moment, her face never revealed any of her discomfort. "And where are you living during all of this?"

"I had moved back in with Dad, but within a couple of weeks, he kicked me out. After a few days of living nowhere, I moved back in with Dad. My brothers and Dad were using drugs. I went back to live with Mom. However, after only a few days, she kicked me out of her house and told me I had to live with Dad."

After three hours of talking with Joseph, the contact visit came to an end. During her drive back to the hotel, Wanda thought about another key person she needed to interview.

Later that month, Wanda called a man she hoped could help to corroborate facts about Joseph's family life. She was driving back from town, taking care of a few errands. These tasks took a little longer than she had anticipated, but she had previously arranged to speak to this contact that day. So, she found herself pulling in under the huge acorn tree at the town park. She lowered the windows to let the still, cool breeze in and dialed the number, her yellow pad ready. Although he had not had any dealings with the Allen Family since 2004, the mitigation specialist had encouraged Wanda to interview him.

"Mr. Ted Marks?"

"Yes?"

"I'm Wanda Draper. I'm working on Joseph Allen's defense team. Do you have a few minutes to talk with me?

"Sure do," Marks responded in a friendly tone. "I can talk now if you'd like."

"I really appreciate your help." Wanda paused briefly before asking, "When did you get involved in Family Services?"

"I joined Family Services in May of '93," he said pleasantly.

"And what was your role with the Allen Family?"

"I was one of their case workers. I provided training for family and foster care workers. There were five of us. And, I was the general case worker manager."

"What can you tell me about the Allen family and their children?"

"You know, they were pretty much left on their own. The boys were regular Tom Sawyers—in a troubled family. They were allowed and encouraged by Terrance to participate in dangerous activities with guns."

"Can you give me an example?"

"Let's see. I took groceries to Terrance the day after James Spencer was killed. While talking with Terrance, he said to me, 'I hope to God they don't turn this into some kind of gun control issue.'"

"Anything else about their gun activities?"

"Their weapons and ammo . . . I thought it was all a recipe for disaster," he commented. "It wasn't the guns as much as it was how they were handled and used."

Wanda switched gears. "Was the family . . . were they active in the church?"

"I heard that James Spencer was named after Spencer Kimball in the Mormon Church."

"And what about Joseph?"

"Never knew him. I'd see him in his black trench coat, even in the summer, walking down the road."

"That's a shame. I was hoping you had had some interactions with him."

"Sorry."

"That's okay. What can you tell me about Terrance and Jenny?"

"She lived in the projects in Melville . . . It's my understanding Terrance didn't care for Joseph. I think this was related to Joseph's adolescent angst. Terrance never followed up on the whereabouts of his children. They were rarely at home—usually on the road and around town, often missing school."

"Did you know the girls?"

"I knew Lydia while I was teaching Junior High in '92–'93. She was in the seventh grade and intelligent. After the family began to disintegrate, I was at the sheriff's office with a narcotics agent, and Lydia and her boyfriend were brought in because they had gotten into drugs while living at Jenny's apartment. Terrance claimed Jenny was a meth-head. 'Course, Terrance himself partied every weekend with drugs."

"What about their daughter Katie?"

"I knew her when she was in seventh grade too—a smart student. But she was older and left home right after high school. Like her older brother, Kyle, they both escaped a lot of the family trauma. Actually, they had a pretty good start because while they were young, their parents were very much in love. By the time they were in grade school, they were strong enough to withstand the emotional bombardment of their troubled family's trauma."

Wanda took a few moments to form her next question. "Did you attend James Spencer's funeral?"

"I did actually."

"What can you tell me about it?" Wanda prompted.

"Terrance and Jenny were both there, but . . . they weren't . . . they didn't sit together. Joseph's older brother Kyle and his wife were there. But I didn't get to talk with them."

"Did you talk with Terrance?"

"He acknowledged me, but had nothing to say."

"What about Jenny?"

"Jenny was pleased I came. I think James Spencer's death was very real to her." *That's interesting,* Wanda thought. *That's the only complimentary statement I've ever heard anyone make about Jenny.*

"Who else was present at the funeral?"

"The children, they were all there. I heard someone in the church had given a burial plot for James Spencer."

"Where was the funeral held?"

"Mormon Church in Melville, Georgia."

"Did Jenny say anything about the family?"

"She appeared to be negative toward DFS. She was skinny—'bout 110-120 pounds. Could be pleasant. But, during our DFS meetings, she was often sharp-tongued. Still, she seemed more nurturing than Terrance. Terrance wanted his wife back and used his children as pawns. I left the agency in 2003 and had no more contact with the family."

Wanda took that last statement as an indication that it was time to wrap things up. "What do you think of Joseph and his situation?"

"I'm not surprised. I'm just saddened by what happened," he replied evenly. "His was an explosive family. He had all the ingredients for a disaster. While they were a religious family, they became drug users. Then James Spencer was killed in front of a couple of the brothers. When the family needed bonding and healing, Terrance was all about himself. Terrance was known to have said, 'I need to protect myself.' Joseph's the outcome of a disintegrated family. Terrance controlled Jenny, threatening that if she left him, 'It'll keep the family from heaven.' Terrance used his distorted religious leanings with the church as a club to control Jenny and the family."

"Did you and Terrance have any conversations other than at the funeral?"

"Yes, through Social Services, we had some interchange. Terrance thought he was my buddy. But, later he threatened to come in and shoot us at work. His angst was exacerbated after James Spencer died. Then on one occasion, we saw each other at a local convenience store, and he said, 'I may as well get my gun and come in there and shoot everyone.'"

There was a moment of silence before Wanda said, "Mr. Marks, if I have more questions, may I call you again?"

"Of course, I'll help any way I can. I'll be willing to testify if I can be of service."

"Thank you. You've been most helpful."

Wanda put her yellow pad down. As she turned her car towards home, she thought about Joseph, remembering one of the first times she met him. It was in his jail cell. The jail either didn't have or refused to provide a private room in which to meet. She remembered being surprised by how neat Joseph was. His cell was immaculate. He kept all his papers fastidiously filed. *He probably went crazy having to live in that ramshackled place of a home with his father,* Wanda reflected.

The sun was quickly setting. Wanda scarcely noticed, her mind still contemplating Joseph's life—all the twists and turns it took. So many of his choices were influenced for the worse by others' actions. *Others' actions and our responses to them do have an impact—often lasting.* The memory of a grade school class flooded back to her.

One spring morning, in sixth grade math class, the teacher called for a volunteer to explain a problem. The twelve-year-old boy, Sandy, rose from his seat in the back of the room. Wanda was seated near the front, and as he walked past her and made his way to the chalkboard, some secret voice inside her head spoke silently, but quite clearly, *He'll always be in my heart.* Wanda never forgot that moment because it was such a strange and unexpected statement. At that stage in her life, there was no boyfriend or even any wish for one.

Wanda and Sandy became good friends, and over the school years, they participated in a variety of shared activities. His parents often gave her a ride to church on Sunday nights. Sandy and Wanda would sit in the back seat. After several months, they began to hold hands. He had a motor scooter that he rode to school. On Saturdays, he often came by her house. She would hop on the back of his scooter, and they would ride through the countryside. For years, she carried a scar on the inside calf of her leg where she burned it when it got too close to the hot intake manifold. They both enjoyed the freedom of riding, feeling the wind blowing against their faces while taking in the familiar scenes of the countryside.

During her junior year, she needed a date for the junior/senior prom, so she asked Sandy to go with her. He was very bashful, but eventually agreed. They double dated with another couple. They had a good time dancing to every song, including the last one, her favorite, "Stardust." After the prom, they began to date, usually with a group of friends. He began driving a Ford Model T and taught her to drive in that old stick shift car. She felt like she could do anything.

By her senior year, Wanda was dating a number of boys, but none tugged her heartstrings like Sandy. During spring semester, she began to think seriously about him. There was always a sense of "music in the air" and "stardust in her hair" when they were together. Although they never talked about their relationship, there seemed to be just the right chemistry between them and a strong connection. They became closer over the months, until something unexpected happened. A girlfriend of hers told her that Sandy told her he really didn't want to go with Wanda anymore. She was completely devastated and just couldn't believe it, but she didn't question her friend's word. She took what she said at face value. If that's what Sandy wanted, Wanda was going to honor his wishes. She never confronted him or even asked about what her friend had told her. Her focus turned to finishing high school and preparing for college. After going out with a few other guys, she began to date someone a few years older. Even then, she confided in another girlfriend that no matter whom she seriously dated, or even someday married, Sandy would always be the one in her heart.

After going away to college, the connection with Sandy ended. She had no information about him because her life took her far away from home. She soon married her first husband, even though she loved him in a different way than Sandy.

Her headlights illuminated the front yard, accented with overflowing flower beds. After turning off the car, she sat there in the driveway, gazing at a home that was several times bigger than the little wooden one where she was born and raised. The grand house that proudly stood before her represented how the river of life wound and flowed through channels and tributaries, taking unknown courses. Although Wanda wasn't someone interested in the road not taken and the words not spoken, she couldn't help but reflect what her life would have been like if her high school senior year had taken a different course.

Chapter 10

April showers gave way to May flowers, and the heat of the Texas summer soon harassed the flowers. Wanda and Catherine were kept busy outside the house, making sure the yard was well-bolstered against the summertime attacks. And, inside they worked diligently on court cases. For the time being, the sisters focused their efforts on Joseph's case.

This was her first experience working on a public defender case that had five attorneys, an investigator, a mitigation specialist, and a paralegal. Mark and Todd, the Florida team, had hired another attorney, Gabriella, from Jacksonville as an assistant and consultant. Todd was the lead attorney of this segment of the defense team.

They had also hired a defense attorney, Ruth Rothman, from Atlanta. Rothman, the epitome of a high-level female defense attorney, was average-size, blonde, and very attractive. She looked like a television newswoman. Having worked with her several years before, when she was a public defender, Wanda had since learned that she was now in private practice with a very successful record. In fact, Wanda didn't think she had ever lost a case. Her strategy was to overwhelm the prosecution with so much data they would often plead the defendant for life without parole to avoid the hours and expense of dealing with the time and paperwork required to go to trial. She was also good in the courtroom—very good. Wanda really liked working with her and her public defender team. They knew how to work a case. No stone was ever left unturned.

Wanda was both surprised and impressed by the number of lawyers involved in this case. When the Florida lawyers hired her, she pulled up the files on Joseph, including his LifePath, and began reviewing records. The Atlanta team, headed up by Ruth Rothman, made contact, and they made arrangements to work together on Joseph's case. While Wanda had never worked with Mark or Todd, she had met Ruth in Tampa while working on this case. The two women traveled to interview one of Joseph's sisters. Riding in the car with Ruth was always a pleasure. They had an opportunity to wrap their minds around this case.

The defense team seemed enthusiastic to have Wanda on board. Both the Florida lawyers and the Atlanta group were aware that Wanda had been scheduled to testify in Georgia on Joseph's case before he was offered life without parole and her work on his case ended. Knowing this, Mark and Todd asked the Georgia defense attorneys for their recommendation. They reported being impressed with the LifePath and suggested Wanda would be a great asset for the Florida case.

Wanda and Catherine worked tirelessly, combing through documents, reports, and interviews. They made any necessary LifePath revisions after corroborating facts from collateral sources in preparation for her testimony in the penalty stage of Joseph's trial. They were making sure that Joseph's LifePath was shored up. The Atlanta office had requested a draft LifePath. They would, indeed, go to trial in the next month or two.

The day before the draft LifePath was due, Wanda expressed her frustrations to Catherine. "I see little hope for Joseph's survival. Yes, I've been hired to present mitigation testimony . . . and there's plenty for me to present . . . I just . . . I just wonder if a jury will be able to view Joseph's plight through his perception and not their own personal versions."

Catherine took a moment before responding. "Wanda, besides giving the jury an eye-opener into this family from hell, I think the key is you have to show them why Joseph is the only one of the siblings to become a killer. These are the questions I think you have to answer: Was Joseph simply more sensitive than his siblings and, therefore, felt more of the pain of neglect, as well as the fear of failure and rejection? Did he abuse drugs just for recreation, or was it to numb himself to feelings of family rejection? Did he need a way to save face in order to start anew, or did he already see himself as a lost soul? Did the other siblings have greater inner strength, or had Joseph become the scapegoat and whipping post for their misbehavior?"

Wanda smiled at her sister's encouragement. She reached for the LifePath again. After a few moments of studying it, she said, "After seeing all these events in his life and seeing he was the only one singled out for such horrible verbal and psychological abuse, is it any wonder where he ended up?"

Catherine was looking over the last page. She threw up her hands and asked, "Why didn't they take away Terrence and Jenny's parental rights?" *Why indeed?* thought Wanda. "You know the LifePath really is key to conveying all these events, circumstances, and influences to an audience," Catherine said in admiration.

"I certainly agree," Wanda said as she smiled. "I think the defense team agrees, too." The Atlanta office had been impressed with the original LifePath that was forwarded from the Georgia office. They had expressed their appreciation for the organization of mitigation facts represented by such a detailed visual diagram portraying Joseph's life. They were eager to see the updated LifePath.

About a week before being called to testify, a call came in from mitigation specialist Tricia, whom she hadn't seen since the Georgia trip to interview Mike, Leonard, Terrance, and Jenny. She was a member of Ruth's group. "We've decided not to have you use the LifePath. Ruth wants to use your data to create a scrapbook approach to help the jury follow Joseph's life. It'll include many photos and captions to capture the emotions of the jurors. We'll convert it to PowerPoint and show it on the huge screen. It'll be impressive. I've already been working on it. We'll give it to you when you get to Duval County. You'll have time to go over it with us prior to your testimony." *What planet am I on? We have a problem,* worried Wanda.

"But, I've prepared testimony based on stepping down from the witness box and standing in front of the jury with the eighteen charts of the LifePath," Wanda countered. "This is the approach I use to educate the jury. This LifePath not only depicts the defendant's life events and critical circumstances, but it's also a very—"

The phone was ringing in the background on her end. "Wanda, excuse me. I have to take this. Hold on a sec, okay?"

Before she could say anything, Wanda had already been placed on hold. And she was on hold for what seemed to be an eternity, clearly longer than a second. The longer she waited, the more the flames of anger and indignation grew.

Tricia finally came back to the phone. "Sorry about that. We—"

Wanda cut her off and jumped right back into her argument. "The LifePath is also a very effective way to point out the expectations and the stressors in each stage of his development. The jury really responds to these aspects. It's a simple yet profound visual way to articulate how Joseph's development brought him to this point and how his behavior unfolded, over time, in a way that could bring him to kill an entire family."

"Yes, and we're using your information. But, let's face it," she lectured, in a slightly demeaning tone, "*you* need to get up-to-date. PowerPoint's more high tech, and your charts are 'old hat.' We think a pictorial scrapbook approach will be a better tool to hold their attention, speak to their emotions, and seek their mercy."

Wanda drew a long, deep breath before continuing. "I understand this is the attorney's call, but I'm not comfortable using PowerPoint. The LifePath is a developmental approach. I'm a developmental epistemologist." Impending silence followed, but Wanda quickly recognized, like a soldier in a brigade, that she was constrained to follow the orders from up the chain of command. "But . . . if this is what the attorneys want—"

"It is what they want," Tricia declaratively interjected. She clearly refused to consider another's opinion or perspective. *She and Ruth are infallible, and they alone know the best course of action.*

"Well, then," Wanda finally spoke. "I'll do my best." *Too late to back out now,* she contemplated. *It wouldn't be fair to Joseph—or I'd be out of this one.* "How soon can I see this . . . scrapbook?"

Since she had conceded, Tricia wasted no time in answering. "We'll have it at the defense house when you arrive. There'll be time to study it." *And how much time is that?* Wanda asked herself. It certainly wouldn't be anything compared to the weeks of working with the details of the LifePath.

"This is the first time in over two decades of being a witness that I feel caught in such an ethical dilemma," Wanda confided to Catherine later that evening. "Other situations were always argued in defense team meetings, often compromised yet with the defendant's best interests in mind." Wanda was still shocked over the lawyer's decision not only *not* to use the LifePath, but also to have her testify using a document she did not prepare herself.

Catherine was irate. She thought the lawyers were insane and told Wanda this in no uncertain terms. "But, no defense attorney ever told me what method to use when testifying," Wanda continued to process. She had always been a firm believer that when you hire someone to do something, you articulate what you want, but never how to do it.

"Of course not!" vehemently agreed Catherine. "After all, this is your intellectual property."

It was spring of 2008. The airport was crowded as Wanda scanned the baggage claim area for Mark, the defense attorney on Joseph's case. She was sure that he said he'd be there, but nobody fit his description.

Wanda hadn't had a good trip. The flight was not the issue. She was suffering from anticipatory anxiety. She was still unnerved by having to use someone else's scrapbook instead of her LifePath.

After collecting her luggage and stepping out on the arrival deck, she noticed a late-model BMW parked curbside, and a young man in walking shorts and flashy sport shirt greeted Wanda by name. She returned Mark's salutation.

The two lead attorneys had leased a big house because they were living this case day and night for three months, and they still had about a week to go. As they drove to the house he had rented for working this case, they exchanged small talk but not about the case. Her intuition, though, told her that something wasn't right. Mark seemed courteous but somewhat aloof. The air seemed a little thick as they talked on the drive. He seemed to avoid talking about the trial and what was happening. As a result, Wanda didn't know what to think. His features were unreadable. Neither of these circumstances reassured Wanda.

Entering the situation room in the defense house with the assumption that all of the defense attorneys had agreed to discard her LifePath in favor of the scrapbook, Wanda was feeling very uncomfortable. They were coming down to the wire and running out of time. The air was getting thicker by the minute.

The only persons present were the three defense attorneys, absent the Atlanta scrapbook side. The room was large and quite attractively decorated. *How did they manage to pay for this place?* Wanda pondered. *Taxpayers, no doubt.* The three attorneys each had private bedrooms and baths. There was a large kitchen, dining room, and living room. The room the team was meeting in had all the accouterments for a working group—a real situation room.

Both Todd and Gabriella were there, waiting for Wanda and Mark. Todd, who was six foot two and in his mid-forties with an athletic build, stood up and walked over to greet Wanda. He was dark haired, with a pleasant face and friendly smile. He then turned and introduced the last member of their team. Gabriella was in her mid-forties, of average height and weight. Her blonde hair was styled to perfectly compliment her attractive face. She welcomed Wanda warmly with a lovely smile.

Even after being introduced to Todd and Gabriella, the air was still heavy. As Todd excused himself, Mark, the penalty stage attorney, picked up the scrapbook and asked Wanda if she had her copy.

"No, I haven't seen it," she answered tersely.

"Didn't you work on it with the Atlanta group?" he asked, confused.

"No," she replied in a guarded and controlled voice. "They called to tell me we were discarding the LifePath and using this as a more high-tech tool since it would be displayed on PowerPoint—not my idea."

"Take a look," Mark said, "We'd better go over it because you'll need time to prepare for your testimony."

"When do you think I'll be called?"

"Day after tomorrow," he announced with assurance.

Mark handed over the scrapbook. This big, black, three-ring notebook, which had to weigh at least fifteen pounds, had everything in it but the kitchen sink. Filled with pictures of Joseph, from infancy through his years of development and throughout his adolescence, the only thing it didn't have were the developmental expectations and stressors.

"I was curious how they found all these pictures," Mark queried. *I am too, Mark,* Wanda thought. *I am, too.*

"Well, when I interviewed his mother, she shared some of these, but I've no idea where a lot of these came from," Wanda added. She paused momentarily before continuing, "Look. I'm trying to be a team player here, but . . ."

Like a kettle of boiling water, she couldn't remain silent any longer. "You need to know I've never used PowerPoint in a courtroom—goes against my style. Everyone uses it for meetings of all sorts, training sessions, workshops . . . Most people are familiar with it. That's why I don't like it in the courtroom. It gets boring."

She paused as she flipped through the tome. Wanda was astonished at how much time and effort had gone into this book and thought, *Too much for a jury to focus on. Disaster.*

No one responded to Wanda's concerns. The room was silent. Everyone was looking at the tome on the table. The LifePath laid on the table next to it, a stark contrast. "Why aren't you using that?" asked Mark as he pointed to a stack of Wanda's LifePath charts on letter-size paper on the table next to the fax machine.

"I wish I could. That was my choice, but Atlanta said no. We have to use the scrapbook."

"We don't like the scrapbook," revealed Mark.

For Wanda, this was getting more and more interesting by the second—or screwier as Catherine would later comment. "I was under the assumption that all the attorneys agreed not to use my LifePath."

"Not so," he replied automatically. "We were told by Atlanta that they wanted to use the PowerPoint, but we thought you were in on the change."

"Only as a matter of information to me from Atlanta—a directive, as a matter of fact."

About this time, Todd returned, and Mark asked him, "Todd, what do you think about the scrapbook in comparison to the LifePath?"

"Of course, you know I preferred the LifePath," Todd admitted, almost defensively. He then shrugged and said, "I assumed this was a mutual decision and Dr. Draper's preference."

Wanda chimed in, "Frankly, I was shocked to get the call that the LifePath was out."

"Why aren't we using it?" Todd asked innocently.

"You know why, Todd," Mark said in a clearly upset tone.

There was an awful moment of silence in the room.

Todd finally turned to Wanda and asked bluntly, "What do you want to do?"

"I prefer the LifePath, of course. I've worked on it for months. I know it upside down and inside out. It's my work. I created it for this case. I'm comfortable using it in my testimony. I'm not comfortable using PowerPoint.

But most important, the LifePath will have much more impact on the jury than this bulky scrapbook." Wanda laughed on the inside. *Can I use "I" any more than I already have?*

Todd took a deep breath, slowly exhaling, "Let's use the LifePath." And then he moved quickly out of the room.

Wanda was both very relieved and very nervous. Relieved because she was back in familiar territory yet nervous because of the fireworks that were likely to occur between Atlanta and the Florida group—and she would be hit with the fallout of angst from both sides. *What will this mean with Atlanta?* They were responsible for her being hired. Now she was caught between a rock and a hard place. Her chest felt like it was bound with leather straps, with water being poured on to make them tighter and tighter.

"But, I didn't bring the enlarged charts. I only have letter-size copies. I used these for review," she replied through pursed lips.

Gabriella said reassuringly, "Not a problem. I'll take them to a nearby copy center . . . get them enlarged . . . have them by morning." *Gabriella. She has the right name,* Wanda thought as she smiled.

Then Wanda stated emphatically, fixing her gaze on Mark, "I'll do this under one condition, that you and Todd talk with Atlanta and tell Ruth about the change back to the LifePath."

Without hesitation, Mark responded, "Sure. Not a problem. We'll talk with Ruth this evening. We'll be meeting about the progress of the trial." Noticing Wanda's apprehension, he added, "Relax. Todd's lead attorney anyway. It's his preference—and his call."

Wanda felt better but still uncomfortable. She knew Atlanta and how they worked. They liked to be in charge. They weren't going to be happy campers. In fact, they were going to hit the ceiling. She locked eyes with Mark and went on to say, "I'll feel better when you both have talked with Ruth and given me a report of how she takes the news."

The pressure was on to get back to the LifePath and prepare for trial. Mark drove her to the motel. Who should she run into in the hallway but Tricia from the Atlanta team, who was so happy to see her. *She won't be happy when she learns what's going on!* contemplated Wanda.

"Ruth and I, we're staying at the other end of the hall. Can't wait to get with you to go over the scrapbook," Tricia said eagerly.

With a big smile on her face, Wanda could only form two words: "Sounds great." It wasn't her place to say anything about the controversy. She was more preoccupied with calling Catherine and giving her a report of the developments and the change of plans. She was going to rely on Catherine's help from a distance.

Exhausted and starving, Wanda unpacked. Changing shoes helped to mitigate the exhaustion. The chain restaurant next door satisfied her appetite. She was relieved that nobody from the Atlanta team was present. All of the lawyers were meeting somewhere. She could only wonder how that was going as she ate her sandwich.

Upon returning to her room, she showered and dressed for bed. While physically exhausted, she wasn't sleepy. She picked up her phone and called Catherine.

After bringing her up-to-date with the day's events and developments, the sisters fell into a comfortable conversation, laughing in turn at each other's comments. Wanda enjoyed the much-needed levity after her day's ordeal.

"Why would a fifteen-year-old kill his parents?" asked Catherine, her mind returning to a current news event. "Have you seen the news? A teenager reportedly killed his parents earlier this week. Talk about a tough case! There are more and more teenagers killing the closest people in their lives. What is going through their minds?"

"Even though every case is unique, there must be some underlying common thread that results in a tapestry designed to give us a clue." Wanda contemplated a notion that kept creeping into her thoughts about this case. "Maybe these kids are simply testing reality."

"Say a little more. What do you mean exactly?"

"Kids see all kinds of violence on TV and some in their daily lives. But maybe some of these kids don't have enough everyday experiences to know what happens to them personally when they push beyond the limits. Seeing violence and hearing about it is not the same as doing it."

"Are you telling me that kids are killing people to learn about what's real and what's not? That's absurd. If these kids can handle school tasks at their age level, they have the logic to figure out what happens when you stick a knife in a person or blow off his head with a shotgun."

"Hear me out. Think about how many kids have had to face limits set by their parents, let alone face the consequences when they violate these limits. Many kids simply talk their way out of consequences. They threaten their parents with love withdrawal or accuse them of unfair treatment. Many parents literally shrink with fear and back off. What happens to a child who can never predict what, where, or when the parent will draw the line? Or what do they do to test their parents to mean what they say or say what they mean? I think some kids will go to any length to discover what it means to face consequences. Most kids are pretty smart. They begin to accumulate guilt feelings about their own behavior but have no way to deal with it. Some will push and push and push to get results."

"So you think this kid killed his family as a way to find out what happens if he breaks the big rules?"

"I'm not sure. But I wonder if he was so caught up in a web of fiction and ambiguity about what was real for him that it didn't take much to make him feel trapped. Maybe his sense of helplessness pushed him over the edge. The only way to break free was to come out fighting. His fears finally got the best of him. And his feelings became so intense that he lost control of his ability to reason. He used guns and knives as weapons because that's what he knew the most about—and they were handy. The more civil means of talking and arguing were not part of his problem-solving skills. Options were not a part of his ammunitions department."

"Kids used to fight with their fists and words," Catherine agreed. "So, do you think we should get rid of all the guns and knives?"

"That's not the solution. It's certainly not practical. What's needed is more parent-child interaction—having fun with one another, talking together, having meaningful conversations. Parents who talk and listen usually detect when their kids need to talk. Kids often have some very good ideas, but they need caring parents to listen to them and acknowledge their intelligence." Their conversation left each of them with a full mind. The sisters said goodnight and made plans to talk tomorrow about how to tackle the LifePath.

While she had forgotten for the moment the day's drama and clashes, Wanda's mind was full of thoughts about her conversation with Catherine and about Joseph's life. As her mind churned, she tried every way to relax, including meditating and breathing techniques. A bed-time snack of crackers failed to lull her to sleep. She despaired of not sleeping, but eventually her mind quieted and sleep found her.

Chapter 11

The ringing of her cell phone caused her to bolt upright. She glanced at the number. It was her cousin Edward, a John Wayne look-alike if there ever was one. He was the same cousin whom she used to chase through the fields when she was five years old. She answered.

"Cuz, what about the Allen case?" Catherine had told him about Wanda's involvement in Joseph's case. He was mortified about her serving as an expert witness for the defense. He just couldn't fathom what she was doing. He had to speak to her immediately. "What's the story with him? I just know he . . . he killed a couple in Georgia and a family in Florida. How could a person do something like that?" Edward emphatically asked. His anger at the atrocity of the crime and revulsion at Joseph was reflected strongly in his voice.

Wanda inhaled sharply. The infuriated confusion of her cousin's words reminded her of her father. Wanda's work as a mitigation expert had been a source of concern in their relationship. E.T. couldn't understand his daughter's desire to work in defense of "the defendants" as she referred to them. He only saw criminals. In his day, they made quick work of these types of people, these plagues to society.

"I'm not trying to get Joseph released from prison—or acquitted. I'm trying to get him LWOP." Wanda tried to explain to Edward about her role.

Much like she tried with her father every time this issue swelled up, usually around trial time.

"No matter what you tell me right now about this man, *nothing* will change my opinion," Edward spat out vehemently. Wanda could hear him squaring his shoulders, planting his feet firmly. He had already made his mind up about Joseph and wasn't about to budge.

Wanda recognized his exasperation. Yet, she pressed the matter a little further, hoping to break through. "My work is not an excuse for behavior and actions; it is simply an explanation for it. I'm trying to give the court a glimpse of Joseph's world, through his eyes, in his shoes. This insight can help them determine if there are mitigating factors worth their consideration as they decide his fate."

"He deserves the death penalty for murdering that family." The wall remained intact. Her impassioned words fell on deaf ears.

"My job is to help provide a picture of him as a whole person—to help illustrate his entire life so they can decide his penalty." Wanda paused, then added solemnly, "If I can help in a situation like this, if I have the ability to help, I must do it."

When she finally hung up with Edward, she felt worse than she already did. Now she definitely wouldn't be going to sleep. As with E.T., Wanda was keenly aware of Edward's disapproval of her choice in line of work. Wanda thought of her father. She was especially and deeply pained to think of any corruption to the high esteem he held his children in.

The next day went quickly for Wanda, working with Mark and Gabriella to make last minute adjustments to the LifePath. Since being told it wouldn't be used, she had not made some entries that would improve the presentation. Gabriella kept the streets burning, dashing back and forth to a nearby copy center.

With intense curiosity, Wanda asked Mark, "How'd Atlanta handle the big change?"

He commented genially, "We'll talk with Ruth at noon today."

Wanda pursed her lips tightly, trying to conceal her shock. "You still haven't talked with Ruth?" she asked in a controlled voiced. She really wanted to scream at the top of her lungs.

"We were too busy last night getting ready for trial. Ruth was preparing to do the direct for the psychologist this morning."

About three o'clock in the afternoon, Ruth knocked on Wanda's door. She greeted her cordially, explaining that she wanted to go over the scrapbook while taking a break from the courtroom.

Mark and Todd still have not talked with her about the change! Wanda mentally shrieked. At that moment, Wanda didn't know what to do, but she thought it inappropriate to tell her about the change.

Wanda acquiesced, going through the motions. While Ruth turned page after page of the fifty-some-odd sheets and talked about how Wanda could articulate Joseph's story on the screen, Wanda saw the disaster growing. *The jury will fall asleep. They'll hate me for keeping them on the final day of testimony for the last stage, listening to the last boring expert. They'll give Joseph the needle because of the scrapbook!* Yet, Wanda remained stoic and said very little.

As soon as Ruth was satisfied, she made her exit. She was eager to get back to the proceedings. Wanda breathed a sigh of momentary relief, only to begin to feel an ambivalent mixture of anger and helplessness. *Why haven't Todd and Mark talked with Ruth about the change? I can't go on the stand unless they talk with her.*

By eight o'clock in the evening, Wanda called Gabriella. "Anything?"

"Anything?" repeated a confused Gabriella.

"Have they talked with Atlanta?"

"They've talked with Atlanta about many things."

"Talked with them about the LifePath," clarified an annoyed Wanda.

"Oh, I'm not sure," she replied, her mind clearly on other things. "I think they might wait until early morning before the trial begins."

Wanda bid Gabriella goodnight. Wanda hung up the phone only to dial another number. She knew she couldn't wait. Time was slipping away. "Good evening, Tricia. Can you come down to my room for a few minutes? It's important."

"Oh, sure. I have Dr. Orman here, and we've been talking about his testimony. He was on this morning and did a great job."

"I knew he would. Bring him with you. I'd like to say hello. It's been a long time since we worked together on another case." They hung up. Wanda went on automatic pilot. *Whatever happens, happens,* she reassured herself.

She greeted Tricia and Dr. Richard Orman, inviting them into her room. She was genuinely glad to see Richard. They were friends, having worked together on several cases. She knew she had an ally. After brief small talk, Wanda pointed to the scrapbook between them on her desk and asked, "Tricia, has anyone talked with Ruth or you about the PowerPoint and this book?"

"No. Why?" she responded, a little uneasy.

"I'll tell you, but you mustn't talk with Ruth. Todd's the lead attorney, and he and Mark will talk with her." Wanda took a deep breath. "We'll be using the LifePath—not the scrapbook."

Tricia's face turned pale white, then blood red. Her eyes immediately welled up with tears. "You . . . you can't do this to me!" She cried. "You can't imagine . . . the hours . . . the days . . . the time I . . . I worked on preparing this book! You . . . you can't do this to me!" Tears began to fall in torrents. Tricia buried her sobs in her hands. Dr. Orman, meanwhile, sat quietly on the sofa next to Tricia.

Wanda gently explained, "Tricia, we can't concern ourselves with how *we* feel. This isn't your case or mine. It's Joseph's. It's his life on the line. We . . . we have to do everything we can to defend him. It's our job. We have to put our egos aside. This isn't an emotional or a personal issue. It's an issue of life and death. Todd has made a decision, and I'm honoring it." There didn't seem to be a foreseeable end to the sobbing. So, Wanda continued, "I've no doubt you've worked tirelessly on this book. It's very . . . I'm sure you've spent many hours collecting, mounting, and writing in this document. But, you and I know it's not my work, not my preparation. It's yours. You and Ruth did a great job. But, I have to honor Todd's decision."

Tricia cried even harder. Dr. Orman joined in trying to persuade. "Tricia, she's right. This is not our case. It is Joseph's. It is his life. We can't let our egos get in the way."

Thank you, Dr. Orman, for supporting our cause. Wanda silently appreciated his input.

"Tricia, I'm sorry you and Ruth haven't been consulted about this," Wanda added, "but time's running out, so I thought you should know. I'm asking you . . . please don't tell Ruth. All of this is between the lawyers. Please keep it to yourself until she's been told."

Tricia glared at Wanda, her eyes and face stained from crying. She stormed out. Dr. Orman left quietly behind her, giving Wanda a supportive handshake and sympathetic nod. Wanda collapsed onto the couch, relieved, but still very uncomfortable.

A banging on her door brought Wanda to her feet from the couch. Tricia had gone straight to Ruth and told her everything. She was not happy. Wanda repeated her explanation to Ruth. "I'm following Todd's decision." Tricia and Ruth were both greatly upset, but Tricia's reaction had been the far more dramatic of the two. As angry as Ruth was, she was a professional and would get over it.

As Wanda locked the door behind Ruth, relief washed over her because Ruth finally knew. She kept replaying the drama in her head. *Those guys should have told her yesterday. I can appreciate her anger.* She ruefully observed, *The handwriting's on the wall—no forthcoming work ever again with Ruth and Atlanta.*

Even though she was exhausted from a full day's work of finalizing all eighteen of the thirty-six-by-forty-eight-inch charts and from the Atlanta ordeal, sleep escaped her. At about five o'clock, Wanda's eyes had finally closed, taking her into a deep sleep. An hour later, Catherine called with her wake-up greeting. The sisters chatted briefly. Nine o'clock was her designated time to testify, and that hour would be here before she knew it. Catherine signed off, wishing her luck.

As Wanda entered the witness holding room, just outside the courtroom, there stood Mark and Gabriella. She asked Mark wearily, "Did you talk with Ruth?"

"Yes, she called me last night." That's all that was said. Based on the ambivalence in his voice, Wanda could guess the tenor of their conversation.

The bailiff approached and said, "Dr. Draper, you're called."

Chapter 12

Entering the courtroom with consternation, she hoped she wasn't visually trembling; she was surely shaking on the inside. For the first few moments after taking her seat on the stand, she feared that she wouldn't be able to speak. She'd never been so nervous—all because of the dynamics between the scrapbook and the LifePath. After the first few questions by Mark, she relaxed, focusing on the task at hand. She silenced all other thoughts, feeling energized and ready. The scrapbook issue was soon put aside.

While responding to Mark's questions about her credentials, her gaze ran across the courtroom, searching for Ruth. She wasn't present. Wanda wondered if she was still fuming. She turned her attention to the jury. She always sought to look each juror in the eye, hoping to make a friendly yet meaningful connection for the duration of her testimony.

Mark prompted her, "Please explain your role as a developmental epistemologist." Questions and responses for the first fifteen minutes are like a warm-up for a Ping-Pong game. This part of the direct examination is aimed at informing the jury about Wanda's professional background and experience and to confirm previous work on capital cases.

Wanda informed the court, "I am a developmentalist. That is, I study and teach about the development of humans in stages." She then went on to explain, as in dozens of trials before, that "the term *child* means the human from conception through all of life's stages, including old age and death. Child development is actually a field of study. It's not a discipline. I chose development because, as a field of study, it encompasses the gamut of behavioral science disciplines: psychology, sociology, biology, and even anthropology."

Mark then asked, "Why is it called child development if it covers the entire life cycle?"

"It really should be called human development. The reason for using child development instead of human development dates back to the 1960s when anthropologists and behavioral scientists mutually agreed that anthropologists would use the term *human* and behavioral scientists would use the term *child*." Wanda could at least leave the stand today knowing the jurors learned one thing that they probably didn't know before.

"Have you ever been disqualified as a witness?"

"No, I haven't."

"Have you ever been impeached?"

"No, sir."

Mark started unlocking the LifePath door. He inquired how many persons Wanda had interviewed to gather information about Joseph. Then he asked if she had prepared any illustrations relative to Joseph's development.

"Yes, I've prepared a LifePath that depicts the major events and circumstances from birth through adolescence."

"Your Honor, may the witness be permitted to step down from the witness box and explain the LifePath to the jury?"

"Yes, she's permitted." He opened the door, and Wanda walked through it.

As she stepped down, the bailiff and Mark stationed two easels directly in front of the jury, turning them at such an angle that the prosecutors would also be able to view the charts. Of course, the defense attorneys were required to turn over copies of the LifePath weeks before the trial. Wanda briefly puzzled about how they would have handled discovery and the scrapbook. *What would they think if they received fifteen pounds of pictures and captions?* However, Wanda was quite sure they knew who put it together—not her. They were surely planning to impeach her if she were to use the scrapbook as part of her testimony.

Wanda quickly returned her thoughts to the LifePath. Mark asked her to explain the legends, the symbols, and all the horizontal and vertical markings. Then she proceeded to bring attention to Joseph's infancy period and numerous factors of vulnerability for Joseph as baby, indicating specific instances with the court-provided pointer. The jurors watched Wanda. The chart, designed as an easy-to-follow visual depiction of Joseph's life, made use of color, shape, and form to move the audience's eyes across the timeline and capture the jury's attention.

Mark guided, "On the first chart, would you explain what you mean by attachment and bonding?"

Wanda composed herself. "Yes, thank you. Attachment is the earliest human connection that a baby makes—first with parents, later with others, such as siblings or grandparents or another primary caregiver. This connection's made permanent by a bonding process. Some infants bond within a few weeks. Some require longer—even a few years for some children. This human bonding is the emotional equivalent of fusing two pieces of cloth together. Except in human bonding, it emotionally and psychologically glues the baby and parent together. During the attachment process, the infant's brain is actually being programed. This forms an internal working model. This is how the structure of the right brain develops."

"Are all attachments equal in quality?"

"No."

"Would you explain?"

"There are basically four types of attachment."

"What are they?"

"Secure, ambivalent, avoidant, and disorganized or disorganized/dissociative attachment."

"Please explain secure attachment to the court."

"Secure attachment is one in which the infant feels safe, comfortable, loved. He feels free to explore both human and physical surroundings during early months and years. The child is confident the parent(s) will be helpful and protective, yet senses their trust in his abilities. For example, some toddlers will either crawl or walk away from their mothers, only to return and make contact and then hurry off again. Once a child feels secure and safe, more exploration occurs. The child with a secure base grows up with confidence, able to cope with life."

"Please tell us about ambivalent attachment," Mark prompted.

"Ambivalent attachment. That's not so secure. This is the toddler who runs from the parent and continues going away until the parent runs to catch up to the child, often admonishing him and returning him to his seat, only to have him run again. Ambivalence does not give the child an opportunity to develop trust. The child's unsure of the parent's love and attention, uncertain whether the parent will be helpful. At times, the child feels close. At other times, the child feels rejected or abandoned, often clingy and fretful. This child grows up with anxiety, struggling with life's challenges, often a victim of bullying." The blonde-haired, blue-eyed child she had observed at the Phoenix airport appeared in Wanda's mind.

"And avoidant attachment?"

"This child doesn't trust the parent to keep him safe and comfortable and, therefore, continually tests reality, trying to live without the love and support of others. The child is often neglected or even abused. This child can be found avoiding the parent, unable to count on help in time of need. This child feels emotionally challenged and may become a bully."

"Finally, disorganized or disorganized/dissociative attachment?"

"This is the most serious and often the most damaging type of attachment. The child is fearful or disoriented, often detached and incompetent, failing at every turn. It's often a result of multiple factors that interfere with bonding. For example, moving a child from one family to another, from one parent to another, or sometimes taking him to other relatives causes the child to feel unwanted. There may be foster placements, hospital stays, or days away from home without the parent's daily contact. Custody changes and child placements, with disregard by a parent, may result in the child's confusion about his self-identity. Severe neglect, family violence, or substance abuse impedes a child's sense of self-worth and dignity. We can expect this child to be disorganized. He is trying but failing to organize his thinking, feelings, and actions in meaningful ways. He doesn't have a foundation for knowing how he fits into a family or community or how to form healthy relationships. He feels detached, unable to cope with life. His internal working model in the right brain is scrambled, disorganized. When the child doesn't know how to express his feelings and his fears, tension builds until he finds a way to expel it, even though the outcome may be harmful to himself or others. The child may grow up to exhibit deviant or even criminal behavior."

Wanda moved to the next two charts while Mark asked, "Does an attachment disorder always occur during the early years?"

"Not always, although it has its roots in the first few years. Joseph's is a case in point. Joseph by age ten was smoking pot. His parents showed no interest in the fact that he was absent sixteen days in third grade or that he had to repeat fourth grade, placing him in the same grade as his sister Lydia. He felt failure and rejection. He felt emotionally empty because neither his mother nor his father provided support. His pattern of school absences, his use of alcohol and drugs, and his failure in school did not concern them. When Joseph was fourteen, instead of his mother bringing him home from doing drugs with peers, she asked the police to pick him up. Her attachment to Joseph was so shallow that she felt no sense of responsibility for him."

Mark added another chart and stated, "He's now a young teenager. What do you mean by the developmental stressor, 'betrayal trauma'?"

"Notice what Jenny, Joseph's mother, said to him." Wanda pointed to the quote she had included on the chart. "To her fourteen-year-old son, she said, 'You're a total loser. I wish I'd never had you.' What a powerful message of rejection for a teenager to hear from his own mother! The Division of Family Services reported the Allen children had no support at home. What kind of role models were his parents? How could Joseph not feel betrayed? His brother Leonard drew a picture of the family but left Joseph out. His sister Lydia added a tombstone with his name on it and told the social worker that Joseph would be dead in a year if he could not change. How could Joseph straighten up when he felt betrayed and when he knew unequivocally that his parents didn't care about him?"

Mark continued, "Let's move to the next two charts. How did Joseph cope with the parental neglect and disregard?"

"He used drugs, skipped school, and sought older teens—all poor substitutes for parental bonding. Jenny left the family and was partying most of the time. By the time Joseph was sixteen years old, he was in a state of disorganized attachment. He was ill-equipped to organize his life, and he was falling apart emotionally as he saw what was happening to him and his family. When the court granted a divorce to Jenny and Terrance, his mother asked the court for Joseph to be emancipated. It was granted. She did not want to deal with him. Jenny took two children, and Terrance took two, but neither took Joseph. After a few months, Joseph took an overdose of motion sickness pills. He was overwhelmed with trauma and feelings of betrayal. He began to use alcohol, weed, and speed. He was having blackouts. He tested positive for marijuana and benzodiazepine. It wasn't long before Joseph was arrested for property destruction. Perhaps, for Joseph, this served as a metaphor for the destruction of his family. His cries for help went unheeded. Neither his mother nor his father wanted to devote the time, energy, or love to help him heal."

Wanda paused to scan the jury and take a moment for the information to settle in. All were intently listening. She continued, "He couldn't avoid the trauma he was feeling. He was admitted to a psychiatric hospital after drug-induced hallucinations. His evaluation included bipolar with psychotic features. These were all signs that Joseph was headed for trouble. In a couple of days, he was diagnosed as having schizophrenic disorder. He may have known right from wrong, but his emotional and psychosocial instability impeded any rational decision-making that would uphold any conscious orientation needed to act in accordance with his concept of right over wrong. We might say that his thinking capacity was like a computer, but his emotions were like the programs that make it run. When the trauma was overwhelming, rational thinking shut down."

Mark proceeded to the next two charts. "How do Joseph's life circumstances, as an adolescent, impact his development? Why can't he simply make a decision to put his life in order in spite of his family problems?"

"By the time Joseph entered middle adolescence, his disorganized attachment had distorted his mental working model. His worldview was distorted. He had reached the point of disorganized and dissociative attachment disorder. He had to detach from a sense of reality in order to survive."

Wanda pointed to the fact that Jenny abandoned Joseph when he was discharged from the psychiatric hospital. She then discussed how Joseph's brother James Spencer was shot and killed in his dad's house when Terrance gave his son and some kids a gun to play with upstairs while he stayed downstairs. She emphasized that neither parent talked with their children about James Spencer's death.

"The courts awarded custody to Terrance because Jenny relinquished all support for the boys. She moved to Florida. Her behavior remained consistently neglectful all of Joseph's life."

As she tracked through the remaining LifePath charts, Wanda hoped it was obvious to the jury that Joseph's feelings of betrayal trauma continued to exacerbate his disorganized attachment. "His life was like an abandoned boat without a rudder, drifting in the murky and stagnate pools of chaos, eventually dropping off the edge of his history into the tumultuous rapids of destruction. He was without a lifeline, without a rescue team, without even the faintest light to guide him through the dark tunnels of despair."

The last charts depicted Joseph committing desperate acts that landed him in prison with a fourteen-year sentence. She pointed out, "He was released in less than two years. Ready or not, Joseph was thrown back into a world that wasn't ready for him, and he certainly wasn't ready for the world."

When she completed all the charts, she returned to the witness box. Mark wanted to clarify some developmental implications.

"Earlier in your testimony, you stated that Joseph had a serious attachment disorder. How would this condition impact his behavior?"

Wanda turned and addressed the jury. "The child or adolescent with a strong attachment feels secure and self-confident. He has an inner strength that makes it unnecessary to misbehave. Of course, all children misbehave from time to time, yet they regain confidence. They're resilient. However, the child who never bonded, or who has an attachment problem, often lives with an underlying fear of rejection and a need to feel safe. Most children would rather have a spanking by a parent than be ignored. The spanking brings the child and caregiver in contact with each other. They connect—even if for the wrong reason. When we look at crime statistics, we find from FBI studies that many criminals have attachment problems from childhood. Their criminal behavior puts them in contact with one or more persons, and they feel more powerful with a weapon in hand. It gives them a false sense of security . . . even if momentarily. They aren't thinking about consequences, even though they know right from wrong. Some criminals also use drugs and alcohol to dull their sense of fear and inadequacy, thereby making it easier for them to commit crimes."

"Are you saying that people who abuse drugs and alcohol are on their way to becoming criminals?" Mark queried.

"Certainly not. There are numerous factors, as we've seen in Joseph's case that converge to impact one's thinking and decision-making. While each person, including Joseph, is ultimately responsible for his own behavior, life circumstances can enhance or impede how one uses his moral compass."

"Your Honor, I pass the witness."

The judge called for a fifteen-minute recess.

As she stood waiting for the jury to file out of the courtroom, Wanda's thoughts couldn't help but envision Joseph's state of mind while he was desperately making his escape from killing two people in Georgia, only to continue deeper down the path of destruction that would end with killing another family.

Court was called back to order. The jury filed in. Wanda returned to the witness box.

The prosecutor approached Wanda. She could tell he was chomping at the bit, ready to pounce.

"Good afternoon, *Ms.* Draper."

"Objection!" Mark jumped to his feet, nearly toppling the chair. "Harassing the witness! Would the court please instruct the prosecution to address her as *Dr.* Draper?"

"Sustained," stated the judge. "Counsel, please use Dr. Draper's correct title."

"Yes. Sorry, Your Honor. I meant no disrespect." The prosecutor struggled to squirm out from under his failed insult. "Good afternoon, *Dr.* Draper."

"Hello."

"Ma'am, are you being paid for your testimony here today?"

"No, absolutely not. I am being compensated for my time."

The prosecutor smiled, trying to recover from his failed trap to find grounds to have Wanda thrown off the stand for bribery. He tried to insinuate that she was a hired gun. "And, ma'am, how many times have you testified as a mitigation expert in a death penalty case in Oklahoma?"

"In Oklahoma, probably thirty to thirty-five times."

"And how many in Missouri?"

"Probably more than that, forty times or so."

"And how many in Texas?"

"Twice in a capital case. Oh, excuse me," Wanda corrected herself. "One of those was not a death penalty case. It was a murder case, but not death penalty."

"How many here in Florida?"

"This is my first."

"So, if my math's right—please correct me if I'm wrong—you've testified in excess of seventy times as a mitigation expert in a death penalty case?"

"That's correct."

"And that would be on behalf of the defendant to show mitigating evidence to the jury. Is that correct?"

"Correct."

"I believe earlier you stated that a severe attachment disorder and the kind of upbringing that Joseph had is a reasonable excuse for his killing behavior."

"No. That's not what I said. I said—"

"And just so I'm clear. You did no scientific testing. Is that correct?"

"Well, it depends on how you define scientific testing. I do my own developmental evaluation. I did not do standardized testing."

"Why not? Don't you think you should have given a standardized test?"

She stole a glance at Mark. He was leaning forward, his face reddening. "That's what a licensed psychologist or an MD would give. There is no license for what I do. I'm in a field of study. And, I'm an educator."

"Did you use any kind of objective testing, as far as some kind of methodology, on Joseph Allen?"

"Much of my work and forty years of experience are all based on very substantial research and study as well as practical application and knowledge and teaching; therefore, as a profession, child development has a scientific aspect to it. My work is not simply an opinion. It's based on information I gathered in conjunction with my own understanding of the defendant's development and my expertise—all the research that I've been involved in and the insights I've garnered from the material."

"Let me ask it a different way. No matter how much research you've done, no matter how much training you've had, you cannot predict human behavior, can you?"

"Well—"

"Yes or no, ma'am? Can you predict human behavior as to what's going to happen in the future?" The prosecutor had just given Wanda a verbal shove, trying to back her into a corner.

Mark sprang to his feet, rushing to Wanda's defense. "Your Honor, I don't think that calls for a yes or no response."

The Judge responded, "If she can't answer yes or no, she can say that."

"I cannot answer yes or no to that."

Ignoring that setback, the prosecutor continued, "And, ma'am, I understand that you've been trained and educated. But, in effect, you're taking that training and education, and you're making what I would call some educated guesses about what might happen in the future. Is that correct?"

"It would be an estimated probability based on information."

"An estimated probability?"

"Yes."

"Doctor, while it's obvious that Joseph had many problems while growing up, so have a lot of people. His siblings grew up in the same family, with the same parents, the same divorce, the same drug and alcohol abuse, and the same living conditions. They didn't become murderers. How do you account for the fact that Joseph was the only one of the children to grow up and kill people?"

Wanda anticipated that question. It was a very good question, a natural one. Throughout Joseph's case, she had recognized the shards that led to the severed lives. She felt compelled to present the unabridged picture of Joseph.

"*Joseph* was the only one that Jenny asked the court to grant her request for him to be emancipated.

"*Joseph* was the only one put out on his own when he was only sixteen. Terrance refused to take him when his mother rejected him.

"*Joseph* was the only one to be admitted as an inpatient in a psychiatric hospital.

"*Joseph* was the only one to overdose on drugs because he felt unwanted.

"*Joseph* was the only one to be diagnosed with several psychiatric and psychological personality disorders, including psychosis.

"*Joseph* was the only one readmitted to the psychiatric hospital for bipolar with mixed manic disorder.

"*Joseph* was the only one with documentation of no support from the parents while hospitalized.

"*Joseph* was the only one diagnosed at the treatment center with schizoaffective disorder and prescribed Depakote and Risperdal daily.

"*Joseph* was the only one receiving no financial support from his parents for purchasing the medications he needed and no help monitoring the administration of them.

"*Joseph* was the only one, after James Spencer's death, who went back to live with Jenny and was kicked out again, told to go live with Terrance.

"*Joseph* was the only one to be kicked out by Terrance—every time he tried to go home.

"*Joseph* was the only one to go to the hospital emergency room to ask for medication that he had previously been prescribed but never received because neither parent responded to his need.

"*Joseph* was the only one of the Allen children whose mother told him she wished she had never had him.

"*Joseph* was the only one whose parents kicked him out on Christmas Day, after he had gone home to be with his family at Terrance's house.

"*Joseph* was the only child in his family who failed to bond with either parent."

"I pass the witness."

The judge asked Mark, "Any further questions?"

"Thank you, Your Honor." Mark stood up from the desk and walked between the jury and witness box. "Dr. Draper, regarding the prosecution's question about why you didn't administer a standardized test to the defendant, Joseph Allen, and your response that you weren't licensed and/or certified to give the tests, have you ever taken the tests to be licensed or certified in psychology?'"

"I've taken the full battery of nine tests in order to be licensed in psychology. And I've passed all nine tests in the 90 percent range. But, the American Psychological Association charges over three hundred dollars for each of the nine licenses. I didn't think it was necessary to pay such an amount for a piece of paper. I have shown that I understand the psychological concepts and material in order to be licensed. In addition, I've taught many training seminars in which I've signed off on countless psychologists' updated licenses."

"Doctor, have you formed an opinion in Joseph's case?"

"Yes, I have."

"Would you state that opinion?"

"Yes. In my opinion, Joseph Allen experienced problems in his early childhood and adolescent years that resulted from the confluence of several factors, all of which significantly impacted his development and contribute to and help explain, but do not excuse, his behavior. These factors are a severe attachment disorder, unresolved and deep-seated emotional pain resulting from paternal neglect and disregard, a constant sense of loss and feeling of abandonment, and a dependency on drugs and alcohol to numb emotional pain and feelings of rejection and betrayal trauma.

"Joseph's perception of himself and the world echo the impact of parental neglect and of the nurturing necessary in building a foundation based on love, trust, and mutuality, together with guidance and limits and the transmission of moral principles. He suffered in his social and emotional development because his formative years lacked both the secure foundation and the major protective factors that mitigate against later aggression. These factors include learning empathy, learning self-control and a conscience orientation, developing capacities for higher levels of thinking, and resisting the effects of substance abuse and adverse temptations in order to prevent the escalation of illegal and violent acts.

"Conscience and empathy, combined with morality and ethics, are not inborn qualities but are learned during one's formative years. Joseph's developing years were filled with attachment issues, unsettled living quarters, multiple school problems, psychiatric issues and hospitalizations, and a lack of parental guidance and limits.

"Joseph experienced neither sufficient environmental opportunities nor adequate personal upbringing to develop the conscience orientation and emotional stability needed to appropriately guide his own behavior."

"I pass the witness."

The prosecutor stood up. He walked towards Wanda, a sheet of notes in hand. He prepared another line of attack to crumble Wanda's testimony.

———

The back and forth interchanges between the defense and the prosecution resembled a tug-of-war match. Each one trying to gain ground, to move the score in their favor. Wanda was the rope, pulled and strained.

The match culminated. The prosecutor glared as he asked, "Is this LifePath, with these charts, your design and the result of your work?"

"Yes, sir. Absolutely."

"Did anyone instruct you in how to do this?"

"No, sir. Absolutely not."

"I have no further questions."

The judge turned toward Wanda and nodded, "You may step down."

As Wanda stepped down from the witness box, she felt the satisfaction of a battle well-fought. Her testimony was long, but it was strong. It wasn't until the door closed that the wave of exhaustion washed over her. Her mind began to replay her testimony, offering critiques. She reassured herself, *I did the best I could.*

Mark, Todd, and Gabriella took Wanda to dinner that evening. Todd couldn't wait to ask, "Can you imagine what the prosecutor would've done had you used the scrapbook?"

"I would've been impeached. Probably never asked to work on another case." Everyone shook their heads, agreeing emphatically.

———

Wanda rushed outdoors to where her sister was weeding a flower bed.

"Catherine! I just got off the phone with Mark. Joseph received LWOP. What a victory!" Wanda exclaimed.

"Wanda, that's fantastic!" Catharine said, jumping to her feet. "An even more spectacular feat since Duval County leads all other counties in Florida for conferring the death penalty. They use the needle or electric chair in their death penalty cases. Duval County, even with its relatively small population, has the highest citizens-per-death-row-inmate rate in the United States." Catherine pumped her fist in exultation.

Wanda and Catherine, giddy with excitement over a job well done, decided to go out and celebrate. The sisters dressed in their skirted finery and drove to their favorite evening restaurant. The two enjoyed their jubilation, reminiscing and replaying the tumultuous journey. They spent the evening sharing experiences, thoughts, and dessert.

It wasn't long before she heard from her cousin Edward, who cut out newspaper clippings of Joseph's trial, highlighting Wanda's contribution, and mailed them to several relatives. He called her to tell her so, expressing his pride in her efforts and the resulting outcome for the case. Wanda beamed inwardly, appreciating the message of esteem and acceptance from her cousin. She picked up her hand shears and headed to the garden. As she deadheaded bushes in the cool of the evening, the earth bathed in shades of lavender and pink against the sun setting in the blue sky, Wanda reflected on Joseph, the one no one wanted, no one accepted. He was discarded, neglected, unloved, and uncared for. He was presented as stone cold, but Wanda contemplated, *His life was sucked from him . . . Every time his family rejected him, disowning any kinship with him, they robbed him of any feelings of compassion, honor, and emotion.* She snipped away at a bush, knowing that removing the spent buds would make way for new, healthy, and stronger growth. A rose beamed at her, and Wanda smiled. A sense of pleasing gratification filled her. *Joseph's jury grasped the fact that early childhood development does indeed have a relationship to adult behavior.* She relished the bliss of knowing one of the very dearest people in her life—her cousin Edward—recognized her differing perspective and learned to appreciate a new view. This case provided the balsam for the inflamed blister in their relationship caused through misunderstandings about Wanda's role in forensics.

PART THREE

Chapter 13

My heart sunk when I realized James would never have his day in court," Wanda told her longtime attorney colleague Ted Holtz over lunch at the Faculty Club. "We never had a chance to put his story on trial." Wanda sipped her cup of hot lemon water as her mind reprocessed James's plight.

"James's case," Ted paused in recollection, "how long's it been?"

Wanda glanced up at the ceiling, mentally calculating before answering, "About five years."

Ted pushed his plate away. "I remember you were very disappointed with the outcome."

"James told me his version of what happened that cold January night in Oklahoma City . . . how grateful he was to the man, Bostwick, who became the victim." Wanda paused. "Yet, I've often wondered about something that was never pursued."

Ted looked puzzled. "What else is there to tell?"

"Harrison reported the security guard at the apartment told him he saw Bostwick and a young man walking toward Bostwick's apartment close to midnight the night of the killing. The guard knew the young man who lived in the apartment complex with his parents. He was rather large and stout and the guard said he wasn't too bright. Come to find out, he was intellectually impaired. The guard thought nothing of it. He'd seen them go to Bostwick's apartment regularly. He thought Bostwick was simply befriending him."

"Why didn't Harrison interview the young man?" Ted leaned back in his chair in surprise. "I worked with him for several years—great investigator."

"One of the best," Wanda agreed. "I also asked him the same question." Wanda shook her head dejectedly, "I remember his words verbatim, 'It takes money to travel, to find someone.'" She looked up at Ted, "Remember, that was a public defender case. There wasn't any money to follow up." Ted nodded in understanding, familiar with the same plight. She paused briefly. "Harrison did say the young man moved with his parents the next day, and no one knows where they went. The security guard thought they might have gone to Michigan or Wisconsin." Wanda then rubbed the back of her neck. She seemed to be struggling with something. "I keep going back to the knock at the door the morning James found Bostwick on the floor. Could that've been the young man, returning to see if Bostwick was alive?"

"Are you saying he was the killer and not James?"

"I don't know. Will we ever really know?"

Ted paused, collecting his thoughts. "Did you and Harrison come up with any theories that might explain what happened?" Ted motioned to the waitress that they would need coffee, and Wanda enthusiastically nodded in agreement.

"I told Harrison that after seeing the police photos and reading the description of Bostwick when they found him . . . I told him we might have a case of AEF."

"Autoerotic fatality . . . Isn't it also called sexual or autoerotic asphyxia, hypoxyphilia, or asphyxiaphilia? Did he agree with you?"

Wanda nodded. "He did. He told me he was thinking the same thing. He had reviewed the literature, and Bostwick fit the description. This intellectually impaired young man from the apartment complex might not have killed Bostwick, but he could've assisted innocently in bringing about sexual play gone wrong. Harrison thought James would've been too sleepy and exhausted to force such a position on Bostwick who was larger and probably a lot stronger than he was. Harrison told me we couldn't go anywhere with this."

"Why not?" Ted fired back.

"He said, 'Frankfort would never let us go there.' He said, 'AEF brings on a moral issue for the media.' I told him I thought we needed to pursue this, but he told me that whether by law or by social edict, this topic's avoided in the press. It's certainly—"

The old grandfather clock chimed, notifying all of the hour of day. As Ted glanced at his watch to verify, a sudden realization seemed to hit him. "I'm going to have to take a rain check on that coffee. Just remembered I have a prelim in an hour," he apologetically informed Wanda. "But, finish telling me what Frankfort said."

Wanda started to gather her belongings. "He said AEF's avoided in the press, and it's certainly never going to be discussed in a conservative Oklahoma courtroom. A couple of cases of AEF caused a stream of 'copycat' incidents in California, and since then, there's been an all-out effort to prevent any publicity on this kind of autoeroticism."

Ted rolled his eyes. "Talk about disconcerting. I wonder if the police investigators even considered such a possible cause of death in this case. Did they even know what this was?"

"An article in one of the prominent Oklahoma newspapers gave an account of the crime. The article described Bostwick as having a record as a homosexual who was accused of picking up young boys and molesting them. He had moved to Oklahoma from Nevada. But there was nothing anywhere about AEF."

After paying their bill, Ted saw Wanda out into the foyer. He was now as upset as she was that James had never had his day in court. Perhaps the search for the truth had never been thoroughly explored and, therefore, had not been discovered.

Wanda continued to reflect on Frankfort's reasoning to persuade James to opt for a blind plea as she returned to work. *Straight life means James might be paroled after serving ten to fifteen years, depending on his behavior and parole plan. But, this was a safe sentence on the part of the judge. He thought James would never be released from the institution. Or, was there doubt in the judge's mind about James's guilt or innocence?*

"They should call a spade, a spade!" Catherine spat out, feeling particularly exasperated with James's case. She sat at the desk in Wanda's office, working another case with her. James's case had established and solidified a partnership between the sisters. They complemented each other well. Catherine emphasized details, insisting not one be out of alignment. Wanda delved into the gray, not allowing concrete perspectives to determine interpretations. Their sister-turned-colleague relationship was a great combination of thought and study.

"This is the truth after all!" Catherine slapped the table, expressing her frustration. While researching the new case, she had come across a recent article discussing sexual asphyxia. It had triggered a flood of feelings for James's case. She demanded to know why the attorneys wouldn't address the issue.

Wanda told Catherine that many attorneys and investigators either didn't know about or wouldn't talk about AEF. Judges wouldn't let them talk about it either and neither would the press. "They weren't going to put before a jury that this was the desire for a state of oxygen deficiency in order to elicit or enhance sexual excitement and orgasm," Wanda further iterated. "They weren't going to allow a witness to explain that the possible criteria for AEF included presence of an asphyxiation mechanism such as pressure to the neck, hanging, asphyxiation devices, or a noose to adjust airflow. They didn't want to have a witness explain further about the illicit act: inferred position of the body during an asphyxiation act (standing or kneeling); the use of safety devices, like having a knife to cut oneself loose; the use of padding to avoid rope burns; or location of the body when found with private, restricted access."

Catherine was ready to let James go and throw the book at Bostwick, even though he was already dead. Her indignation was fueled by numerous newspaper articles reporting Bostwick's history of molesting young boys. This was intolerable to her.

Catherine let the subject drop. She closed the file before her and pushed back from the table. Working with Wanda had inspired alterations in Catherine's thinking about defending the accused. She learned how to piece the puzzle together to form the bigger picture. Catherine, now, fascinated with human development, initiated many long discussions about society's attitude toward children and, later, their adult behavior. Yet, she was a moralist who saw things primarily as black or white, without gray areas, allowing no excuses for illegal or immoral behavior.

Both she and Wanda contemplated James's plight, each upset by the injustice. Walking over to the file cabinet, she exclaimed, "Tell you what!" A wiry grin appeared on Catherine's face. "Crime does pay! Think of all these high-dollar paychecks to the prosecutors, the defense, the other professionals! Think of all the motions, orders, medical tests, and the psychological evaluations. All those people have to be paid! I wonder if people even realize what a booming market crime is." She reached for a file and continued, "I'm going to have seminars for people who are going to commit murder," Catherine started shaking the file for emphasis, a playful spark in her eyes. "I'll start with six rules." She held up her fingers. "Rule one, never make a statement or agree to talk with the police without an attorney. Rule two, never make a confession unless you've had some sleep. Rule three, never confess to something you didn't do, thinking that in court 'the truth will set me free.'" Her voice rose an octave in remembering what James had said. "Rule four," she continued down her fingers, "never count on a 'partner in crime' because he'll turn on you if it's to his advantage. Rule five, never believe you can get away with a crime, and rule six, never commit a crime without taking my seminar first!" Then she said emphatically, "It's cheap, and we always have refreshments!"

"Sign me up!"

The sisters simultaneously broke out in laughter.

One day, five to six years after James's confinement in the forensics hospital, Wanda received a letter from him. Over the years, she had heard from him occasionally. She filed most of the letters after copying them for his Grandmother Matilda, who always sent copies of his letters to her. In all of the years that James wrote to Matilda and to Wanda, he never blamed anyone for his plight. *Much like John Carlyle,* she remarked to herself. But, he always did maintain his innocence. He began studying the Bible while at Vinita, and prayer had become a daily part of his life.

This particular letter caught Wanda's attention because it was postmarked from Lexington, a less-secure facility for prisoners with nonviolent crimes or for those considered very low risk. Wanda decided that when she was in that area of the state she would go and visit him. She wrote and asked him to put her on his visitor list. He seemed very excited that she should still be interested in him.

Driving up the road to the Lexington Correction Center, Wanda was impressed by the farms and surrounding land areas worked by the inmates. The sidewalks and entry area were filled with well-groomed lawns and beautiful flowers. *What a change from the big prison,* Wanda thought. The lobby was so out of character it seemed surreal. Three large chandeliers hung from the ceiling. *Where in the world would one find such decor in the lobby of a prison?* she pondered. Officials and guards worked with efficiency, and Wanda was processed with courtesy.

A female guard led her to a large visiting area filled with small tables and comfortable chairs. Soft drink and snack machines lined one wall. There were several men and women seated with their inmate spouses. A large viewing window showcased inmates' visiting children enjoying a sparsely furnished but attractive playroom.

James came into the room dressed in crisp-clean gray pants, a buttoned shirt, and immaculate sneakers. He was all smiles. His hair looked professionally styled. They sat at one of the tables, and James's first words were kind-hearted. "How've you been? I was surprised you'd come to see me."

How nice, Wanda thought. *He's still so cordial, friendly, and concerned about me. Just like his letters—genuinely friendly. He ends them all with a sunshine face!* Wanda assured him, "Every opportunity I have to come and see you, you know I will."

They had a good visit, and when Wanda left, it was her belief that James finally had a purpose in life. He had several friends. It seemed like he had somewhat of a family. He had a good relationship with the chaplain and had been studying the Bible and participating in daily devotionals. He had been given a job in the prison television studio. He earned seventeen dollars a month while learning to operate the video cameras.

When dignitaries and politicians came to inspect or visit the facility, James videotaped their tour and conferences. He earned the rank of trustee. This was such a change from James, the escapee on the way to the dentist.

A few months later, Wanda returned for a second visit because James had written to ask if she might assist in helping him prepare for a parole hearing. This visit proved to be almost shocking.

James was not only vibrant and looking like a mature young man, but he seemed settled and serious about his work. He was now in charge of the video studio. He created the format for the daily devotional, menus, and activities that were funneled over the closed circuit system to all inmates. He used pictures of flowers and other exterior points of interest as he developed each day's visuals.

She was impressed that he selected verses from not only Christian sources but other faith literature as well to accompany the daily devotionals. He was allowed to show a sample of these to her, and his plan for a career possibility upon parole was clearly evolving. He expressed sincere interest in this work.

During their visit, James told Wanda he had been trying to locate his half-sister, Stella. She was Bruce Balzo's daughter by a marriage after James moved away to live with Amanda and Albert. Matilda had encouraged James to contact Stella, who currently lived in the Las Vegas area.

James also told Wanda, "I've finally let go of Molly because . . . when I was in Vinita, I didn't think I'd ever . . . ever get out of the, um, there."

Wanda sat there quietly listening. She didn't inform James that Molly had called her during his confinement. Although sad, she was pleased that he had come to the realization that their feelings for one another would likely never manifest beyond those first days together in Minnesota.

Wanda changed the subject. She again encouraged James to write his life story. "It would be therapeutic for you to share such an unusual life history at such a young age."

Wanda returned home from her visit with James. Her husband Edwin presented her with a stack of mail and telephone messages. She was pleasantly surprised by the message from an old classmate inviting her to a high school reunion, the first one since graduating forty-two years earlier. Wanda excitedly looked forward to visiting with old friends. *What will he look like after four decades?* Her thoughts inadvertently turned to Sandy. *Please let him be fat, ugly, bald, and boring.*

As Sandy walked through the door of the large room where they were all congregating, Wanda's heart stopped. He looked about the same as he did forty-two years ago, only more mature and handsome. *Darn it!* Wanda was mentally vexed.

He gave her a big hug. She felt like sparks would go right through the top of her head. He introduced his wife to her, and she was, indeed, lovely and beautiful. *Matilda and Roy were right,* she noted. *She does greatly resemble Elizabeth Taylor.* They visited a while longer, but soon dispersed, moving on to see other old friends.

During lunch in the old cafeteria, Sandy approached Wanda, asking if they could talk. They headed to the auditorium where pictures and memorabilia were posted. Wanda wondered at the synchronicity that "Stardust" would be playing over the speakers at just that moment. After learning about Sandy's family, Wanda told him his wife was lovely. He said she really took good care of him.

"Why'd you leave me?" he demanded out of the blue.

Wanda, shocked at the question, answered evenly, "Our mutual friend told me you didn't want to go with me anymore." She had never expected him to bring up the past.

"That's not true," he replied defensively. "Not true. The only reason she told you that was because she wanted to go with me."

Glancing away, Wanda remained poised and displayed no emotion. Inwardly, she was a train wreck. She was speechless. Eventually, she returned her gaze back to Sandy, looking directly into his blue eyes. She smiled, "I think you and I will always have a very special relationship."

"I sure hope so," he sincerely replied.

The moon had made significant progress across the star-speckled sky. Wanda, still excited over the revelations earlier that evening, sat outside on her hotel's balcony. She gloried in feeling and smelling the familiar Gulf air. Catherine was on the phone, delighting in Wanda's retelling. As the stars twinkled above her, she marveled about life to her sister. "Here I am, at age fifty-eight, still learning things about myself and the world." She recognized that because she believed at face value the selfish falsehoods of a friend without confrontation her life had taken a different path. Yet, she also conceded that her life might otherwise not be what it is now, so she could not regret this seemingly tragic incident.

"I can't believe the twist of fate," Catherine remarked, astonishment evident in her voice.

"At one time in my life, I wanted nothing more than to be a farmer's wife," she reflected. "Yet, now, I am content, satisfied."

"You don't wish to undo the past?"

"Just suppose I had married Sandy. I wouldn't have had the opportunities for all that I've had the privilege of experiencing." Though she had three marriages and two divorces, she regretted nothing, cherishing the good times she had with each husband, as well as the periods of singlehood in between. Wanda elaborated, "To me, relationships are complex and dynamic, not stagnant. I choose to focus on the positive experiences, letting them grow and nurture my own development." She smiled up past the stars in thankfulness. "'Life is a mystery to be lived, not a problem to be solved,'" she quoted a line from a dear friend.

Wanda's next visit to Lexington was even more exciting than the last. Not only was James continuing his video work, but he was also now one of three inmates selected to design a children's program to be implemented in the play area adjoining the visiting area. He helped order and place the furnishings. Then, they ordered additional outdoor play equipment for the children of inmates to enjoy during visitations. The icing on this cake was that all equipment, both indoor and outdoor, was purchased by inmates donating their earnings. They felt like this was their contribution to their families since they were unable to be at home supporting their children and spouses. James was modestly pleased to have a leadership role in this monumental effort. And, in addition, he was one of the three selected to play with the children while parents visited in the adjoining visitation room. Wanda was so impressed with him. She thought, *He will make a great employee for a television station or even for helping design children's centers or filming children in various settings.* She found this work situation to be an excellent background for his parole request plan.

Before their visit ended, James told Wanda he had been corresponding with Stella and how thrilling it was for him. He expressed with elation finally feeling part of his family. Unity was becoming a reality. James also told Wanda that Matilda was his mainstay for keeping the faith and staying strong. He didn't know at that time that Wanda and Matilda had corresponded or that Matilda had been diagnosed with cancer.

Wanda often wrestled with how much to disclose to James about Molly and Matilda. At the same time, she didn't want to do anything to shake his newfound faith. He was doing so well.

Wanda sat at Matilda's kitchen table enjoying a freshly baked apple pie. Wanda was traveling to present a two-day workshop on human development at a university in East Texas, and she arranged to stop by Matilda's.

"This is the best apple pie I've ever eaten!" Wanda enthusiastically complimented as she took another bite. Sipping her coffee, she added, "Absolutely superb!" The two women visited for a couple of hours, Matilda talking about James's mother, Lisa, and how she loved James when he was a little boy.

"Lisa told me James was very loving and affectionate," Matilda remembered. "He was extremely sensitive and often climbed in her lap to hug her as if to comfort her. He had no idea his stepfather was engaged in an affair. Even so, I think he sensed his mother's sadness."

Wanda nodded in agreement.

"James was devastated when he found his mother dead," Matilda said. "I want to live long enough to see James pardoned or paroled," she confided. "Then, I will be resigned to my own fate."

Wanda's next visit to see James was for the purpose of discussing his parole plan. Ted Holtz agreed to collaborate with her, both working *pro bono* to facilitate this process. With only a couple of months to make the deadline, they met at Lexington and entered the facility. Wanda told herself, *If I have the capability to help in a situation like this, I must do it. If I can, I must.*

As they exited Lexington after their visit, Ted told Wanda, "I think James has a really good shot at being paroled. He's got a good prison record—no behavioral write-ups and excellent work experience." Wanda's spirits lifted. *Ted's such a good guy—a really seasoned attorney.*

Wanda put down the latest letter from James to answer her phone. He had written to express how impressed he was with the attorney. He also said that Stella was planning to visit him. The letter was filled with optimism. His words practically jumped off the pages with enthusiasm.

"Wanda?" came a weak voice from the other end. It wasn't until the voice identified itself that Wanda knew who it was. She didn't recognize the strange, garbled voice.

"Yes, Matilda. How are you doing? What's going on?" Wanda sensed her distress.

"I got a bad report . . ." Matilda's voiced faded out, overcome with the pain of reality. "Would you talk with James? I don't want him to be surprised—not again." Her voice broke under the strain of sadness. Wanda readily agreed, already mentally packing for her trip to Lexington.

James was visibly shaken. His loving grandmother and his surrogate support from his mother was all slipping away. James, through tears, declared he would communicate with Matilda through a video.

"That's a brilliant idea and such a noble gesture," Wanda encouraged him.

"I'm sure that was such a comfort," Wanda replied on the phone call from Roy. She reached for a tissue to wipe away her tears. Matilda had died. Roy was delivering the sad news.

"You should have seen her face when she received that video from James," reminisced Roy. "It was a forty-five minute 'face-to-face talk' as James labeled it. He told her how much she meant to him and how thankful he was for her years of support. Then he described his video studio work and the children's program." Roy's voice gave out briefly. "Matilda was so thrilled to hear that the playroom was complete and that James was selected as one of the three inmates to interact with the children."

Wanda expressed appreciation and pleasure for James making the effort to create the video and to get it to Matilda in such a timely manner.

Roy continued talking a few minutes, enjoying the brief respite from mourning, "James told Matilda that he would be up for parole soon and that he would forever be grateful for her love and her many letters of encouragement." Roy swallowed tears. "She died the day after watching James's video."

In Wanda's next visit with James, they embraced in the large visiting room. Both felt the loss. Wanda shared Roy's story about Matilda and the video.

"You know I had to break a rule to get the video sent by express mail," James admitted. "But I'm glad I did it. No one said anything." James's reputation at Lexington was one of being friendly, responsible, and working with integrity.

"I'm sure they trust you," Wanda comforted.

James smiled, "Several guards and inmates gave me their condolences when they heard about my grandmother's . . ." James couldn't bring himself to say "death."

Wanda smiled and said reassuringly, "She loved you dearly." Then they talked about his parole plan. He really liked Ted and expressed gratitude for his willingness to help. James was also pleased that Stella was finally coming to visit him.

———————

"Pardon me. Who'd you say is calling?" Wanda was reeling.

"The US Marshal. Calling from Oklahoma City. I believe you're acquainted with James Fields?"

"Yes," she replied, her pulse quickening. "As a matter of fact, I've been working with an Oklahoma City attorney . . . preparing for his parole hearing."

"Well, James has escaped from Lexington. We think he may be headed your way. You haven't heard from him, have you?"

Wanda paused for a moment, trying to gather her swarming thoughts. "No, I haven't." She was utterly surprised. It was only three weeks since her the last visit to Lexington. "But I don't think he'd come here. He knows it would put me in a bad spot."

"We don't know if he's dangerous or whether he has a weapon, but we can't take any chances. If you hear from him, call me immediately." He paused before advising, "I think you should leave your house and stay some other place for a few days until we find him."

"Will you please call me when you do?"

"Yes. We'll stay in touch." He hung up. Before she could decide what to do next, the phone rang again.

"Wanda, it's Roberta. Just saw the five o'clock news." Roberta was one of her close friends in Oklahoma City. "James has escaped. They showed his picture. He doesn't look like a criminal. Actually, he looks like he could be in the movies," she said, surprised and momentarily distracted. "What do you think happened?"

"Roberta, did they say how he escaped or give any details?" Wanda was devastated.

"Apparently, he and another inmate walked into the parking lot in mid-afternoon and overtook a woman in her van. They were reportedly seen traveling toward Oklahoma City." Wanda thanked her for the information and signed off, explaining she needed to make another call.

"Ted, you heard about James?"

"I was just about to call you. They found the woman and her van halfway between Lexington and Oklahoma City. She said they were nice—didn't hurt or threaten her. But, they did tape her mouth with duct tape. She said James thanked her, then disappeared. They left the van with the keys in the ignition. There's an all-points bulletin out on him. I'll let you know if I learn more."

Wanda told Ted about the US Marshal's call. "You think I should leave my house for a couple days?"

"Better to be safe than sorry, but like you said, I don't think he'll head to your place."

"I think I know where he's going," she surmised.

"Don't tell me. Call the marshal. Just keep in touch."

Wanda called a friend to ask if she had a room at her bed and breakfast that might be available for a few days. When she gave her a report of what happened, her friend was only too glad to help.

Before Wanda could call the marshal, he called her again. "Any word from him?" he asked urgently.

"No. But, I . . . I think I know where he'd go."

The marshal was definitely eager to hear since they were at a complete loss. They had him posted all over national television as "Most Wanted—May be armed and extremely dangerous."

However much Wanda disliked this characterization of James, she didn't show it in her voice or say anything about it. Instead, she opted to say, "He won't come here. You'll likely find him in the Bryan-College Station, Texas, area. His grandmother lived there . . . She died recently. I think that's where he'd go." As she hung up, she thought, *If only the public knew James as a whole person, they'd realize he is one of the least dangerous people around.*

———

"We're tracking a man who fits his description, driving a compact car, going about ninety miles per hour down I-35 South," the marshal called again and reported. Wanda was just settling into the room at her friend's bed and breakfast.

"He wouldn't drive that fast," Wanda informed the marshal. "But, let me know if that's him." They signed off. *Whatever possessed James to escape when he was so close to his parole hearing?* Wanda wondered. She picked up the phone again and made another call.

"Ted, have a minute? I'm very concerned about James. This is so unexpected."

"I know. What do you think sparked his escape?"

"My hunch is Stella had something to do with this."

"The marshal said James had two hundred dollars on the books that was taken out a few days prior to his leaving. Where'd he get that kind of money? He had no outside sources."

Wanda went on to say, "Had to be Stella. I think James . . . I think he became enamored with the idea of reuniting with a family member. Hasn't been that long since Matilda's death. Stella visited him since you and I were there, and I think she gave him the money. I really do. I also think she helped him plan his escape."

Ted and Wanda both drew long breaths. Then, Ted asked, "You know how to contact her?"

"No, but I'll find her."

The Lexington facility gave Wanda Stella's phone number from their visitation register. She had a Las Vegas address. Stella answered, conceding that the US Marshal had called her and asked if she gave James any money.

"He told me that I may be guilty of aiding the escape of a prisoner," Stella confided, distressed. "I hung up on him . . . I was scared they might arrest me."

"Did you give James money?" persisted Wanda.

"I don't want to get in trouble," she evaded. In a burst of rebellion, she declared, "I think James should not have to stay in prison because he's not guilty." She then hung up when Wanda further pressed her about the money.

Wanda shook her head, indignantly frustrated by Stella's words.

Amanda Fields then called. *I'm really burning up the phone lines*, Wanda thought as she listened to Mrs. Fields pleading to know what was happening. The US Marshal had called the Fields soon after James escaped, thinking he may have tried to call or go there. But she told Wanda that they had not heard from James.

"I don't know, Amanda," Wanda admitted. She mentally lamented, *Oh, James, why? You were so close.*

Wanda returned to her home after a couple of days in the bed and breakfast. She was confident that James would not come to her house. After eleven days, he was still on the run. She hardly finished bringing her groceries in when her phone rang. She glanced at the phone as she answered. The voice stunned her.

"James, are you all right?" Wanda asked, unable to hide the concern in her voice.

"Yes," he sputtered.

"What . . . what are you going to do?"

"I, uh, I don't know." He paused, breathing heavily. "I just had to be free . . . for a while. I've had eleven days of freedom. That's eleven days I never would've had in prison." His voice rose in elation. "I . . . I hope I haven't caused you any trouble," concern returning to his voice. "I really hope I haven't. I, uh, really appreciate all you've done for me." James paused again. "Um, I've gotta go now."

Wanda looked at her phone, bewildered, noting the area code. She dialed the US Marshal and informed him about the call, telling him about the area code. It was the Bryan-College Station area.

———

"We found James asleep on the roof of one of the university dorms," the marshal told Wanda when he phoned the next day. "He didn't resist. He said, 'I just wanted to be free for a while.' We really appreciate your help."

Wanda drew a sharp breath as she contemplated James's life. *His work and life as a trustee had no chance of survival.* Her train of thought turned to Stella. *She will never know what impact her two hundred dollars and her influence had on James's future. His parole plan just went down the toilet.*

PART FOUR

Chapter 14

Bob, we got a hit on the Anna Stanford case," stated Officer Tom Wyn enthusiastically. A chestnut-eyed, young, energetic rookie, he excitedly typed and clicked on his computer, pulling up files.

"Finally, a new lead to work with," replied Detective Bob Lacey, relieved at making some forward progress on a cold case. Little more than a year old, the Cold Case Unit in the St. Louis Police Department was eager to prove their merit as well as justify the grant they had acquired. Other divisions had their eye on the tidy little sum provided by the federal government.

"CODIS flagged—"

"What's that again, Tom?" interrupted Bob, who still felt left in the dust by the rapidly advancing technology and all the acronyms that marked its progression. Detective Lacey had been serving the community of St. Louis diligently for twenty years. He was cast from the old mold, where officers relied on their intuition and common sense.

"Combined DNA Index System," replied Tom.

"Great! Who's our perp?" excitedly asked Bob.

"Um . . . let's see." Tom scanned the computer screen. "A Quentin Mathews. Printing his file now." Tom had long since realized that his partner preferred a tablet of paper rather than a tablet with digital paper or a computer screen. He handed the printout to his partner.

"Mathews is already servin' a term for stealing and burglary," Bob announced. "Any other corroborating evidence?" he then asked as he continued to peruse the file, collecting another page from the printer.

"There's a note on the file that the lab's reviewing the case's evidence . . . Maybe they have something." Tom snatched up the phone and dialed the lab's number. The rookie affably inquired about the progress with the case and then graciously waited on the line while the technician checked.

"He has a history of stealin' since he was young," noted Bob as he continued to scan Quentin's file. "And it is sure a rough part of town where Quentin lived."

"So, it looks like he's a thief . . . Doesn't really fit the MO for a rapist . . . Yes, yes, I'm still here," Tom assured the technician who was back on the line. Tom then gave the tech his undivided attention, only to ask, "That's the only evidence? . . . Oh, okay. Thanks." Tom placed the receiver back on the cradle and glanced up at Bob. "Lab said a handprint from the back door leading to the outside is a positive match for Mathews."

"Looks like our guy. The crime occurred . . ." Bob paused as he checked the document. "Three years before Mathews was picked up for stealin'. That fits the time frame."

"What about motive?" asked the rookie. "And pattern? This doesn't fit his pattern. He's a thief—and a non-violent one at that. Thieves aren't usually rapists and murderers."

"But things go wrong," replied the seasoned detective. "I've seen plenty of cases—plenty—where a simple robbery went wrong, and a victim ends up at the morgue."

Tom considered this. "'Okay, I see your point there, but Anna Stanford . . . She was raped, beaten, and strangled," Tom said as he cited details from Stanford's file. "That's not a robbery gone wrong. That's a rape crime," argued Tom.

"Listen, we got his DNA," declared Bob, a devotee of DNA evidence. He believed in its infallibility. "And a handprint. Two." Bob held up two fingers and continued, "Those are corroborating pieces of evidence at the crime scene. Mathews . . . you know my motto: if it walks like a duck and quacks like a duck . . . he's startin' to sound like a duck."

"DNA's not omnipotent," declared Tom emphatically. "I attended a seminar on it as evidence while in school. The presenters discussed DNA being much more complex than we think, especially when it's involved in forensics. It's not like what you see on one of those crime TV shows, where DNA evidence is foolproof. DNA, as it's used in criminal investigations, is more about the statistical probability that a person's genetic makeup matches the crime scene DNA. There are major questions and concerns about subpopulations and genetic variability," explained Tom. Bob, however, saw DNA as some type of molecular fingerprint—just a matter of swirls and loops.

Unfazed, Bob continued to make his case, "He has a history of violence towards elderly women." Bob pointed at an incident under the criminal history heading on Mathews's file. "At age seventeen, Mathews was arrested for assaultin' an eighty-two-year-old woman."

"She was knocked down—or fell—when he snatched her purse," retorted Tom.

"Her hip was broken," Bob simply responded. "This isn't about violently attacking little old ladies. I can see that may have been an 'accident,'" Bob gestured quotes with his fingers, "but it shows he targets old women who are frail and would be less likely to put up resistance." Tom didn't respond, but Bob made a good point. "And," Bob continued, "he's currently servin' time for breakin' into ladies' offices at the university and stealin' their purses. Again, it shows he prefers females. Mrs. Stanford was a sixty-eight-year-old homemaker, a grandmother who loved to bake and spoil her grandchildren. She was found by her husband when he returned home from helpin' a friend. They were going to go to their church's choir practice that night."

"But, Mathews doesn't have a sexual violence history," challenged Tom, still not quite convinced.

"That we know of. He might be a serial rapist but never got caught. We only know for sure what he's been convicted of. Look at his jail behavior record." Bob motioned toward that section of the file he just grabbed from the printer. "The notes show he's a problem in prison. Could be that some aspect of his personality isn't right." Bob held Tom's gaze. He could tell that he was making headway at removing the rookie's doubts. "Consider how long it took for Anna Stanford's case to get to this point. She was murdered on February 3, 1995, and it's now June 2007! There might be other victims we don't know about, that haven't been linked, or . . ." Bob paused a moment and finished in a quieter tone, "Or, that we haven't found yet." Tom's shoulders slumped in resignation. He trusted his partner's experience. Bob made sense on many levels. However, even though Tom gave in to Bob's argument, he couldn't help but think, *Something still doesn't add up with Mathews and this case.*

––––

On a bright, sunny day, Wanda climbed into her Jeep Grand Cherokee at Larry's Hardware and Garden Center with several flats of flowers to plant. She usually went there for some home maintenance items, but more often than not, she got distracted by the gardening section. Her cell phone suddenly jolted her back to reality from fantasies of gardens full of color and scents.

"Todd, sure I remember you. We worked that Willis case together a couple of years ago. How are you?" Wanda greeted him as she started her car. She always used a hands-free device for her phone, preferring mobility and the ability to use hand gestures.

They talked a few minutes, catching up since that last case. Then, Todd switched topics. He asked, "Would you like to take on a rather unusual case?" Todd truthfully added, "But, it has some problems we may not be able to overcome."

"Sounds familiar," Wanda replied merrily. "When has there ever been a case that didn't reek with problems? Tell me about it. I assume it's developmental, my kind of case." Wanda pulled over under a shade tree in Larry's parking lot. At the word "case," she recognized that she would need to free her hands from the wheel as well. She grabbed her yellow pad and pencil, items she always kept handy in the Jeep.

Todd chuckled in agreement with Wanda's remark. "It's developmental, all right. The defendant—Quentin Mathews—has fourteen siblings. Father left when our guy was two. Lots of family changes and moves. Mother died when Quentin was a teenager." While he was well-experienced with the more gruesome cases, he still paused in awareness of the heinous nature of the crime. "He's accused of strangling a woman with a vacuum cleaner cord after raping her in her home."

Wanda's face reflected the dreadfulness of the crime. Yet, she only voiced empathy, joining in Todd's apprehension. "What happened? What were the circumstances?" Wanda was expecting the usual drug or alcohol involvement.

Todd paused again before explaining to Wanda that twelve years had passed between the crime and the city incorporating a new DNA database comprised of convicts' and victims' DNA samples. "Quentin was in the system because he's currently serving a twenty-year sentence for stealing and burglary. His DNA matched a sample found on the victim. They also matched his palm print to a print taken from a door in the victim's home."

Wanda was curious to know what the complication was and how she fit into it. "You mentioned problems we may not be able to overcome."

Todd hesitated, searching for the best way to explain the situation, "Quentin, he . . . he won't talk to anyone. Not even his attorneys." Todd honestly elaborated, "Five professional experts have been up to see him at the state prison. He won't utter a word. He won't even talk with us—not to anyone. He's never spoken with anyone. How we can represent him . . . I'm not sure."

"I'm not sure either, Todd," Wanda admitted in a concerned tone.

He drew a long breath before asking, "So, do you even want to get involved? I certainly understand if you don't. The DA knows about the problem and seems somewhat sympathetic but wants to get on with the case. The prosecutor knows he won't communicate with us . . . not verbally or in writing."

Wanda silently contemplated the situation. *If I get on the stand as an expert for the defense, the prosecutor will go after me with both barrels loaded. The prosecutor may seem sympathetic now, but in the back of his mind, he sees this problem as a way to win his case.*

"What about family? Any family members available to talk with me about Quentin's life?" she inquired, looking for a back door. As an expert witness, she could use hearsay to form an opinion. She was hoping that someone who knew Quentin would be willing to help his case.

"That's another problem," Todd said in a tone of defeat. "Evidently, Quentin's given them orders not to talk with us or anyone in any way connected with the case."

"Can I have the names and phone numbers of the family members anyway? Let me see what I can find out. Then, I'll decide if I can help."

Todd gave her the names and numbers that held the most promise. Wanda scribbled down the names and numbers.

"But, don't count on anything," he warned. "They refused to talk with me . . . Doubt they'll talk with you."

"I'll call you in a couple of days," she promised. They signed off.

Still parked underneath the tree at Larry's, she decided to call a couple of Quentin's sisters. One sister, Abby, stayed on the phone long enough to tell her not only that the family would never talk with anyone but also to warn Wanda not to try and talk with Quentin.

"I think youse trying to get information to get my brother convicted," another sister angrily accused her and then hung up.

Wanda shook her head, a little amazed, and tried to regroup mentally. *Seems like every new case is worse than the last. But, this is a first—no one is willing to talk.* After a moment to check the time, Wanda pulled out her address book.

"Hi, Ted. Got some questions about a new case I've been asked to take on," Wanda said as she got straight to the matter at hand.

"Fire away," responded Ted good-naturedly.

After she informed Ted of her problem, he matter-of-factly replied, "If you haven't talked to the guy, the prosecutor will impeach you and have the judge throw you off the stand. You won't last more than thirty seconds. You'll also ruin your reputation by taking such a chance." Ted added sincerely, "I'd turn this one down, Wanda. Don't do it."

"Okay, that's what I thought you'd say. Thank you. I'll let you know what I decide." After they disconnected, she immediately dialed another attorney in St. Louis, Quentin's home territory.

"Hi, Megan. How are things going in Capital?" greeted Wanda.

"Good. Busy. You? How's your garden?" responded Megan. Wanda smiled. Megan was a no-nonsense, pragmatic attorney who, like Wanda, loved flowers.

"Staying busy. I have a car load of flowers to plant," Wanda chuckled. "And a question for you," she continued. Before Wanda could finish explaining her dilemma, Megan cut her off.

"Drop it! You don't want to jeopardize your credibility by making a fool of yourself—if you even get to the stand. It'd be professional suicide to go anywhere near the courtroom without having interviewed the defendant. I'd turn this down and work in your garden."

"Okay. Thanks, Megan. Tell everyone I said hello." Wanda punched the end call button. She pulled out from under the tree and headed out of the parking lot. She took a few moments to look out over the Rio Grande Valley farmland. She had officially moved from the Texas Hill Country to the Valley full-time to be near Catherine, who had been diagnosed with cancer.

Catherine had moved to the Valley to help care for their elderly aunt. Yet, now, due to Catherine's illness, Wanda started taking over more of their help with Aunt Denise, who lived next door to Catherine. Wanda wiped a tear away as she thought of her younger sister. She wanted to be near her and do what she could to make the last years as pleasant and comfortable for Catherine as possible. She wanted them to have every opportunity to be with each other.

As she drove back to her La Feria residence, she tried to comprehend Quentin and his family's silence. *Quentin's sisters are so adamantly against talking—their very vehement hostility obviously shows they care about him. Yet, the sad thing is their silence will cost him his life.* Like an off-key instrument in an orchestra, something was blaringly wrong in the case. She then turned her mind to her colleagues' responses. While she was not surprised by their sound and logical analysis of the potential consequences, she was nevertheless struck by their advice.

Wanda unloaded the tropical foliage, luscious exotics, and intoxicating blooms from her Jeep and planted the colorful new additions. As she studied her yard, she realized she had, through meticulous and dedicated efforts with shovel, spade, and elbow grease, transformed the typical suburban, carpet-grassed yard into her own botanical paradise. After giving the newest members of her garden a drink, she sat down underneath the pergola and decided to make one more phone call, a call to one of her most-trusted friends, Howard in Oklahoma City.

After describing the Quentin dilemma to him, Wanda asked, "What do you think? Could this case be my professional suicide?" Though Howard was several years younger than she, his thoughtful questions and insightful observations gave him a maturity and wisdom beyond his years. He could have been a successful and, no doubt, highly sought-after professional psychiatrist. But instead, he chose to work with the hearing impaired and had rapidly moved up the ladder to become the vice president of the State School for the Deaf and then to the State Office for Children with Special Needs. Wanda knew she could talk to Howard about anything from philosophy to practical everyday issues, and they often had over coffee at CJ's Café when she lived in Oklahoma City.

"Sounds like you're at a crossroads. One path could lead to, as you said, professional suicide, and the other to—"

"Job security," Wanda interrupted. "The preliminary details I know clearly show developmental implications. I wouldn't be turning down the case because of my inability to help, but because of my lack of willingness to help at the risk of my professional reputation."

"It reminds me of when you wrote to that inmate at McAlister many years ago . . . Oh, gosh . . . what was his name?"

"John Carlyle."

"That's right! John Carlyle. I thought it was a bad idea at the time, but you went ahead with the correspondence."

"Hmm. Are you suggesting I slip into a predictable pattern when someone tells me not to do something?" Wanda asked with a wry grin as she looked down at her muddy boots.

"Well, you know. You jump right in," Howard chuckled. After a pause, he continued in a more serious tone. "But, Wanda, it's more than some sort of stubbornness rooted in your family DNA. It's about honoring life and yourself through respecting others. It's like not wanting to help someone change a tire on a rusty, mud-laden clunker because the helper wouldn't want to smudge her dress. Seems to me like you're wrestling with the idea of turning a blind eye in order to not get your hands dirty."

Wanda reflected. "Well . . . I don't know about that." Even though she was on the phone, she looked down at the brick-paved patio floor and then up through the sky-lit openings of the pergola, contemplating.

"And, I've never known you to shy away from a little dirt. You wouldn't have such a beautiful garden if you did," Howard playfully added.

"These lawyers don't have anything to lose by telling me not to pursue the case," Wanda further pursued the issue. "But, they fall into the same trap that jurors often do."

"The IT, the identity trap. I remember you warning me of it."

"Exactly, the person thinks that everyone should think like he does: 'If I were her, I'd stay away from taking a chance like that,' or 'The accused is a bad apple,' or 'I sure wouldn't do that.' Howard, I'm approaching my own life from a developmental point-of-view. At the end of the day, if I have the capability to help in a situation like this, I must do it. If I can, I must!"

"Well, I think you've already made up your mind. There's nothing more for me to say."

"Todd, Wanda Draper." She took a deep breath before giving him her answer. "I'm willing to take the case if you can get me into the prison. I have to make a good-faith effort to talk with Quentin. Also, I want to find some family members and gather some background information."

Todd swallowed nervously and said, "Well, I can tell you the state's not going to want to pay expenses for what they consider a dead-end effort. But . . . well . . .

we really need you, or we have no case." There was a brief moment of silence. "Let me see what I can do. The state knows you've worked on other cases for us, and we can't keep delaying."

"I have to make an attempt to meet Quentin. Otherwise, there's no way I can do this." She paused and added, "Is there anyone at all in your records who might be available for an interview? School teacher? Minister? If I can get to someone, I may be able to work my way into the family and ultimately talk with Quentin."

"I'll dig in the records and get back to you. In the meantime, talk with Allie in my office and make flight reservations. I'll let you know about the expenses and approval for your services. Frankly, you're our last hope. Trial's less than four months away."

She sighed within as she hung up. *Four months away! What an expectation! Will the State come through with expense funds? If I can just talk to Quentin a few minutes, I think he'll respond. Maybe, just maybe, I can get through to one of his sisters.*

A few days later, Todd called again. "We're in luck! Because the state knows you've worked for us before, they've agreed to bring you in if you can talk with some of the family. And, they said you can try to see Quentin at the prison. We'll get the flight plan and ticket out to you right away. Can you travel next week?"

"There's so little time! I'll clear my calendar and get there ASAP. Please send me all his school documents, medical reports, police and prison records—everything. I'm going to need as much as I can get to prepare for this case and be ready in four months. I can't emphasize enough how much I need to read about every detail related to your defendant and the crime. I don't want any surprises." Wanda mentally added, *If I can even get on that witness stand!*

Todd called back the next day to give Wanda the name of a man who had tutored some of the Mathews children when they were in school years ago. "Maybe he has some vague recollection of the family," Todd suggested hopefully. Encouraged and armed with the name of one stranger, Wanda prepared for a long shot.

The arrangement was that she would fly into Lambert-St. Louis International Airport at eight at night. Then, she would proceed to the Country Manor Inn at Union Station in downtown St. Louis. Todd planned to arrive at seven thirty the next morning to drive her to the prison to see Quentin.

At ten, her plane arrived in St. Louis—two hours late.

It was ten thirty by the time she retrieved her luggage and hoofed it to the motor-vehicle transportation area. She went to the taxi line, where she learned that the airport taxi service was limited. The driver wanted forty dollars plus a tip to take her to her hotel. *Supply and demand,* Wanda thought as she politely declined the offer.

She decided to take the Metro and inquired at information how to get there. The gentleman, proudly wearing a blue uniform and donning a cap that gave him a sense of importance, told Wanda to head to the third level through the parking garage. After fifteen minutes of scrambling and searching for the elevator, she found it in a nondescript hallway as a small sign directed her. *Thank goodness!* she mentally sighed in relief. There was no way she could climb three flights of stairs carrying all of her luggage.

Around a quarter of eleven, she reached the third level. The station was dimly lit. A sign firmly stated, EXACT CHANGE ONLY. She had no idea how to procure tickets to ride the Metro. She looked around, exhaustion weighing heavily on her. The only other people at the station were a couple of young women, each weighing about two hundred and fifty pounds. At her wit's end, she asked these intimidating women for help.

To her surprise and relief, the two proved very helpful. After assisting her in acquiring change, they told her which train to take, talking in a friendly manner while they waited for another train. Thankful relief engulfed her. To her untrained eyes and lack of familiarity with the area, it was impossible to tell which train was going toward downtown and which was heading out of town.

Once on board, Wanda waved her thanks to the two hospitable women. She sat on the well-worn seat and watched the scenery speed by as she tried to get her bearings. She studied her surroundings, like one who is studying hieroglyphics, trying to determine which was her stop and when it would be approaching. Suddenly, she sensed someone breathing on the back of her neck. She was at the edge of panic, her anxious distress clearly visible. A middle-aged, bearded, dark-skinned Middle Eastern man touched her shoulder and pleasantly said, "Looks like you need help." Relief flooded through her at the sight of much-needed aid.

Thanking him and telling him where she was headed, he said, "I tell you when to get off. My stop's the one before yours."

He waved her off when he stepped off the train. He signaled to her to remember to get off at the next stop. She smiled and waved her thanks. She faithfully followed his directions and exited the train where instructed.

But as soon at the train's doors closed behind her and the train rushed off, she realized this was not the correct station. She had been to Union Station before and stayed in the same Country Manor. This was not where she needed to be.

It was eleven thirty at night, and she was totally lost. Like a brown suit at a black-tie affair, she did not fit in. She asked a few of the exiting passengers if they could help her find her way.

One middle-aged man, very thin and scruffy, said benignly, "Come with me, Miss. I'll show you hows to get to the Country Manor."

They walked and walked and walked. Exhaustion permeated every feature of her body. She was hungry and felt weak in the knees; her bones ached.

The Samaritan suddenly said, "Stop. You don't wanna go down this street no farther. See those dudes lazin' on the sidewalk?" She nodded, as he further explained, "They're all drugged out. I'll go with you 'round this block."

"Thank you so much," she said with a smile, though she was sure he didn't notice that her hands were trembling, still dragging two loaded luggage caddies.

After about half a block, he said, "Miss, I gotta be on my way. But," he pointed down the street, "if youse go down this street another block or so, you'll see some people at another hotel. They'll show you the way to the Country Manor." He paused and then said, just before leaving her, "Miss, youse gonna bes just fine because them angels is with you all the way." And, then he was gone. She followed his directions and sure enough the attendants at the hotel pointed the way to the Country Manor, which she then recognized.

At midnight, she dragged her luggage up the steps to the night door, only to find it locked! She banged on the door, pleading in her mind, *I've come too far now!* Finally, the desk clerk opened it. She checked in, asked for a six o'clock wake-up call and fell into bed. Too exhausted to be scared, skeptical, or upset, she fell fast sleep.

Todd arrived at his expected time the next morning. They drove for two hours to reach the prison. According to protocol, Wanda and Todd had to go through a

TSA-style screening before entering the doors to the inner prison. When Wanda went through the metal detector, the alarm rang.

"I have four long metal screws in my left hip," she explained to the female guard.

"Let's see the letter from your doctor," the jobsworth inquisitor demanded.

In an incredulous tone, Wanda replied, "That was twenty years ago."

"Next time, bring the letter, or you won't be going through," Miss Vitriolic replied curtly.

"Thanks. I'll be sure to remember," Wanda replied, letting the guard's remarks roll off. As she approached the elevator, she contemplated, *Let me do this with least effort, with grace, and in a sacred manner.*

A cordial guard then approached and greeted her, "I have your paperwork." He proceeded to lead her through two locked doors, each slamming shut with a loud bang as though alerting all personnel that someone was coming through. They continued down the long corridor flanked by gray enameled walls and a cement floor. No windows were in view. Heavy doors broke the monotony on both sides. *So depressing*, thought Wanda as she followed the guard to the contact room where Quentin was to meet with her. Wanda reflected on how more and more jails were being built in this country. *Not one of those new jail cells will remain empty—if we build them, we will fill them.*

The guard told her to push the buzzer just inside the door when she was ready to leave and he would come to escort her out. She waited there, alone, for several long minutes, only Quentin never showed. Another guard finally opened the door on the opposite side of the contact room and swaggered in saying, "He won't talk with you."

Wanda pleaded with him, "But I'm from out of state. I really need to talk with him. Can't he just come out and meet with me for a few minutes?" *If I can just shake hands with Quentin and introduce myself, maybe he'll talk with me,* she thought. *If not, at least I can say that I spoke to him.* "Please, go back and tell him I'll wait here until he comes."

The guard reluctantly stepped out of the contact room. He returned to tell her adamantly, "Quentin refuses to talk with you or anyone else." She wondered if this guard even made an attempt to get Quentin. He didn't seem interested and wasn't at all helpful. His tone gave the unspoken message, "You're wasting your time and mine."

A defiant Wanda told the guard, "I'll wait a while longer in case Quentin changes his mind. Please tell him I'm still here." After an hour, Quentin hadn't appeared. Her imagination guided her down the hallway to a cell where Quentin lived. *Why won't he talk? Is he mentally ill?* She shifted her thinking to the records she had been reviewing. *There must be something yet to be discovered that can shed light on this mute force.* She stood, slid her notepad under her arm, and pushed the buzzer. She was relieved but disappointed as she journeyed back down the gray hallway through the banging doors to the lobby where she met up with Todd, who was waiting for her. As they departed in the state car, Todd wasn't surprised when she reported her failed attempt to see Quentin.

The name of the one person Todd had found in St. Louis who knew Quentin's family was sixty-one-year-old Andrew Ericson, who had been a school teacher and a community advocate for children. Currently, he was tutoring students in a college not too far from the airport. Todd gave Wanda Andrew's name and phone number.

The next day, she rented a car, determined to find Andrew and investigate. After numerous failed attempts, she finally reached him on his apartment phone. He said he'd meet with her, and she agreed to pick him up on a designated corner by the college student center. Andrew gave her explicit directions, and when she turned the corner on campus, she spotted him. He was an older, scruffy-looking man, wearing an old, torn jacket; his frizzy hair poked out of a baseball cap. His jeans were two sizes too big, but he had a grin on his face that was immediately reassuring. Because of the description she had given him of the rental car, he easily recognized her. As she stopped by the curb, he slid in. They shook hands as they introduced themselves to one another. Wanda then commented, "I'm starved. Why don't I buy you lunch, and we can talk?" He told her about a steak house close to campus.

"Feel free to order yourself a steak," she encouraged him. "That's what I'm getting." Setting the pace, she ordered an eight-ounce rib eye, her favorite.

"Oh, my teeth. They're not strong enough, um, to chew it. I'll, uh, um, just have a . . . let's see . . . a . . . a chicken salad."

When their lunches arrived, Andrew was very careful to eat only half of his. It quickly became clear to Wanda he wanted to take the rest of the chicken salad home for supper.

Andrew was easy to talk with, and Wanda was impressed with his apparent education and his interest in working with students. He may have been dressed like a homeless vagabond, but he was courteous and articulate. His fund of knowledge was admirable. They talked briefly about Quentin. He was familiar with the case, having kept up with the news.

"I don't think Quentin's guilty," Andrew firmly declared. "Yes, he was a thief, a compulsive thief, but I don't think he could ever kill anyone. He wasn't one to use drugs or alcohol. I know he had a foul mouth, but that doesn't make him a killer."

When Wanda asked if he knew much about the family, Andrew eagerly offered, "Oh, yeah, I know all fourteen kids. I used to tutor Quentin and his brother Evan when they were in junior high. I know them really well." He paused before adding, "I'll do whatever I can to help Quentin because I believe he's innocent of that horrible killing."

Andrew confirmed the list of siblings Wanda had named from her search of social services records before coming to St. Louis. She turned to the list on her yellow pad: Alice "Rosie" Carson, Phyllis Mathews, Thomas Mathews, Lilly Mathews, Tristan Mathews, Quentin Mathews, Evan Mathews, Melody Mathews, Daniela "Nell" Mathews, Abby Mathews, April Mathews, Nathaniel Mathews, Noah Mathews, and Dylan Mathews Baker. After hearing the names, he said, "I know all of them." Wanda was impressed. *That guy last night was right. My angels must be working overtime.*

As they reviewed the list, Andrew commented, "I know where most of them are." He added helpfully, "I also remember their birthdays—year and month." He looked down, shaking his head. "I just can't believe Quentin would . . . could kill anyone." He took a deep breath before offering, "Like I said, he's a thief and has been most of his life. But he's not a killer."

Wanda didn't ask Andrew specific questions. Consistent with her style, she simply encouraged him to tell whatever he could about Quentin and his family.

"Quentin was Virginia Lee Mathews's sixth child," he divulged. "Born on December 4, 1957. She wasn't quite fifteen when she had her first child and was twenty-four when she had Quentin."

"Six children in nine years!" Wanda exclaimed.

"As you can see," he pointed to her list of fourteen names, "there's more to come."

How would Virginia Lee have been able to provide the nurturance and physical care to assure that each of her newborns would meet normal expectations? Wanda pondered. She asked, "Was there the same father for all of these children?"

Andrew shook his head. "Thomas Mathews Sr. was the father for her first five children. But, Mr. Eastland was Quentin's father."

"How long was Mr. Eastland in the picture?"

"A few weeks after Quentin was born, he took off. Then, Thomas Mathews Sr., who was acting as a surrogate father to Quentin, took off when Quentin was two."

"So, who was the father of the other eight children?" she was curious to know.

"Donnie Baker was the father of Evan and Melody. Then, Tony Coleman . . . he was the father of Daniela, Abby, April, Nathaniel, and Noah. Thomas Mathews Sr. then came back into the picture and fathered her last child, Dylan. Three months after giving birth to Dylan, her fourteenth child, Virginia Lee died of a heart attack. Quentin was fifteen."

"Let's back up a second," she asked of him. "Was Quentin born in St. Louis or someplace else?"

Andrew sounded like a recording. "The first six children, including Quentin, were born in Magnolia, Arkansas. They moved to Memphis, Arkansas, to find better housing. When Quentin was four, they moved here to St. Louis to once again find better housing. Even though what they found was minimal, they felt safe in the neighborhood." He then smiled at her. "You have to remember. St. Louis didn't have so many gangs or high crime back then."

"What about Virginia Lee through all this? Was she considered a good mother?"

"From everything I know, she was a kind and caring mother who wanted the best for her children. I just think it was really overwhelming for her." Then, after a deep sigh, he added, "All those kids."

"I can't even imagine what it must've been like for Quentin," Wanda concurred. "In his early years, he experienced childhood with the absence of his father and stepfather figures, and he had an extremely busy mother raising all those children—that must have been really rough. How could he get a handle on language and speech skills, emotional stability, and appropriate social skills?" She took a few moments before she went on to query, "What about Quentin's education?"

"He went to three different kindergartens in St. Louis. He never really adjusted and began having learning problems."

Wanda wondered aloud, "Is it any wonder Quentin was lacking academic skills? Who helped him with study habits? Who checked his homework? With one father figure in and out the door and a mother caring for so many children, he hardly knew his own family members. How could he form new friendships with peers?" She then asked for clarification, "I'm assuming the family was on welfare?"

Andrew nodded. "They were. It was meager but necessary to feed and house that huge family. With so many siblings and cousins in and out those doors, Quentin's family could lose one or two and never miss them."

By this time, the waitress had brought a to-go box for the remainder of Andrew's chicken salad. While he carefully scooped the salad from his plate into the box, Wanda continued peppering Andrew with questions.

"When did you become involved in Quentin's life?" she inquired.

"When he was twelve. I was a tutor at the Fellowship House After School Tutoring Program. I helped Quentin and two of his brothers with their homework and took them on field trips and got them involved in sports. Plus, I had always been a family friend of the Mathews. That's how I know all this stuff about them."

Wanda grinned. "I was about to ask that, Andrew. You're better than an encyclopedia. Were you able to spend a lot of time with Quentin?"

"Not as much as I would've liked to. I was mentoring several other students and couldn't devote the time needed to keep Quentin on track."

"How long did Quentin go to Fellowship House?"

"Three years. But, like I said, he needed a lot more than I could give him. He needed a father, friends. He just needed so much more."

She took a moment to catch up on her notes before asking, "And then his mother died, correct?"

Andrew nodded. "Virginia Lee was only thirty-nine."

"And did you attend the funeral?"

"Yes, I went."

"How did everyone behave?"

"Everyone was overwhelmed with the loss. Even with the tears and grief, they all were well-behaved. But, Quentin . . . he wailed and cried and couldn't control himself. You know he was only fifteen at the time, right? Between you and me, that's where it really started to go downhill for him. He just couldn't deal with it."

After losing two father figures earlier in life and now his mother, Quentin had to face the reality of no living parent. Wanda thought how those early years had to carry a lot of trauma for Quentin. *Complex trauma, perhaps developmental trauma disorder,* she listed in her mind. "Am I correct in assuming Quentin's performance continued to worsen?"

"Correct. After Virginia Lee's death, he just couldn't function in high school. He was admitted to Missouri Hills School, a program for special needs students."

They approached the register so that she could pay the bill. As the cashier made change, Wanda looked at Andrew and commented, "You do know that all the family members refuse to talk with me, yes?"

He responded in a surprised tone, "I just can't understand why."

"Is there a person on this list you think might talk?" she was anxious to know.

Andrew immediately said, "The older sister, Phyllis. She's the one who took care of Quentin and the others after their mother died. She might talk to you."

"Let's give Phyllis a call," Wanda suggested. She had the phone number that Todd had given her earlier. "Luck is with us," she whispered to him as a woman answered.

"Hello. Phyllis?"

"Yes, I'm Phyllis."

"My name is Dr. Wanda Draper. I'm working with Quentin's lawyers on his case. I'm in town. I was wondering if I could come by for a few minutes to talk with you. I went to see Quentin yesterday." She didn't tell her he refused to talk with her and that she hadn't even met him. But she had been to see him. He just wouldn't see her.

There was stone silence on the line. Phyllis then skeptically responded, "Okay. Come on over."

Andrew agreed to ride with Wanda because she had no idea how to get to Phyllis's house. She was relieved he'd go. *I would never be able to go without him,* she thought.

Phyllis's neighborhood was in the middle of the St. Louis slums, right on the edge of Ferguson. It took about a half hour to get there. When they arrived, there were four cars, older model Cadillacs and Buicks, with at least two African American men sitting on the hoods of each car. Four women, apparently sisters, were sitting in the front yard, and Phyllis was standing in her doorway. Wanda knew Phyllis must have called to let them know she was on the way, and they weren't about to miss this for anything. The yard was very small, no grass, just hard dirt, with one large tree and not one flower. As soon as they started up the yard toward the door where Phyllis stood, Andrew evaporated. Wanda looked around, confused and surprised by Andrew's disappearance. She finally spotted him behind the big tree at the yard's edge, safely tucked away, hiding. *Thanks a lot, Andrew.*

Quentin's sisters, Lilly and Abby, immediately exuded hostility, and Wanda began to feel unspoken messages of "Get the hell outta here and leave us the f--- alone." She wasn't sure why the sisters remained outside in the front yard, but Phyllis, Virginia Lee's second oldest child who acted as the "mother figure" for the clan, guarded the open doorway, and Wanda knew then they were not inviting her inside.

Wanda took a seat in an old, dirty white plastic yard chair. She could see everyone from this angle—Phyllis blocking the door, the sisters seated in lawn chairs as they glared at her, the guys sitting on the cars, as well as Andrew hiding behind the tree. Wanda felt the tension in the air thickening every second with hostility.

Where's that handsome private investigator, Michael Westbrook, when I need him? she mentally wished. He was the PI who had worked with Wanda on a capital case that involved going in the early morning to do an interview on the dangerous side of Okmulgee, Oklahoma. As she was about to exit Westbrook's SUV, he said, "Hold it a minute." He reached under the driver's seat, pulled out his revolver, checked it, and stuck it in the back of his belt, pulled his leather jacket on and continued, "I never go into one of these complexes unarmed." But, he was not here. She had no ally. Wanda took a silent breath, repeating her personal mantra: *Let me do this with least effort, with grace, and in a sacred manner . . . with least effort, with grace, and in a sacred manner . . . with least effort, with grace, and in a—*

"Youse only here to get our brother put to death!" Abby's yelling brought Wanda out of her mantra.

Wanda didn't try to convince them of anything. The only strong statement she made was, "If you don't talk with me, the court will put your brother to death. I'm the only chance you have to save your brother. I'm here to help Quentin."

Only then did Phyllis seem to be a little congenial. But, the others continued to make menacing remarks asserting that Wanda wasn't really there to help. "We know what youse up to. Youse not goin' in that court to help us—or Quentin. Youse up to no good. Stay away!" Again, Abby led the others in their chants of accusations. The guys on the cars remained vigilant. They never moved. They just glared.

"Quentin akst us not to talk to nobody," Lilly said harshly.

Wanda could see where they were coming from and why they didn't want to talk. They were scared to death. They knew nothing about the court system, what a death penalty case was, or the difference between the prosecution and the defense. They didn't have a clue about the guilt-innocence stage or the penalty stage. At this point, Wanda decided she had only one possible way to get through to these people.

She finally asked, "Did any of you visit Quentin when he was in the hospital?"

Abby snarled, "He wasn't in no hospital. We woulda known. Whatcha talkin' 'bout?"

"When was he in the hospital?" Lilly fiercely interrupted. "What happened? Tell us what happened to Quentin!" she demanded.

The air was loaded and primed, the slightest spark would set off a blaze. Wanda remained undisturbed. "I've been through the hospital and prison records. It's all there." The atmosphere suddenly set the yard and the participants apart from the rest of the neighborhood.

Wanda proceeded to tell them about the records from Quentin's previous jail term and what she had discovered. She sensed some of their body and facial expressions softening. Now, they were more inclined to listen and maybe to talk. Phyllis led the charge by asking, "So, whaddya wanna know?"

"Tell me about Quentin when he was a boy," Wanda requested as she began to put pencil to paper, her yellow pad eagerly waiting to become a repository for their stories.

The sisters all looked at one another, all waiting to see who would comment first. The eyes of Abby and Lilly darted to Phyllis. They clearly didn't feel comfortable answering until the "mother figure" responded. She would set the tone for the types of answers they would provide. Phyllis finally offered, "He was real easy-goin' and liked school. But then he began havin' problems. He needed help to learn."

Lilly jumped in on the defensive. "He was real funny, though. Could make us all laugh."

The sisters nodded, laughing and repeating in unison, "That's true. That's true."

"Did you all get along growing up?"

More nodding in unison. Abby added, "We played together. Took care of each other. We loved each other. Still do." More strong nods from the outdoor congregation.

"Besides the good times he had with all of you and your mother, were there any other bright sides to Quentin's life?"

Lilly piped up with a smile. "He enjoyed sports, 'specially baseball. Quentin . . . he'd take me to Busch Stadium to watch the Cardinals play. He'd often shine shoes at the stadium—"

Phyllis interjected, "To earn money for food for the family, he started shinin' when he was seven years old. There were lots of mouths to feed. He seemed to know how to help."

Lilly then said thoughtfully, "To this day, I owe my love of sports, 'specially baseball, to Quentin."

Phyllis then jumped in, "But, Quentin, boy did he have a mouth on him."

Abby was quickly back playing defense, "But he meant no harm. He just mouthin' off." The other sisters nodded. She carried on, "It was his way of feelin' big—he was so small for his age . . . his mouth was big though."

During Wanda's interview with the sisters, Abby occasionally walked back and forth—from her chair to one of the cars to whisper to one of the hood-sitters. She was very well dressed in a tan pantsuit, high heels, and a good-looking hairdo. Wanda assumed she was on her way to work or to meet someone for dinner. But there was no small talk to be had in this crowd.

Wanda treaded carefully with her next question. "After your mother's passing, which I know had to be really hard for you, how did you all manage?"

Phyllis gave the final answer on that one. "We all stuck together."

The sisters all joined in, like it was some revival. "That's right. Stuck together."

Abby started giving Wanda the evil eye again. "Youse sure Quentin was in the hospital?" She turned to Phyllis to ask, "Why didn't none of us know 'bout that? Quentin would've called us."

They all turned to Phyllis, who eventually shrugged and replied, "I didn't know 'bout it."

Wanda assured them that she was telling the truth. But, she could tell that by this time she had worn out her welcome. Abby spit out the words viciously, "I just know youse settin' Quentin up for a death sentence. I just know it."

Lilly echoed her sister's sentiments, "I know it, too."

Wanda could tell they didn't trust her. And their suspicious eyes let her know it. She attempted to shake hands as she thanked them for letting her come to talk with them. But, they wouldn't shake hands, and they didn't say thanks.

As Wanda and Andrew drove back to the campus, she asked, "What do you think, Andrew? Think they understand about the court system and what Quentin is going through?"

Andrew replied in the negative. "They don't have a clue. I'm sorry I wasn't more help. It's been a long time since I've had close contact with them."

Wanda offered to buy Andrew dinner, but he said his box of chicken salad leftovers would be plenty. She thanked him profusely as they approached his curb where she had met him earlier in the day. As he climbed out of the car, Andrew assured her he'd help in any way he could. She felt his sincerity. He still refused to believe that Quentin could end anyone's life. She verified his cell and home phone numbers, knowing she would be contacting him more than once as she prepared for Quentin's trial.

It was dark now, and she was relieved to be heading to the Country Manor, by rental car this time and not the Metro. Her mind was whirling with the day's events, the fifteen miles to downtown St. Louis seemed like only a mile. Wanda mentally reviewed the information Andrew offered and the details Quentin's sisters provided, trying to distinguish the pattern created by the interwoven threads of each one's narrative of Quentin. While Wanda gained valuable and good information, there were still gaping holes in Quentin's life. *According to Andrew, he lost track of Quentin when he left home and went to live on the streets. Quentin's sisters also had little to offer once Quentin left home and they began living their own lives. Oh, how I wish Quentin would help in his defense!* Wanda was frustrated by the limited findings and Quentin's refusal to talk.

She walked into her nicely made-up room. The bathroom was restocked with fresh towels, inviting her to enjoy a hot shower. The bed tempted her to rest. Yet, she couldn't wind down her mind. She continued to strategize about how she would approach presenting Quentin as a whole person. *I'll have to depend on the records and any more information Andrew shares to discover as much of his history as possible.* Wanda switched the television on, hoping it would distract her and allow her to start relaxing. *The LifePath is the only way to illustrate Quentin's life to the jury.* Wanda's thought was interrupted by a scene on the television that caught her attention. The screen showed a couple of inner-city men, clothed in the epitome of gang attire, down to the bandanas and chains, sitting on the hood of a car parked in front of a house that had seen better days. A sense of *déjà vu* enveloped Wanda. The scene looked almost exactly like the one she had just encountered with Quentin's family.

"Trouble is waiting is the message that these men are sending," declared the narrator. The television had Wanda's full attention now. "According to one of the foremost cultural anthropologists, this is an intimidation tactic. This behavior lets everyone else know one or more of the following: they are ready for a fight; this is their territory; there is illegal activity, such as drug sales or gang activity occurring in that location. It's an indicator of their power and wealth or success, especially when displaying a car decked out with all the trimmings. It also shows their affiliation with a gang or clan." Images flashed on the screen that looked as if they could have been taken that afternoon during Wanda's interview with the Quentin Mathews siblings. Wanda froze as the reality and full extent of the dangerous situation she had unknowingly and brazenly entered hit her like a ton of bricks. *No wonder Andrew ran and hid,* Wanda exhaled in astonishment. She turned the television off, half fearful that it might reveal more dangers unbeknown to her.

Wanda went to bed, thankful for the divine protection that shielded her from her now-known foolhardy actions. *It's unbelievable that I made it alive from the airport to the Country Manor, didn't get robbed driving through the St. Louis slums, and didn't get run off by Quentin's sisters or the intimating hood ornaments.* Wanda shook her head in amazement. *And Andrew! Talk about angels and synchronicity. Andrew's got to be the key to saving Quentin. What are the chances that I would meet someone who tutored Quentin many years ago, knew the family, and is willing to help?'*

Chapter 15

Wanda pulled her suitcase to the curb of the airport's arrivals area. While the flight was uneventful, she still felt the fatigue from the trip. She was relieved to see Catherine pull the car up to meet her. After giving her sister a welcome-home hug, Catherine took her sister's luggage and placed it in the trunk of the Jeep.

No sooner had Wanda clicked her seat belt when Catherine handed her a notepad full of messages. "Two lawyers, each with a different court trial. Both capital cases," Catherine said as she pulled away from the curb. Wanda had been preparing expert testimony for each case. One was guilty; one she was sure was innocent. "Then there was a call from an associate in Vancouver, BC, with interest in publishing one of your manuscripts. There were four calls from your office from frantic parents about their children's learning disabilities," Catherine rattled off.

"Looks like I can't get away from work, doesn't it?"

Catherine chuckled, shaking her head.

"Oh, Belle says to call her as soon as you can." Catherine smiled at the grimace Wanda made. "It looks like Jackson's case is going to trial."

"I'm surprised that they didn't plead him out." She shook her head, making sympathetic utterances.

Catherine nodded. "I know we started working his case two years ago. Swift justice, again, I suppose." She cleared the intersection, pulling out of the airport. Traffic was moving; people were rushing back from their lunch break. "I have all the documents at the house, ready to go."

"You're too efficient!" Wanda cried jovially.

"Do what I can for the good of the order," Catherine said and winked.

"How about we find something good to eat?" Wanda smiled. Catherine laughed and directed the car towards a favorite restaurant.

"Okay, what did Jackson Dell do, again?" Wanda asked. They were seated at her kitchen table. Again, they were surrounded by stacks of papers. Quentin's case was put back in the file cabinet for the time being. "I need a refresher."

"He allegedly raped and strangled a ten-year-old girl. She was a family friend and stepdaughter to Jackson's best friend, Ethan. After he killed her—"

"Allegedly killed her, right?" she amended.

"Right. After he *allegedly* killed her, he dropped her into a thirty-foot, dried-out bayou bog, into a bed of leaves." Catherine leaned back in her chair and whistled. "You have to admit . . . It sounds smart. No one would ever find her in such a remote area, in the swamplands of Louisiana."

"Oh, yes!" Wanda expressed as the case came rushing back to her. "He confessed to killing her . . . as did his friend, the girl's stepfather." Wanda found the LifePath and started studying it. "He had a horrible childhood." She turned the page and then the next one. "He was sexually abused—maybe even raped—numerous times between ages five and eleven years by relatives and baby sitters—both males and females." Wanda straightened up in her seat. "A childhood such as this . . ." Wanda gestured to the LifePath. "Is it a surprise about his adulthood?"

"No surprise," Catherine agreed. She picked up her notes on the interview DVDs that the public defender's office had provided along with mounds and mounds of reports, records, and evaluations. The sisters had sat through several hours of watching various police personnel interrogate Jackson. "Something stinks in the State of Denmark, if you ask me. There are still way too many questions."

"I know." Wanda cringed at the thought of sitting there watching hour after hour of interviews. "There's more answers than questions. I tried to talk to the defense team about that."

"What happened? What did they say?" asked a curious Catherine.

Jackson Dell's defense team sat around the conference table with coffee mugs and electronics. The meeting was aimed at preparing for the penalty phase of the trial, thereby justifying Wanda's presence as the mitigation witness. The lead attorney for first stage and the investigator were also there to prepare for the penalty stage, together with the second-stage group.

Rick, the penalty stage defense attorney, was as much known for his excellence as a defense attorney as he was for his artistic talent of turning the sea-beans that he picked up along the coast into beautiful art pieces. A tall six-footer, Rick was slim and always smiling. His demeanor was low key. During long meetings, he sometimes exited for a few minutes to take his blood sugar because he was a severe diabetic. But, he never mentioned this, and he never complained. Belle was also in attendance as she was the one who coordinated the experts with the attorneys.

They had all agreed that a LifePath was needed to help the jury form a picture of Jackson's unfolding trauma, from early separations to adolescent mental health issues to failures of interpersonal relationships in adulthood. Unless the jurors could see Jackson as a vulnerable person, growing up in broken and disintegrating families, with trauma at every turn, they might miss the mitigating factors that could save his life. They'd be entering the penalty stage of the trial carrying visions of the distorted body of the ten-year-old girl thrown into a thirty-foot bayou bog after being brutally raped and strangled. The jury would have all of the dirty pictures in their minds. Wanda had to grab the jury with the human side of the case.

A huge obstacle for Wanda was that Rick and Belle agreed with the community that Jackson was guilty of kidnapping, raping, strangling, and throwing the little girl in the bog. They really believed he acted alone, and that Ethan, his friend and the girl's stepfather, wasn't involved. In their eyes, Jackson's behavior was that of a guilty, unremorseful psychopath. Wanda disagreed. "It wasn't premeditated," she told Rick and Belle. "Jackson doesn't have the developmental background of a sexual predator-killer, even though he does have lots of sexual deviant behavioral issues and alcohol abuse, among other family issues."

However, Jackson's antics in the jail, disobeying many policies, disrespecting the guards, and distinguishing himself through misbehavior did not invoke any sympathy. Neither did it provide support for a differing opinion. Wanda shook her head as Belle related how he had made a pass at her. Belle was furious, and Jackson was vehemently unremorseful. She sympathized with Belle's exasperation. However, Wanda recognized that Jackson could make people uneasy. *His mannerisms are like an Oliver Twist who asks for more attention in very wrong and misguided ways.* Wanda thought about how Jackson was incomplete, caught between boyhood and a full-grown man: *This unnatural combination of boy and beast makes him a brute. And, Jackson's brutishness is his most egregious crime. Whispers and suspicious glances have always followed him throughout the community. Is anyone surprised that Jackson is connected to this horrible murder? No. Did anyone expect anything less from him? No.*

During their strategy meeting, discussion about guilt or innocence naturally occurred. While everyone recognized that guilt/innocence was irrelevant to Wanda's testimony, they still appreciated her perspective.

"Okay," she began, "for example, how could Jackson, drunk and staggering, lift a sleeping ten-year-old off the floor without waking her?" Wanda began. "And why was she on the floor? Could she have already been dead? Or, how could he have carried her down the stairs without falling and without waking her? Could she have been drugged? How could she still be asleep while he carried her out of the house and placed her in the truck without waking her, and why didn't she scream or try to get away? How could Jackson drive a vehicle after consuming enough beer and hard liquor to fill a dozen people at a drinking party? How did they find DNA evidence from his semen when he had a vasectomy? Why did Jackson and Ethan give the same confession? Why would either of them confess to something if they didn't do it? Which confession was accurate? Why was the little girl allowed to be in the house with a group of men having a drinking party? Where was her mother? Was this child a victim of sexual deviant pleasure for several men that night? Is Jackson taking the fall for this crime? I believe he'd take the fall for Ethan, but would Ethan take the fall for Jackson? Maybe Ethan knew how drunk Jackson was and planted the idea of Jackson as sole perpetrator. Why did Jackson say in his confession that it seemed like he was standing aside looking at the crime? Why would Ethan confess, too? Where's

Jackson and Ethan's friend Sid in all of this? All these questions leave me . . . to quote Jackson . . . 'bum-puzzled.'"

Rick tried to break into Wanda's endless questioning. "I think you're—"

"It seems in many of these small communities, if there's a warm body and a confession, the attitude is 'let's go to court,' without always conducting a full-blown investigation."

The group sat in silence. Belle and Rick exchanged corner glances at each other. None in the room expected Wanda's monologue. A moment later, the three smiled and shared a hearty laugh.

Wanda put her hand up like a crossing guard stopping traffic. "Okay, I'm finished. I'm going to talk less and listen more."

"No one thought any of those questions were good ones?" asked Catherine at the end of Wanda's story.

"No. I had hoped that these comments would spark and inspire further examination. At least I tried. If I have the capability to help in a situation, I must do it. If I can, I must."

Catherine drew a sharp breath and gazed directly into Wanda's eyes. "I don't understand how someone could hurt someone they love. Like with Jackson, he really liked Rachel. I mean, the documents say he cared about her. Why would he hurt her?"

Wanda responded, "I think there are two reasons. One, he was heavily inebriated, which lowered his inhibitions. But, the other has to do with the deeper need to connect with another person. You see, Jackson was never able to make an authentic human connection. Look at his history of failed connections. His mother was more interested in her preoccupations than to take the time to hold, cuddle, feed, and comfort her newborn. From infancy on, there was a pattern of neglect that prevented Jackson from making those meaningful connections with his mother and father."

Catherine fired back, "But he got adopted by a family that wanted him!"

"I see I need to back up further. Have you ever heard the word, *gemeinschaftsgefuhl*?"

"God bless you," Catherine was quick to respond.

Wanda couldn't help but laugh. "No, not *gesundheit*, but *gemeinschaftsgefuhl*. Have you ever heard of that?"

She shook her head, puzzled.

"A human's a social creature. We have, as the Germans say, *gemeinschaftsgefuhl*, or 'with-ness,' the need to be connected to others. That's what makes us human. We have to feel connected. Man has to feel connected to the ultimate, to the universe, to God. And when man doesn't feel it, he may go to any length to get it."

Catherine was spellbound, looking at her sister with deep interest.

Wanda, encouraged, explained further: "How does this begin in man? It begins at birth. When the newborn is connected to the mother. We call it bonding or attachment. First, through the umbilical cord, which is cut. That's the first separation experience. The infant now has a yearning to reconnect. The reconnection experience is with the mother. That's natural. The infant bonds with the mother and makes the attachment-connection permanent. Anytime attachment is broken, the child has a need to reconnect—ultimately to the universe—like the womb of life. As the child grows and develops, there are feelings of security, safety, and exploring possibilities when there is a permanent connection to the mother. And, the same goes with the connection to the father. Every time the child is moved from one mother or father figure to another, there's a deep-seated subconscious yearning for retaining that original connection. As the person grows into childhood and adolescence, if these connections aren't adequately repaired, there will be a continued yearning that the person isn't even aware of."

After digesting what Wanda had to say, Catherine asked, "So let me see if I have this right. Jackson had to distort his reality in order to survive?"

"Yes. He changed his name because he wanted so much to connect with Dave, his foster dad. He therefore initiated taking on a name that would bind him to that family. This was another way of assuring and securing a connection. Then, when Beth and Dave divorced, he was, in his mind, discarded. The connection was broken."

Catherine stared at Wanda incredulously. "A seven-year-old can really think all this through?"

"It's not a matter of being intellectual about this. It's a matter of trying to satisfy a very deep need that isn't being fulfilled. The person may become so desperate to make the connection that he's willing to do almost anything—raping, strangling, shooting, or impregnating—and, in the process, reconnecting through blood in the ultimate distortion of reality. This is an emotional and psychologically-based behavior and not one that would be expressed intellectually with words. That's why it's referred to in the literature as an 'internal working model.' Jackson was desperate to make a connection, and he did it the only way he knew how. Even though it was a distorted expression of love, I believe Jackson raped Rachel to make a connection with her. Was it horribly wrong? Absolutely. But, it was a *connection*. The need was so deep, it overshadowed any rational thought he might have had for her well-being or his own behavior. If we could get the jury to understand that, how could they not have some empathy for Jackson?"

"Wow. Is the lawyer going to ask you that on the stand? That's powerful stuff." Catherine was fascinated with the new concept.

"Unfortunately, no. I brought up the subject, but Belle and Rick said that the jury won't understand—they just don't have the time to process. So, I can't talk about *gemeinschaftsgefuhl* on the stand. I will not get to go there with the jury," Wanda stated, somewhat disheartened.

Chapter 16

D r. Draper, would you agree with the statement that Jackson was deteriorating with each passing year, up until the time of his arrest?"

"I would agree with that statement." Wanda sat erect in the surprisingly comfortable chair of the witness box. She had arrived just the afternoon before in Shreveport, Louisiana. That evening she found out that the lawyer had decided to have the LifePath bound instead of blown up to posters to set before the jury box. She accepted the decision. It was beyond her control. *This sounds like the scrapbook scenario all over again,* she mentally foreboded. "Developmental stressors became paramount and began taking a toll on him. You will notice on page one of your notebooks, in the lower portion of the page, that there are developmental expectations on the left and stressors on the right." Since the notebook was new to her, she had asked Rick and Belle to have a copy of it on the stand so that she could lead the jury to certain pages where they could find important development information regarding Jackson.

Looking directly at the jurors, she said, "You will also notice on page one of the charts in your notebooks that Jackson was deteriorating as a result of being taken from his parents when he was only six months old. He had been placed in two different foster homes until, at seven months, he was placed with the Dell family." Wanda turned the page. "And on page two, you will see that Jackson was separated from his five siblings and had to adapt to four other children besides new parent figures. Then on page three, note that his foster sister, who took care of him and with whom he began to form an attachment, suddenly died in a car accident. By the time he was almost two-years-old, Jackson had to be hospitalized with unexplained high fever. A diagnosis of febrile seizures was listed several times in his medical records during his infancy. And his biological mother, released from prison, wanted to visit him while he lived with his foster parents."

"During Jackson's preschool years, what stressors impacted his development?"

Wanda quickly glanced down to find her place in the notebook. "Looking on page four, we see that his birth mother was arrested and returned to prison. His birth father, while released from prison, had supervised visits with him on two occasions. This was confusing for Jackson because he was finally beginning to make attachments with his foster parents. By the time he entered kindergarten, he was having behavior problems. He was already feeling betrayed and separated from people he wasn't sure of. 'Who are my parents?' and 'Whom do I belong to?' 'Why did they give me away?' These were questions he could not find satisfactory answers for. In over three decades of my involvement with thousands of children and parents, I've witnessed the fact that the strength of the roots of morality in the first three years will manifest during the teenage years. Young people with strong family ties and moral underpinnings may stray while experiencing the larger world, but they eventually return to the values transmitted by their roots."

"What was significant in Jackson's sixth and seventh years? On page five?"

"After a visit with Ralph, his birth father, Jackson felt betrayed when his father went back to prison—with no explanation." Wanda reflected a moment before continuing, "Many children think it's their fault when a parent leaves. 'What did I do?' 'What's wrong with me?' 'Why did he leave me?' At this time, Jackson decided he wanted to be adopted by the Dell family since he had lived with them for seven years. But, Mr. Dell had second thoughts about adopting Jackson. And Jackson received no explanation for the adoption delay. Finally, the adoption was approved. Also, this was the year the courts terminated parental rights for both biological parents."

"What happened in his eighth year?"

"On page seven, you will see his adoptive parents began having marital problems. They separated, and Jackson shifted back and forth between them. He wasn't feeling accepted by either. Fears of rejection and abandonment mounted when he realized that his adopted father didn't have time for him."

Wanda and Rick continued to guide the jury through the thirteen pages of LifePath saga in Jackson's life. Although Wanda wasn't missing a step with her testimony, she couldn't help but contemplate, *If I was showing all of this on the large charts of the LifePath while standing in front of the jury, it would be that much more effective and powerful.*

"What impact did these many life changes have on Jackson by the time he was a teenager?"

"A sense of loss, coupled with separation anxiety, propelled Jackson toward behaviors unacceptable to his parents and society. But this was Jackson's way of retaliating and compensating for his own inadequacies in being unable to handle all the changes and sense of betrayal that he felt."

"Would you explain the betrayal?"

"Betrayal trauma for Jackson was a never-ending feeling that everyone he was supposed to be connected to had deserted him. These feelings became more deep-seated, and disorganized attachment led him to a disposition of *assumed disability*. If he couldn't succeed at socially acceptable expectations in family and school life, he could succeed in misbehavior.

"I believe that Jackson was falling into an emotional trap that wasn't of his making. It has been well documented in the experiences of hundreds of thousands of infants and young children that attachment and bonding begin at birth. Every time a baby loses a parent or consistent caregiver through death or other separation, there's a sense of loss. Many infants suffer anaclitic depression, which occurs when a mother is unavailable to her newborn, either through absence or neglect. This can also be seen in orphanages and institutions that house and care for displaced infants."

"And Dr. Draper, do you have first-hand experience observing these displaced infants in either orphanages or institutions?"

"Yes, I do. I was invited and accepted an offer to travel to Romania as a visiting professor in the College of Medicine at Athenaeum University in Bucharest to teach doctors, nurses, and caregivers in the orphanages. There, I witnessed hundreds of children, ages two to seven years, with severe physical, mental, and emotional problems. Most of these children couldn't walk. Even at six years, they'd be in their cribs. When they were out on the floor, they walked on all fours, like dogs. Their knees were all enlarged from having so many injections of antibiotics. The lack of bonding and attachment was obvious, causing all kinds of developmental problems. By age six years, those children who could not yet talk were placed in outlying orphanages and caged like animals for the remainder of their lives. As I worked with the medical professionals, I emphasized more than any other teaching that these children are the result of inadequate or broken attachment and bonding with parents when they were placed in the orphanages. These professionals finally opened their eyes to what happens when children are not attached. Most of these children were too far gone to rehabilitate and were experiencing developmental and betrayal trauma."

"So, how had the impact of developmental trauma affected Jackson by the time he entered high school?"

"The impact of developmental trauma from early childhood has left fixed structures of habit patterns, beliefs, and expectations. It would be increasingly difficult, without long-term therapy and a support system, for Jackson to transform his personality after early childhood or to change his behavior, thinking, and emotional patterns during adolescence.

"The effects of betrayal trauma in his early childhood carried over into Jackson's adolescent period, precisely because it mounted in a one-time-only period of developmental growth. This resulted in his failure to adapt to consolidation of his personality and self-identity during adolescence. He became stifled in his emotional growth and his social adaptability."

As Wanda continued to articulate Jackson's life, she could see the jurors doing exactly what she knew they would, thumbing through their notebooks. Some of them were moving beyond the time lines.

"And would you please explain to the court the idea of emotion regulation?"

"Emotion regulation . . . ahem . . . it begins in infancy. This means having relatively automatic reactions to distress by crying and to pleasure by visual attention and smiling. If the infant has repeated success in coping with mild and brief episodes of fear and anxiety, self-regulation . . . it's enhanced. However, in the case of Jackson, his infancy was filled with . . . ahem . . . with early neglect and multiple changes in caregivers and surroundings."

Wanda unobtrusively slipped a cough drop from her suit pocket into her mouth. "Emotional stress as an infant prevented Jackson from learning to modulate internal feelings of fear of the unknown and the unfamiliar." Wanda paused, taking a moment to scan the jury. She was trying to speak to them, make a connection. But, their eyes were fixed on the notebooks.

After a moment more, she continued, "Jackson's early experiences became lasting sources of unmanageable distress, with failure to learn how to regulate the body when experiencing fear of the unfamiliar."

"Can you give us a specific example of this from Jackson's infancy?"

"Certainly. The medical professionals could never explain the cause of Jackson's high fever on several occasions during his infancy. This fits the scientific explanation of his inability to self-regulate. Both emotions and bodily feelings were compromised early on and carried forth into adolescence.

"His pain of family disintegration added to the betrayal trauma that plagued Jackson. He hated school because he knew he was a failure. He never developed the inner strength and self-discipline to practice a routine for study or to acquire the skills for rising above his emotional turmoil."

"Jackson faced new challenges when he was fifteen, is this correct?"

The prosecutor was quickly on her feet. "Objection. Leading the witness."

"Rephrase, Counselor," instructed the judge.

"Yes, Your Honor. What were some of the developmental changes that impacted his behavior?"

"Jackson was shuffled between his biological mother and his adopted parents. He went to spend time with his birth mother, Val, because Mrs. Dell was unable to cope with him. But, his stay of only a couple of months with Val proved to be a disaster. He described this home as 'horrible.' Val had numerous verbal altercations with Jackson and told him that he had to leave and could never come back. She banned him from her home after her husband, according to Jackson, sodomized him."

Wanda heard the gasps and whispers from the courtroom audience and noticed that the jurors finally looked up from their notebooks on that one.

The judge slammed the gavel down. "Order, please."

When silence returned, Rick continued his questioning. "As you indicate in your charts, Jackson was admitted to the psychiatric unit of Harrah Hospital, correct?"

This is where Wanda's combing through every Social Services and mental health record paid off. "Yes. Jackson stated in his initial evaluation, 'I'm destructive. I can't get along with other people.' This was a clue Jackson was open to getting help, but no one in his family responded."

"And what were the hospital diagnoses?"

"Intermittent explosive disorder, dysthymia, major depression-recurrent, parent-child problem, academic problems, conduct disorder, solitary-aggressive type. Academically, Jackson was diagnosed with developmental expressive writing disorder. Physiologically, he was diagnosed with rule out intracranial lesion and—"

A spectator's cell ringtone suddenly started playing some rap song, igniting laughter from the court and prompting the judge to bang his gavel once again.

"Order…order, please. As you all know, phones must be turned off in the courtroom—and that includes texting. Any further disturbance, and I will request that any ringing phone be turned over to the bailiff."

As the spectator *slowly* made his exit into the hallway, Wanda was personally appalled. She wondered what happened to the early days of cell phones when judges never allowed them in the courtroom. *Now, everyone's phone is constantly going off, and the judges don't usually say a thing—How times have changed*, she thought.

The judge instructed, "Please continue, Dr. Draper."

"Thank you. Physiologically, Jackson was diagnosed with rule out intracranial lesion and functional nocturnal enuresis. He was still wetting the bed at age eight or nine years—often a sign of having been sexually abused. He also carried the psychosocial stressor of divorce of parents. His ability to function was at a low score of thirty-five."

"What does this low score of thirty-five imply?"

"It's a score out of a possible one hundred. It means possible illogical or obscure speech at times and major impairment in such areas as work or school, family relations, judgment, thinking, mood, defiance, and school failure."

Rick paced in front of Wanda two or three times before arriving at his next question. "With all of these diagnoses, was Jackson also diagnosed as 'a danger to himself or others'"?

"He was diagnosed as '*Not* a danger to himself or others.' Clues were obvious Jackson had lots of problems. Yet, none of his parent figures seemed to have an inclination of how to help him beyond admitting him into the hospital. The follow-through and interfacing with those professionals was absent."

"When was Jackson released from the hospital?"

"Two months later, with the recommendation for outpatient psychotherapy through county services. But, no one took him to the sessions."

"And what happened two months after that?"

"Jackson applied for homebound study when the psychologist, Dr. George Simmons, recommended he repeat ninth grade. He stated Jackson needed to be more stable emotionally before reentering a high school environment. 'Otherwise,' he stated, 'Jackson would have devastating results.'"

"Where did Jackson live following his time in the hospital?"

"Jackson went to live with Mrs. Dell. By summer of the following year, he had to move in with Mr. Dell and his new wife, Bernice, and her daughter, Edith."

"How was his relationship with his new family?"

"During the stay with his adopted father, Jackson engaged in altercations with Edith and Bernice. But Mr. Dell also had problems with past-due child support for Jackson, so Jackson had to move back to live with Mrs. Dell. While in this setting, Jackson was taken to the county sheriff's office, where he admitted to assaulting his stepmother and an eleven-year-old boy. This resulted in probation and house arrest, with a state commitment for three counts of class C misdemeanor, third degree assault, second degree property damage, and one count class B misdemeanor.

"Jackson, he . . . he continued to be shuffled back and forth, even after his adoptive parents had been separated for seven years. He continued to live, off and on, with his stepmother and his adopted mother. And then, finally, with no one." Wanda felt like she was reliving Joseph's situation with his parents, Terrance and Jenny, all over again.

"What did all these changes do to Jackson?"

She continued, walking through the doors that Rick opened. "All these changes . . . each with unpleasant interactions . . . brought about internalized anger in Jackson toward his family. He felt betrayed, rejected, abandoned, and humiliated. After Mr. Dell rejected Jackson yet again, he, um, he became even more defiant and destructive. His self-image was one of failure, and he was . . . unable to balance what he felt like doing with what he knew was right or wrong."

"What happened to Jackson next?"

"After living with Mrs. Dell for less than a month, Jackson was admitted to the Division of Youth Services because he violated his parole. He was sixteen when he left Mrs. Dell's to enter the Youth Center in New Orleans. The court order included his entry into the school program there. Jackson was evaluated by use of cognitive and health assessments, The Woodcock

Johnson, vocational testing, and the Jesness Behavior Inventory. His overall goal was to earn the GED, but he continued to be angry, viewing himself as unwanted. His evaluations showed multiple issues, including under-socialization; lonely, scared, and confused; feelings of rejection; poor hygiene; immature behavior; low scores in writing, social studies, art, music, and literature; drug and alcohol problems; nervousness; depression; allergies to penicillin; and seizures."

"How did Jackson adapt to institutional expectations?"

"Not well. Fear of failure, a poor self-image, thoughts of confusion, and feelings of loneliness made it difficult for Jackson to adapt. He was distraught over having no place to call home, and feelings of abandonment continued to plague him while he felt forced to live in the Youth Center. His early life history continued to add to his feelings of loneliness. He had been separated from birth parents, siblings, adoptive parents and siblings, stepparents and siblings, and his home settings. His feelings of confusion—"

Wanda was interrupted by a female spectator who developed quite a coughing fit. As she finally excused herself into the hallway, Wanda backtracked and continued. "Jackson's feelings of confusion and loneliness made it impossible, in his view, to experience close and loving relationships. About the time he began to build trust in a parental figure, he would be moved. By the time he reached the Youth Center, his inner resources were too damaged to make new attachments or connections for establishing fulfilling emotional relationships. His self-confidence and inner controls never manifested because he never felt the parental support and guidance that grounds an adolescent. Jackson was never successful in maneuvering through the myriad obstacles and opportunities that confront teenagers."

When Rick referred to his notes, this gave Wanda the opportunity to scan the jury. As before, the jury members were peering through the binders in their hands. Wanda couldn't determine if they were all on the same page. She quickly centered herself and waited for Rick's next question.

"What happened when Jackson turned eighteen?"

"He began to search for his birth father, Ralph. This reflected his deep-seated need to reconnect. He was reaching back into his past in an effort to regain an element of certainty about himself. This was a manifestation of his need to patch up his identity."

"In searching for emotional ties, what did Jackson end up settling for?"

"Sexual intimacy. His personal life was in shambles. He kept reaching for connections through sexual encounters. He engaged in consensual sex with his stepsister when he was twenty-three. By age twenty-four, he had fathered three children."

"In your opinion, was Jackson prepared for parenthood?"

"No, Jackson's failure in family life was another reflection of his developing years in which his own parent figures were ill-prepared to care for him or to set the models he needed in order to experience success in relationships. The disintegration of his families set the stage for continuing changes and inconsistent guidance. As a child and young adolescent, each time Jackson began to trust his parents enough to attempt a close relationship, he would be moved to another family setting. By adulthood, Jackson didn't have a foundational pattern for building trusting, intimate relationships.

"It is my belief that the family in today's society is the foundation for this democracy and republic. The family is the cradle of development for the child, and the everyday world is the proving ground. The cycle of parent-child bonding and attachment—either weak or strong—will continue when these children reach adulthood and have children of their own."

"And how did his relationship with the Dells manifest over the years?"

"Mr. Dell had become quite ill in his later years, and Jackson managed to help with his care. He really wanted to have a close relationship with him when he was a young child but felt rejected and abandoned when he was forced to go live with Mrs. Dell after the Dells divorced. But Jackson still loved his adopted father. By helping care for him in his later years, Jackson was able to experience some of the closeness for which he had always longed."

"Jackson was desperate for some form of acceptance, wasn't he?"

The smartly dressed prosecutor once again leapt to her feet. "Objection, Your Honor. Leading the witness."

The judge glared at Rick. "Sustained. Rephrase your question, Counselor."

"Yes, Your Honor. Dr. Draper, how did Jackson deal with his need for intimacy?"

"He turned to having sexual relations with a thirty-one-year-old woman and her fifty-one-year-old mother."

More gasps from the spectators once again brought the judge's gavel down. "Order, order in this court."

As silence returned, Wanda continued, "Jackson also claimed he had sex with prostitutes. When asked why he got involved in these relationships, all of which were void of love and sincerity, Jackson stated, 'I got to where I didn't care because when you care, you get hurt.'" At that moment, Wanda was sure Jackson would have agreed with John Carlyle's opening line in his initial letter to her: "'People, people who need people, are the luckiest people in the world.' This isn't true."

"Did Jackson suffer any losses in his family?"

"He lost ten family members in the period of five years, including his real mother, Val, and his adopted mom, Mrs. Dell. He also lost his wife, who divorced him."

"What was the result of the accumulation of all this distress?"

"It caused Jackson to lose any semblance of emotional stability. Attachment was disorganized, as he had no significant attachment figures to care about him. He again turned to alcohol as a crutch and an ill-perceived sense of satisfaction."

"But Jackson was a grown adult. Shouldn't he have been able to handle these emotions?"

"Jackson's behavior in adulthood reflected years of pent-up feelings that had no outlet for healthy relief. He carried within himself a culminating snowball effect of his growing up and adult years of unexpressed pain and anger. Jackson carried into adulthood the psychological pain from loss of family relations, unresolved and internalized pain of rejection, betrayal trauma, and dissociative/disorganized attachment recycling since his earliest years. By the age of thirty-two, he was overindulging in alcohol and losing control of any reasoning. His behavior had become erratic and pointless."

Cross-examination began, and the female prosecutor finally had her chance to grille Wanda with questions.

"Dr. Draper, would you agree with me that a lot of kids don't get a proper education?"

"Many don't."

"And would you agree with me that a significant amount of kids have parents who drink and use drugs?"

"That's correct."

"And would you agree with me that there is a significant amount of kids who have to suffer through a divorce?"

"That's correct."

"And would you agree with me that there is a significant amount of kids who are moved from place to place or sent from foster home to foster home?"

"Yes."

"And do all of the kids I've mentioned in the previous questions turn out to be killers?"

"No, but—"

"Thank you, Dr. Draper. Let me now ask you, are you against the death penalty?"

Wanda replied confidently, "That goes against the scope of my role as an expert witness."

"Do you have an opinion regarding the death penalty?"

"No, I do not have an opinion in this instance."

The prosecutor had no further questions. Wanda was dismissed from the stand.

As Wanda walked out of the courtroom into the hallway, she noticed that Ralph was sitting there, looking like a replica of his son. In this case and many others, Wanda had often wanted to say to the parents, "If you want to save your son or daughter, you need to get on the stand and say, 'It is because of me, the mother, the father, that my child is on trial today. I should be on trial—not my child."

The judge called for a recess. Rick and Belle met Wanda in the hall, and they briskly walked outdoors. Rick admitted, "You were right. We should've used the big charts. The jurors got lost in their notebooks."

Wanda nodded slightly, careful not to betray her inner thoughts. *I really like you, Rick, but it's too late now. The jury made their decision in the first stage. Plus, they were ready to go home to their families, to their children's ball games, to their weekend activities.* Her only response was, "Hopefully, we'll know before the week's out."

Belle called Wanda on Monday morning to tell her the jury gave Jackson the death penalty.

"I'm surprised," admitted a baffled Catherine when Wanda relayed the verdict. "I thought they wouldn't give him death, not after you explained how he never had anyone to model a caring and loving relationship."

"But, even with all the mitigation, raping and strangling a little girl was surely the deciding factor," Wanda replied. "If only I had been able to efficaciously use the LifePath and really delve into *gemeinschaftsgefuhl,* maybe the jury would have given Jackson LWOP," she lamented.

Catherine shook her head, sympathizing.

Wanda continued. "I think the jurors weren't able to put aside their own perceptions about life and what they would or wouldn't do. Many are unable to put themselves in the defendant's shoes in order to see things from his point of view. Most people think that someone is either born good or bad. They think, 'I would never do that,' so the accused is automatically guilty. They fall into what I call the 'identity trap,' the IT. They can't let go of their own reality to understand what his reality is . . . or was. Jackson was just an unwanted brute in their eyes."

Catherine commented, "I guess the next step for Jackson is his appeal. Will you be involved?"

"Not likely. I may be contacted by the lawyers handling his appeal. They would want to know if I would have done anything differently. The appeal is complicated and can take many months or even years."

Catherine shook her head in disbelief. "Do you carry the emotions of a case for a long time after? Doesn't it take its toll on you, emotionally and psychologically? How can you keep doing this work?" Catherine's eyes betrayed the strain of such cases.

Wanda considered the questions before answering. "I guess I'm blessed with the ability to let go when a case is over. I'm into it all the way while preparing and testifying. I'm focused on little else. When it's over, it's over. I did everything I could to the best of my ability. Now, it's out of my hands, out of my mind . . . and out of my heart. Perhaps it's in my spirit but only as a means of helping me know that I don't have to take it personally. I leave the case, the defendant, the family, and the dynamics. I let it all go. I put the files in storage and get ready to start the next one. I go to work in the rose garden for a couple of days, and this seems to be very therapeutic, refreshing, and invigorating. Sometimes, I just sit here and relax in mother's rocking chair. Then, I'm ready to take on the next case."

Chapter 11

Wanda loaded her car with the boxes of documents mailed from the St. Louis Public Defender's Office. The Valley morning sun was bright, already warm, unlike mornings in Oklahoma City. The La Feria Post Office did not deliver packages. She was impressed with how fast the public defender's office was able to get her the case material. She said to herself after placing the fifth and final box in the trunk of her Jeep, *Wow, they are so efficient!*

Wanda jumped in her car and dashed back to her little cottage. She was eager to get home. The boxes held the first clues to Quentin Mathews's life. What Andrew and Quentin's sisters wouldn't or couldn't tell, maybe the pages and pages of records, documents, and reports—from the day he was born until now, including prison behavior records—would tell her. The task now was to extract what happened to him in his childhood and how those events cast their lifelong shadow over him. As always, she was glad for Catherine's assistance.

The sisters spent the rest of the day opening box after box of case material and then reading, marking, and writing notes, page after page. Wanda reached for her interview notes. "I'm going to call Noah, one of Quentin's younger brothers."

"Oh, ask if he ever saw Quentin hurt anyone," Catherine prompted.

Noah answered on the first ring.

Wanda introduced herself and asked if he would be willing to answer a few questions. She emphasized that she really wanted to help Quentin and that she needed input from as many siblings as she could get. Noah said that he was just a toddler when Quentin left home, so he didn't really know him. "We had different fathers. My dad was Tony Coleman. I don't have any childhood memories 'cuz we was thirteen years apart."

"Can you tell me if Quentin talked a lot?" she queried.

"I do know, well, my older sisters and brothers told me that he'd talk up a storm when he was young . . . That was before he went to prison. But I didn't have any personal contact with him after that."

"What about your sisters? Did he talk with them after he went to prison?"

"Yeah, Abby and Lilly did call him, but he told them he just had a few minutes to be on the phone. I'd ask about him, but they said it was the same ol', same ol'."

"Were you at his hearing in the summer of 2008?"

"Yeah, but that was a disaster. Lilly got Quentin stirred up. She tried to tell him what to say. He got all riled up, and they removed him from the court room."

"Did you have contact with him after that?"

"Wasn't much contact with anyone after that. Tell the truth, there really wasn't much contact with Quentin ever since he went to prison in 1980."

"Do you know why?"

"No. Never knew why. Quentin just stopped communicating with all of us. Then, a few years ago, my sisters started calling him once in a while. And when he was charged in this case, they called, but he wouldn't talk. Well, he did say one thing. He told them not to talk with anybody about him. Abby and Lilly thought he was just depressed." Wanda thanked him, and they finished their phone conversation.

Catherine, tapping her pencil on the stack of Quentin's juvenile records, suggested, "Why don't you call Melody? She was just five years younger than Quentin. Maybe she remembers something you can use."

"Good idea," Wanda agreed.

Melody Mathews reported that her father was Donnie Baker and that she really didn't have many memories of her childhood with Quentin. "I mainly remember that the kids were all close," she trailed off. "I was only ten when

Mama died. It was really hard for us after that," she repeated what Wanda had heard many times before.

After hanging up with Melody, Wanda suggested that she and Catherine make the forty-five minute drive to South Padre Island for dinner. Their favorite place was a seafood restaurant, overlooking the Laguna Madre, that specialized in fried shrimp and catfish. They changed out of their work clothes and dressed for an evening on the Island.

Catherine could still drive, and this gave her a sense of some control over her life. Wanda enjoyed looking out the window, not having to watch the road. The sisters took pleasure in the present moment of quiet togetherness.

"I still think you're crazy for taking this case with Quentin not speaking to anyone!" Catherine's empathic words caught Wanda off guard. "Then again, you've done crazier things before. Go for it! What's the worst that could happen?"

"I can get thrown out of court, lose my reputation, never be able to work a capital case again, and look like an idiot." Wanda ticked them off on her fingers, laughing. "The list goes on and on, but I'm in too deep to stop now."

Catherine facetiously replied, "Tell you what. If all else fails, you can plant more roses!"

Throughout dinner, the sisters laughed and teased, each taking true pleasure in their evening together. Yet, a somber shadow followed them. Both knew this would likely be their last time to come to the island together. Catherine was getting weaker by the day.

After a Thanksgiving-turkey-sized platter of fried shrimp and fish, Wanda and Catherine left the restaurant, feeling gastronomically satisfied but in need of a short walk. They decided to walk to the other side of the restaurant where there were a few benches. The sisters sat on the benches, basking in the evening light. The waves lapped against the shore.

"How is Sandy doing?" asked Catherine abruptly.

"Great, I had coffee with him the other day," answered Wanda. "He's excited that rain came just at the right time. Looks like he'll have a great crop." She smiled, recalling the pleasant morning sitting at one the town's old mainstays, visiting and exchanging stories.

"How can you be satisfied with your relationship with Sandy?" queried Catherine. "If the connection is true—genuine—shouldn't you continue and strengthen it?" Catherine's mind reflected the churning of the water. Something was on her mind, waiting to break loose.

"We have a connection—yes—it is genuine. The connection will always be there. There is no worry of it disappearing or weakening . . . A true connection cannot be broken." Wanda paused to collect her thoughts. The waves languidly rolled onto the beach, humming to themselves, not caring if anyone heard its song. "A relationship is not like a highway. It's more like a river—it makes its own path in its own time. We can't push destiny around . . . And when we try to, we put obstacles in the path. Marriage is not the ultimate way to show the connection."

"But isn't there pain and agony knowing that you will never have more than friendship?"

"Perhaps it's pain and agony that brings to light the depth of feeling and attachment. In friendship there is an underlying peace of mind, knowing that we share a genuine relationship. "

Silence descended on the sisters. Each contemplated the twist and turns of their lives while watching numerous boats return from the Gulf. Each took deep breaths of the salty air. Each enjoyed the moment, taking pleasure in the other's company.

Catherine stopped before the red light as an intersection changed. She visually cleared both directions and proceeded to turn right onto the main boulevard. The two sisters were surprised to see the red and blue lights flashing behind them. Neither saw the little sign that said, "No Turn on Red." The officer gave Catherine a ticket for two hundred dollars, following the letter of the law. No mercy for the two "criminals" who were so reckless.

Catherine immediately drove to the police station in order to save time later by paying the fine now.

"Let me give you a hundred. Half of this was my fault. I sure didn't see that 'no turn' sign." Wanda felt awful as her sister had very little money.

"No way!" Catherine firmly argued. She determinedly grabbed her purse and indignantly walked up the steps to the police station. She insisted on paying the fine and leaving no mark against her character. Despite Catherine knowing she didn't have that long to live, she refused to leave the ticket unpaid. Wanda admired Catherine's still-strong sense for dignity of life and integrity. As long as she was alive, she would live every moment, honoring herself with each breath. Wanda watched her and thought, *She still looks attractive, her short-cut blonde wig beautifully styled and her soft, pale complexion perfectly complemented with a dab of makeup. I'm glad she's living with cancer and not dying with it.*

A few minutes later, Catherine came out and said she had made her case. "Unfortunately, they weren't at all sympathetic."

Despite her explanation, the officers were unmoved and unmerciful. They demanded their pound of flesh. She paid the fine, irately scribbling out a check. As she was leaving, she turned and said to the police officers, "This'll be my last visit to the island. Thank you for making it so special!" Then, she pulled off her wig, smiled, and walked out. She had lost all of her hair because of the chemo. Speechless, they just stared at her.

Wanda and Catherine then toured South Padre Island and parked by the seaside to watch the waves ebb and flow. The sound of the ocean had a calming effect. On the drive home, the two grown women laughed and giggled like two little sisters.

Weeks later, in the midst of finishing Quentin's LifePath, Todd called to inform Wanda that the prosecutor on Quentin's case was telling the press that he believed that the cruelty of Anna Stanford's death warranted a death sentence.

"Quentin Mathews put four loops around her neck and pulled tight. He's a rapist, a killer, a *bad* human being." Todd quoted the prosecutor.

Wanda shook her head disapprovingly at what the prosecutor had told the press. *Playing judge and jury to the public even before the trial begins.* She countered, arguing, "One reason I don't think Quentin is a killer is because he had a strong connection with his mother during his first fourteen years and a strong attachment with his sisters. He didn't have a deep-seated need to kill, but he did have a need to steal. He became a compulsive thief—not a killer or a rapist."

"Okay, so you think that you have enough information to counterargue? You can offer a professional opinion to that effect?" probed Todd. Wanda assured him that she did and could. He was pleased and told Wanda that he would let her know about the trial date soon.

Wanda returned her attention to the LifePath. Catherine sat at the other end of the table and heard every word.

"What makes you certain that Quentin isn't a rapist killer?" Catherine picked up where Todd left off.

"Because he had *gemeinschaftsgefuhl*," responded Wanda.

"Explain, please," requested Catherine.

"It is evident, for example, by how Quentin went out to shine shoes and gave the money to his family. He used his shining shoes money to take his sister Lilly to the ball game to make her feel good. Also, he felt close to his tutor Andrew and made some close friends in the Fellowship House experience."

"He did steal—that's criminal. I've heard of people robbing people and killing them and even raping them. It's not mutually exclusive. What makes Quentin different than . . . let's say . . . Jackson Dell?"

"Quentin is a compulsive thief . . . He has been a thief since he was a child. Yes, he stole. But, he stole food to help his family. So, he developed a pattern of stealing." Wanda straightened up in her chair as she continued. "They had a good attachment, even though he didn't have his father as a role model."

"What about raping?"

"Rapists generally have a history of being sexually abused when they were young. They also have a history of betrayal trauma and disorganized attachment. Quentin doesn't have that history. His mother and all of his siblings were kind to one another." Catherine listened intently.

"He doesn't have a history of assault either," Wanda continued. "He has a foul mouth, but that doesn't make him a killer."

"So, ultimately, you're saying he cared about people?" Catherine clarified.

"Yes," Wanda confirmed. "I must help the jury recognize the consequences of attachment disruptions during childhood that often impact adult behavior. Quentin was not born mean or bad, but his stealing set him up for a negative perception by the police and now possibly by a jury that will determine his fate."

Chapter 18

Wanda entered the courtroom, curious to see the setting where she would testify in a few minutes. The only people present were the defense and prosecution attorneys, as well as frail, middle-aged Quentin dressed in his orange jumpsuit, looking like a lost soul. This was Wanda's first view of him. He was small in stature with a "little boy" face and several random cornrow pigtails sticking straight out of his scalp that was covered with crimped hair.

Todd greeted Wanda and asked if she would like to meet Quentin. He would be escorted out before court commenced because he had chosen not to participate in his trial.

"Of course," she responded. "I'd be grateful for the opportunity."

She walked over hastily, adorned in her classic-cut Christian Dior suit. It was her signature courtroom garb. She sat down beside Quentin and said earnestly, "I'm so glad to meet you, Quentin." She extended her hand to him, and he returned the favor. "I really wish I could have talked with you. I wanted to learn more about your hospital incident. I was so sorry to read in the records that you had such a horrible experience."

He remained expressionless for several seconds. Then, he smiled meekly and said in a whispered tone, "I really would've liked to talk with you, too." She smiled within. He struck her as a young teenage boy, even though she knew he was fifty-two years old.

Quentin's comment rekindled Wanda's skepticism about her visit to interview him in prison. She had been told by Todd that the guards hated Quentin because he "shot off his mouth" to them every chance he had. She, again, wondered whether or not those guards wanted him talking to anyone, especially a potential witness on his behalf. *There is something so innocent-like about Quentin and something so wrong about this entire case.'*

Her conversation was brief with Quentin. The guards removed him from the courtroom as the penalty stage of trial was about to begin. Wanda stood up to exit. The rule, not permitting any witness to be present during the court proceedings, had been invoked since the onset of the trial. As she also left the courtroom, she was keenly aware that both prosecutors had been watching her talk with Quentin.

While sitting on a mahogany bench in the hall just outside the courtroom, waiting to be called to the stand, Wanda began mentally reciting her mantra, trying to unwind. She was soon approached, but not greeted, by Quentin's sister Abby who sat down beside her and frowned into her eyes.

She barked, "Don't youse testify. We know youse settin' our brother up to get the death penalty. We know what youse tryin' to do."

"I'm sorry you feel this way," she said tersely. "My only concern is to do everything I can to save your brother from the death penalty. I intend to do my very best."

At this point, court was resuming, and Abby jumped up and growled, "Don't do it!" She marched in, leaving Wanda there in the hallway, wondering what drama was about to unfold.

While continuing to wait, several of Quentin's siblings paraded past. They had been with Abby in Phyllis's front yard a few months before. They didn't speak, much to Wanda's relief. She thought that the males who entered with them may have been brothers or husbands. *Hood-sitters, for sure,* she speculated.

For Wanda, waiting to testify is always the most difficult part of any trial. It's too late to review and too tense to focus on anything else. But it's never too late to pray. She often thought there's more praying going on in courtrooms than in churches—especially when it's a matter of life and death. *Let me do this with least effort, with grace, and in a sacred manner,* Wanda internally repeated to calm herself.

After the jury returned from the break, the bailiff ushered her in, and Todd called her to the stand. She was sworn in by the judge and invited to sit in the swivel chair in the witness box. The direct examination began by reviewing her credentials.

She already knew what was coming. She expected the prosecution would try to disqualify her as a witness. Before Todd could begin, the tall and confident brown-suited prosecuting attorney, the same man who identified Quentin as a bad human being to the press, jumped to his feet. *I bet he was a college basketball player. And, he still likes to play center*, was the thought that ran across her mind.

"Your Honor, I object!" cried the prosecuting attorney. "This witness needs to be disqualified. She's not qualified to testify in this case."

This is it. Either this is my last court case, and it is time for early retirement, or I'm about to testify by the skin of my teeth, Wanda thought.

The judge declared, "Overruled. You'll have your turn."

Todd, standing at the dais, ready to begin the direct, quickly asked, "Dr. Draper, have you ever been disqualified as a witness?"

"No, I haven't."

"How many capital cases have you testified in?"

"Over one hundred."

"Have you ever worked on any federal cases?"

"Yes, I have. And I've never been disqualified on those either."

Preliminary questions were asked and answered for about half an hour. These centered on Wanda's education, work experience, publications, and preparation for this case. Then, Todd asked that she be certified as a witness.

There were clearly inner judicial politics going on here. The prosecution wanted to disqualify her because she didn't interview the defendant, and the defense wanted her to have an opportunity to present her findings. The judge didn't want to be the one judge in over one hundred cases to disqualify her. He wouldn't look good.

Soon after being certified as a witness, the real work for Quentin commenced. Every word uttered would have to carry weight if Quentin was to be saved from the needle.

In preparing to testify, Wanda had created Quentin's LifePath from birth to age twenty-one. This required eight charts, the objective being to illustrate the significance of the early years in Quentin's development and how these life experiences influenced his adult behavior.

In order to effectively use the LifePath, Todd requested permission from the judge, with approval from the prosecuting attorneys, that Dr. Draper be allowed to step down from the witness box and stand in front of the jury while explaining Quentin's life.

As Wanda was taking her place in front of the jury box, she could see the same question in the jury members' eyes that she observed in case after case, "Do we have to listen to all this? Let's get on with his punishment!"

I wonder how many jurors understand that in a death penalty case there must be mitigation testimony—it's the law of the land, Wanda exasperatedly contemplated. Her face showed no emotion. She stayed calm and focused on presenting Quentin as a human being, a whole person.

Wanda stepped to one side of the easels, and Todd stood on the other side. The jurors had full view of the LifePath charts. As Todd placed the charts two at a time on the easels, Wanda used a pointer to direct the jury's attention to the visual illustration of Quentin's first twenty years of development.

It was important to give the jury a mental picture of Quentin in his family in a poverty-stricken neighborhood: one of fourteen children, with a father who was in and out of his life before he was two years old and then gone forever; a mother who had several men enter and exit her life, many babies to bear and care for; and then her own death when Quentin was a young teenager. The charts identified the years and dates of the children in Quentin's family during his early years and that his mother was only fourteen years old when her first child was born. The jury needed to see that the significant breaks in his life line—illustrated by broken lines on the chart and caused by coming-and-going father figures, a young, single mother, an increasingly large family, and his mother's untimely death—all influenced Quentin's development.

Todd strategically asked, "Why is it important to view these early years, since Quentin is now fifty-two years old?"

Wanda talked about how love, trust, and mutuality are the roots of morality and are grounded in the first few years of life. "This requires time and attention. Some children are more sensitive than others and require more close contact with the parent. Quentin's first five years," Wanda spoke as she gestured to the first chart, "clearly illustrate how difficult it was for his mother to give him attention with so many babies and young children to feed and care for. There were already five siblings before Quentin was born. By the time he was four years old, the family moved from Arkansas to St. Louis, and another brother, Evan, was born. When Quentin was five and a half, another sister, Melody, was born."

The second chart showed that Quentin attended three different kindergartens in one school year. Wanda continued to contrast how the circumstances in Quentin's life—the repeated disruptions in his first educational experiences, the male figures coming in and out, the continually growing family, and the increasingly overly burdened mother—disrupted normal development, leaving their mark on his behavior.

The third and fourth charts were placed on the easels. The third chart showed that between Quentin's sixth and eighth years, two more sisters were born. The fourth chart reflected his school attendance and the birth of another sister, April. Wanda pointed out that by the time he was seven years old, Quentin began shining shoes to earn money for food for his family. "When he was eleven, Quentin was tutored by Andrew, who became a close family friend. His mother bore two more children, Nathaniel and Noah, by the time Quentin was thirteen years old."

Todd then asked, "And what is significant on chart number six?"

Wanda, pointing to the center of the chart, replied, "Quentin, by age fourteen, was reading only at a third-grade level. He emancipated himself from the family in order to work and buy food and provide money for them. Because he was living on the streets, he was picked up and sent to Mission Hills Group Home, where he attended school and scored a full scale IQ of sixty on the Stanford Binet LM. But, he continued to struggle in school and simply couldn't focus enough to make his grades. He finally dropped out in the ninth grade."

Chart number seven was placed on the easel while Todd asked, "What is so important about this stage in Quentin's life?"

She explained, "Even when Quentin was living in the Group Home and on the streets, he would go home to see the family, especially his mother. She had another baby when Quentin was fourteen. And three months later, she died. According to reports from Andrew Ericson and some of Quentin's siblings, he was devastated. Mr. Ericson reported that he attended Virginia Lee Mathews's funeral. He recalled that while the entire family freely expressed their sorrow with crying and moans of grief, Quentin could not contain himself. He sobbed uncontrollably, and several siblings had to restrain him."

She pointed to the notation at the lower part of the chart, "It was after his mother's death when his pattern of stealing began. By the time he reached his sixteenth year, he was picked up for trespassing. One year later, Quentin was charged with stealing and placed in the State School for Boys for two years."

Todd stared directly at Wanda. "This brings us to the last chart of Quentin's LifePath. What does this tell us about him?"

Again, Wanda emphasized Quentin's pattern of stealing. "It was obvious that he lacked socialization and regard for societal laws. He was in and out of confinement as a ward of the state throughout his adolescence until he was twenty-one." She paused, scanning the jury. "But, we've only seen evidence of stealing. He was on his way to becoming a compulsive thief, but he never assaulted anyone."

Wanda was directed by Todd to return to the witness stand and be seated.

Todd queried, "How did his mother's untimely death impact Quentin's development?"

As she brought the jury's attention back to Quentin's fifteenth year, she stated that his emotional and psychological development was actually stifled when his mother died. "He never recovered from the loss he felt. This brought about feelings of betrayal, resulting in developmental trauma. With no father and now no mother, Quentin felt alone, even in the midst of his large family. Everyone was out for himself. Siblings went their ways, and so did he. This is when he began to steal, a psychological manifestation of feeling like his mother had been stolen from him. This is not unusual behavior for children who have been taken from their parents and placed in foster homes or put up for adoption or, for some, children who lose their parents in death. Without consistent support and understanding, many adults never realize that children who steal may be trying to get something of value, something that represents the idea of value they treasured in their loved one—value now missing that they were yearning to reclaim."

Todd continued the questioning. "Was Quentin already having problems before his mother died?"

"Yes. He was having problems in school. He was struggling. He lost his motivation to study when he was placed in the school for boys and made a ward of the state. As long as he was able to shine shoes and do odd jobs, he felt he was helping his mother and his siblings, especially the younger ones. But after his mother died, he gave up. He felt he had been robbed. His mother had been taken from him. His worldview changed."

"Please explain," Todd requested.

She fixed her gaze on the jury members, wanting to connect with each one. "Quentin's perceived image of himself formed the organizational core of his beliefs, of his expectations and his motivations. This worldview and his inner convictions began to guide and shape his sense of self. That is, how he saw himself and his role in relationships in everyday life. He formed his own inner eyeglasses and created an image of himself based on how he felt and what he believed others thought of him. If he couldn't be a success at anything else, he could be a success as a thief. He seemed to be able to maintain self-confidence when he was stealing. He was gathering value. He never learned to get along with others except when he could share the stuff he stole. His view of the world never seemed to broaden beyond that of a teenager who couldn't quite step out into the real world. Society's rules never seemed to apply to him. After all, he believed he was helping others. Deep down inside, Quentin's feeling of having his parents stolen away from him seemed to be the driving force that made him want to steal from the world. His focus was set on thievery as a way of life."

Todd wanted her to keep talking, so he prompted her, "From what you learned about Quentin's development, why did he have such a rough time in prison?"

"Unfortunately, Quentin was arrested time after time and lived much of his life in jail or prison. His greatest problem while incarcerated was his foul mouth. His way of lashing out at others, especially the guards, seemed to be his only means of expressing his frustration and anger, which was motivated by underlying fear. As a child and young adolescent, Quentin never had the models or the guidance to help him develop social skills and the ability to resolve problems and make transitions from behaving like a child to adapting like an adult. He carried a heavy load of emotional baggage, and because he never developed the coping skills for handling daily challenges, he habitually reacted by lashing out with verbal obscenities. His unexpressed power from within—his trapped life energy—needed an outlet. The tension would build until his tongue seemed to be his only ally."

Todd returned to the table to consult his notes. This gave Wanda a short respite. However, her mind was still turning.

His words are the key. Medical reports, interview notes, and incarceration records replayed in her mind's eye. She ascertained that Quentin's mouthing off became almost lethal for him. She, through the prison records, followed his vitriolic orations and profanities; they spewed out like water from holes in a dike.

And then, abruptly, the verbal outlet stopped spewing. Wanda was perplexed. She wanted to know why he would cease the only outlet of expression he had. She had searched through hundreds of pages of prison records, looking for the missing link. Suddenly, an epiphany—it was like being struck by lightning. *This might just save Quentin from the death sentence!* Excitement at her discovery radiated throughout her body. She wanted to take the document and wave it in victory. If she could excite the jury's sense of mercy and sympathy, perhaps the defense could prevail.

Throughout the case preparations, she had expected someone to bring this fact up. Yet, there hadn't been the slightest allusion. She now believed that neither the defense nor the prosecution had gone to the depth of searching the records that she had. Neither side had the complete story of Quentin. She felt like this was a pile of gold out in the open, and no one but she could see it. Now, it was up to her to convey the whole story, the whole person to the jury. She was nearly euphoric about concluding her testimony.

Wanda's hopes sank as Todd suddenly announced, "I pass the witness."

How will I ever be able to convince the jury to consider the most important mitigating circumstances? Wanda was horrified. *Will I have another opportunity?*

The judge called for a short recess. The jury needed a restroom break. Wanda stood to revive her legs. She glanced at the prosecution table and saw the lawyers chomping at the bit. She peeked at the defense table from the corner of her eye. There was no way to let Todd know that she wasn't finished. Once court started, Wanda, like all witnesses, could not speak with her side's attorneys at all, not even during a recess. She was careful not to look directly in their direction, so that no mischievous legal assistant could insinuate foul play. Wanda lamented, *Is this the end? What about Quentin? There's still one aspect . . . one fact that needs to be known!* Wanda could read the writing on the wall. She knew how and where the prosecutor would attack. *Maybe I am finished . . . for good this time!*

Court soon resumed. As the prosecuting attorney moved toward the dais, a tinge of anxiety bore through Wanda as if a vice was squeezing every cell in her body. She knew what was coming, and she braced for the storm.

The judge asked, "Is the prosecution ready to cross examine?"

"Yes, Your Honor," he replied. Like a child opening the long-awaited presents on Christmas morning, he tore right in. "How is it that you can testify on the defendant's behalf when you have not even interviewed him? Isn't it true that you have not interviewed the defendant?"

"It is true. I have not."

"Isn't it true that you spoke with the defendant only this morning . . . in this courtroom for only thirty seconds?"

"That's correct."

"Then please tell the jury how . . . how can you form an opinion in this case?"

"I collected data from multiple records, and I talked with family members and friends."

"You mentioned earlier in your testimony that the defendant grew up in a poverty-stricken neighborhood. Are you saying that all poverty-stricken kids become murderers?"

"No, I am not." She was unfazed and elaborated, "Many children grow up in poverty-stricken neighborhoods with drug-infested surroundings and violent role models, yet they succeed in school and become engaged in careers and community life with interest and enthusiasm. Many grow up to face challenges with sound decision-making abilities. However, these successful individuals, with few exceptions, are the result of caring and nurturing parents who consistently provide emotional support, guidance, limits, and models of appropriate behavior. Children, with the benefit of at least one parent who is consistently emotionally stable and reliable over the course of their infancy, childhood, and adolescence can usually withstand the pressures, crises, traumas, and misfortunes that bombard them. But, many children who grow up like Quentin, without a stable childhood and without secure attachments, are vulnerable. From the beginning, the effects of traumatic experiences often lead to self-serving motivations, including the potential for illegal behaviors.

"Quentin was virtually robbed of his natural childhood and adolescence through the loss of his parents, and he, in turn, began to steal from others—thus his cry for help to assuage his deep-seated feelings of having his parents *stolen* from him. This was the evidence of a psychological need to recover his losses."

"Well, I'm not sure you'd know anything about poverty," he replied, making assumptions that because she had a PhD and worked in a medical school she grew up with a privileged life. He set his trap. His goal was to cast Dr. Draper as some ivory-tower royalty—too lofty to understand the common man.

"Actually . . . I grew up poverty-stricken," she enjoyed correcting him, "in the Depression." He was stopped cold in his tracks.

Wanda took pleasure in the hidden compliment paid by the prosecutors' inability to distinguish her true age—Wanda never looked old enough to have lived through the Depression. Several times Wanda felt a tinge of pity for the prosecutors when they made that attack. It exposed their mud-flinging tactics.

This cross-examination continued for over an hour. Wanda withstood every attack, both legitimate and underhanded. She parried insinuations by referring to various records that were court provided. She blocked false assumptions and manipulative inferences, bolstered by her twenty-plus years of experiences in death penalty cases. The prosecutor finally finished and passed her as witness.

The judge addressed Todd, "Do you have further questions for this witness?"

Please have some more questions for me. Please—we need them! Wanda mentally urged.

Todd rose. "Yes, Your Honor."

Thank God! Relief washed over her.

He then began his redirect. "Is there any further compelling evidence, in your opinion, that you wish to share with the jury?"

"Yes, there is." *This is my chance! My only chance! What luck—or is it?*

"Please proceed."

"I discovered that several years prior to Quentin's arrest for murder, he was in jail for stealing. While serving time for various acts of stealing and robbery, his medical reports showed that he had severe burns on one entire side of his body. From his hand and arm all the way down the left side of his body to his foot."

At this point, the jurors were suddenly moved to attention. She stared fixedly at them. "As I read the medical reports, I could visualize only one way such severe burns could occur. He had to have been dipped in scalding water." She paused theatrically before proceeding. "While going through the hospital records, I remembered a few years ago when I literally got lost in one of the state prisons. The guard had given me directions on how to leave the contact room and head to the exit floor. But, after descending two floors, I couldn't find the elevator to the ground floor to exit. It was like a maze. I finally took some stairs."

"Objection! Irrelevant!" stormed the prosecutor.

"Overruled. Please continue," stated the judge.

"While walking down the stairs, I realized I was entering the basement, the laundromat. Several prisoners were manning a huge trough of boiling water, with sheets and towels being stirred with large paddles." Now, she had the jury's full attention.

She looked straight at each of the jurors and asked pointedly, "'How?' I asked myself. 'And why?' While considering these records, I began to imagine what might have happened. If Quentin were dipped, it would have taken several men to hold him, and yet there were no records indicating any such incident."

The prosecutor bellowed, "Objection! Irrelevant!"

The judge, with a slight edge in his voice, said, "Objection sustained."

But, the jury already got the picture, and that's what Wanda wanted.

Todd came to her rescue, "Please continue with the facts. "

So she did. "The burns, according to the physician's notes and the chart records, were so severe they became infected, and Quentin was admitted to a local hospital for treatment. Yet, his family knew nothing about this trauma." Now her confidence was building. She spoke clearly as she deliberately panned the members of the jury, looking each in the eye. Her intent was to make a connection with the jury. She was well aware that to truly grab a jury, one must make them laugh—or cry. There were certainly no laughs in Quentin's case. Yet, she hoped to touch and move some of them to tears.

For only what seemed a split second, Wanda's eyes shifted to the audience. There were the sisters, holding on to one another. They looked like stone statues staring straight at her. *What must they be thinking?*

But she didn't focus long enough to make eye contact. *Better to not.* She proceeded with her testimony.

"The sheriff took Quentin to the hospital. Deputies were posted around the clock. But Quentin was so severely burned that there was no way he could have escaped. According to medical records, he was heavily sedated. He couldn't walk and couldn't use his left arm or leg. He had to maneuver in a wheelchair and was in tremendous agony. He had to be given pain meds around the clock. After several weeks in the hospital, he was finally released, and the sheriff arrived to take Quentin back to jail. He was weak but able to travel in the sheriff's van."

Wanda paused long enough to let the images of Quentin and his plight sink in to each juror's sensitivity. Then, she continued, "About six weeks after returning to jail, the burned areas became infected again, and Quentin had to be taken back to the hospital for more severe treatment. Not only for infection but also for plastic surgery and skin grafting. They had to use his other hip for the graft."

Another quick glance at the audience found one sister wiping tears. Another sniffled. One of the brothers patted Phyllis on the shoulder.

Wanda, hardly taking a breath, wanted to keep up the momentum of her message without lawyer interruptions. "I knew in my mind that Quentin had good reason not to talk with me or anyone else about his case. I had no doubt that his foul mouth got him into trouble with the guards as well as with other inmates." *And I know my mouth is about to get me into major trouble with the prosecutor,* her thoughts interjected. "I can easily imagine that when Quentin was dipped into scalding water, probably in the prison laundry, he was told that if he ever spoke one word about how this happened that he would be dipped again on the other side. Is there any wonder why he told no one and why the guards didn't want him to talk with me or with anyone else for that matter? Also, Quentin had good reason to order his siblings to talk to no one, even though he never told them about the burn episode."

The prosecutor leaped to his feet. "Objection, Your Honor! This is complete speculation by the witness!"

The judge took a second, then instructed, "Overruled. I'll allow it. Please stick to the facts, Dr. Draper."

"Yes, Your Honor."

She moved on. "According to hospital records, undergoing two surgeries for a traumatic hot water scalding of no less than 20 percent of his body resulted in second- and third-degree burns and a long, difficult recovery. This experience further exacerbated Quentin's poor self-image and did not lessen his underlying fear—and anger. No one in his family knew about this trauma, and consequently he received no support from them during two periods of hospitalization. How could he not feel traumatized and abandoned?"

Todd asked, "Do you have an opinion about other developmental findings that could influence the defendant's behavior?"

"Yes, I do."

"Please state your opinion."

"Quentin Mathews has no early childhood manifestations that point to mental or personality disorders, although it is apparent, in my opinion, that he has suffered for many years with developmental trauma disorder—both during childhood and adulthood. And, he does not meet the criteria for sociopathic or psychopathic behavior. The most productive time of Quentin's formative years was when he had a tutor with imposed structure, both for studying and for sports. He responded positively to the structure while in middle school, but it was not enough to ameliorate his poor intellectual capacity. Then, his mother died, and he became stifled in his emotional and psychological development. To this day, his behavior reflects that of early adolescence. But,

Quentin has learned to live in a structured and secure environment, and he has the capacity to conform to the rules and confinement of prison life." *And he won't be talking about his plight, and I hope the jury thinks about that in their deliberations.'*

"Thank you. I pass the witness," Todd stated, as he triumphantly plopped down in his seat.

The judge asked the prosecutor, "Do you have any further questions?"

The prosecutor sighed and said resignedly, "No, Your Honor."

As she was dismissed from the stand, Wanda held her breath, hoping the jury would keep the image of Quentin being dipped in scalding water imbedded in their minds. As she briskly walked through the double courtroom doors into the hallway, her eyes were focused on the courthouse exit. She wasted no time heading that way.

But there, just inside the door, stood one of Quentin's brothers, Evan, obviously waiting for her. She recognized him from the front yard visit at Phyllis's house on that memorable afternoon several months ago. He had been sitting on the hood of one of the cars. *Uh-oh. What am I in for now?*

Today, he was dressed in a black outfit with a black leather jacket, black boots and a long chain hanging from his waist to his knees. His crimped hair was cut close. *How did he get through security wearing that metal chain?* She wondered if he was going to follow her out of the building—or escort her. *Who else might be waiting for me?* The fear inside her grew. She thought about heading toward one of the offices—or back into the courtroom. But then she let go of her fear, squared her shoulders, and made a beeline for the hood-sitter.

As she approached him, he surprised her when he extended his hand. They greeted one another with a firm handshake. Evan said, "I wanna thank youse for your testimony. I know youse did all youse could to help Quentin. I was closest to him all the years we was at home. But, when momma died in Quentin's arms, he, yeah, he, uh, changed. He told me, 'I don't care what happens to me now. My life's over.' I thought he'd never stop cryin', but then he left home again, and I lost my favorite bro. But yeah, thanks for all youse did." Wanda thought her heart had just stopped.

In a croaky voice, she said to Evan, "I, uh, I didn't know your mother died in Quentin's arms. That . . . that had to be a terrible shock for him."

"Yeah, 'cuz he tried to get her to 'wake up.' He didn't know how to help her," he admitted thoughtfully.

"I hope you and your family will keep in touch with Quentin. He needs your support—and your love."

"We will. We understand things now that we didn't before today."

"Thank you for sharing this with me. Take care, and I'm glad to have met you." As she flung the doors open and headed down several blocks to the Westin where she was staying, she couldn't stop thinking: *If I had only known that Quentin's mother died in his arms, I could have made a much stronger case for the jury's mercy. Maybe there would have even been a few tears in the jury.*

When Wanda reached her hotel room, it was just the way she left it. One of the two double beds was still covered with her last-minute notes from early in the morning. Now, overwhelmed with exhaustion, she disregarded the entire day's events as she slipped off her heels and jacket before lying on the other bed and staring up at nothing. *Now, it's time to wait for the verdict. How long will it take?*

It was four o'clock. She had been on the stand almost all day—though it felt more like three days. She thought about packing her files and getting ready for the next day's flight, but her exhaustion made it easy to let go of that idea. She had talked with Andrew before court and asked him to call when there was a verdict. She promised him, "If we win—that is, LWOP instead of death—dinner is on me." He replied that he was going to remain in the courtroom to hear the closing arguments and wasn't about to leave until a verdict came in.

She tried to watch TV but couldn't focus. She began rerunning her testimony. She kept returning to the same thoughts: *If only I had been able to use the circumstances of Quentin's mother's death. If only I could have said more about Quentin's scalding incident. If only . . . if only . . . But, it's too late for that. Stop beating yourself up, Wanda!* She then said aloud, "Now, I wait."

———

At seven o'clock, the phone rang. She answered it, only to hear an excited voice. "Andrew?"

"We won, we won, we won!" he exclaimed with joy.

She could hardly believe what she just heard. She said immediately, "Meet me in front of the hotel in ten minutes. We're going to dinner." She quickly ran a brush through her hair, donned her suit jacket and shoes, and hurried down to the lobby.

Andrew was standing there in his oversized overalls, plaid shirt, baseball cap, and an old, battered denim jacket. Despite the day's events, she still looked like she was ready to step into a limo and head for a meeting with dignitaries. There was such a pronounced and stark contrast between the two, but she didn't care. *What a pair we make!* she told herself. They trekked down the street to one of the most famous steak houses in St. Louis. Anyone who was someone dined there. In Wanda's eyes, Andrew was a *Someone.* Without him, she wouldn't have been able to represent Quentin from the witness box.

The host smiled at Wanda, then stared daggers at Andrew. With an upper-crust superiority, he asked, "Do you have a reservation, please?"

She replied in her most polite and legal liaison voice, "I don't have one, but we'd like a table for two on the veranda." He hiked his eyebrows at the strange-looking couple, as if to say, "Who in the world is this?"

He eventually acquiesced and ushered them on to the veranda. Wanda wondered what this host thought. She speculated that he perceived Andrew as an actor of some sort, just coming from a performance.

While Wanda and Andrew perused menus, Andrew quickly said, "I'm not hungry. I'm still too excited about the verdict." Wanda's eyes focused on the sixty-dollar steaks and surmised that was why Andrew was suddenly not hungry. Even the soup was thirty. But, she didn't think she could digest much either, so she suggested, "How about sharing one of these shrimp scampi appetizers?" He agreed, and they enjoyed replaying the courtroom drama.

Wanda told Andrew, "I never could've worked this case or testified without your help. You were absolutely crucial to making this case turn out the way it did. You've won this case as much as I have. I only wish that Quentin could know how helpful you've been. I'll always be grateful, Andrew."

In a relieved tone, he replied, "I always knew Quentin was a good person. I still don't believe he could kill anyone." She thought to herself, *Neither do I.*

A few weeks after the trial, Wanda received a letter:

Dear Miss Draper,
*   I wish I could have talked with you. Thank you for helping me.*
*   Everybody loves you. God loves you, and I love you.*
*   Quentin Mathews*

PART FIVE

Chapter 19

Imagining the crickets were birds chirping early morning greetings, Wanda switched the lamp on beside her bed. It was only midnight. She rose from her futon. Giving up on sleep, she reconverted her bed to a sofa. When she had her little four hundred twenty square foot studio built as an addition to her La Feria cottage, she didn't want to take up space with a bedroom. Wanda with a smile replied, when Catherine had asked her why no bedroom, "It doesn't matter where my bed is . . . my eyes will be closed. This is going to be an efficiency studio." Wanda's postage-stamp-sized dwelling consisted of one large area, divided by furniture for specific purposes. Wanda was very pleased with this little space, enjoying it immensely. Snuggled in between two oversized designer pillows on the bed-turned-sofa, Wanda began sorting through the mail in her lap. She was hoping the plethora of bills and junk mail would lull her back to sleep. Yet, she was filled with surprise and curiosity when she saw the return address on a plain white envelope. She eagerly swiped it open with an antique letter opener.

Dear Wanda,

How are you? I hope you are doing well. I am so sorry that I haven't corresponded with you sooner. But, I have been unable to send or receive mail for sixty days; I've been in solitary confinement for the last several months.

I am now in the big prison. It's very different than Lexington. I think about Lexington a lot. I have good memories there. I found and met my half-sister, Stella, there. I hope she's doing well. I haven't heard from her since I was there, but I am going to try to get in touch with her. I want to make sure she's okay. I did really like it there. I wonder how their program is working. I plan to write to them to offer help. I think I can still make a contribution.

I am doing very well. I have developed a routine that keeps me disciplined. I exercise vigorously several times a day: running in place thirty minutes at a time, push-ups, sit-ups, etc. I can now easily do thirty to forty push-ups at a time. I feel very strong. Also, I get along with the guards really good; I have excellent behavior, and I never talk back to them or make off-handed remarks. I try to treat them with respect and courtesy. I think they like me.

I am also faithful to reading the Bible and praying every day. Studying passages of scripture really helps me; it is my only way to survive.

I will end this letter here. I need to write to a few other people tonight to let them know why I haven't been able to communicate. I will write again soon, and I look forward to your response and talking with you one day soon.

> *Much love and sunshine,*
> *James*

After Wanda put the letter aside, her mind reeled from the question provoked by James's letter. Sleep long forgotten, she leaned back against the futon. *Why did James call me when he escaped from Lexington?* As she relived that fateful phone call, she pondered, *James is smart. He must have known that I couldn't—I wouldn't—aid and abet him. He must have known that I would call the authorities as soon as he hung up with me.* This unspoken dialogue continued within Wanda. She was at a loss to grasp James's ulterior motive. *After all, behavior always has a purpose.* Wanda knew this was fact. Her years of experience verified and re-verified this truth. *Yet, what was James's purpose?* She thought about his development: the broken attachments, the abuse, the neglect, the rejection.

The blaringly loud ring of the phone interrupted her internal discourse. Wanda glanced over at the clock on her desk. It was two in the morning.

Before Wanda could say hello, a frustrated and exasperated voice said, "Can you believe Auntie wants me to come and check the lights upstairs? Who in the world changes a light bulb at two in the morning?" Wanda wasn't surprised by Catherine being awake. She hadn't been sleeping the entire night for many months now. But, she was startled that Catherine would call her at such an hour. Regarding her sister's questions, Wanda knew Catherine and Aunt Denise were like flint and iron. When the two interacted, sparks always flew.

"Catherine," Wanda said gently, but firmly, "you have to read between the lines. She's afraid—"

"Afraid of what?" Catherine scornfully interrupted. "What does she have to be afraid of? It's not like she's facing death." Bitterness had crept into her voice. "Oh, and she even threatened me she'd change the bulb herself. I told her to go ahead and do it. Then, I hung up on her."

"She's afraid of being alone," Wanda soothed. "She wants someone to be there for her." Wanda could understand her aunt's fear. Denise was nearly one hundred years old and still very much in her right mind. She recognized that both her nieces were independent and capable. She recognized that she, herself, was now dependent.

"I can't wait to move," Catherine said, changing subjects. "It's so aggravating living next door to her. She's always keeping tabs on me, wanting to know what I'm doing and why." Catherine vented her frustration. "I'm thinking of moving back to the Hill Country. It actually has a winter. A mild one, but at least it'd be a change."

"Yes, it is nice there," Wanda agreed. Catherine further talked of her plans to move from the Valley once her chemotherapy was completed. She was undergoing a new treatment regime. Her oncologist had told her to get her dancing shoes on. She would have a fun life ahead of her.

A quarter of an hour later, Catherine and Wanda's conversation came to an end. As Wanda sighed, she flipped her phone open to make the time appear on the screen. She checked it against the lightening sky outside and the clock on the desk. Wanda looked back at the desk clock and muttered in defeat, "Too late to go back to bed now." Instead, she headed to her compact kitchen.

Against the sound of the electric coffee maker, gurgling and sputtering, and the aroma of brewing coffee, Wanda's mind was still turning over James's letter. She picked up the letter. She hadn't mentioned it to Catherine as she needed a little longer to process it. She skimmed it again, hoping the answer would somehow be revealed. *His running pattern turned destructive . . . once again.* Like a boomerang, the questioned returned—it plagued her: *Why did James run from Lexington? He was sure to make parole.*

Once again, "all behavior has a purpose" echoed through her mind. She could see this truism manifest itself with her aunt who didn't want to be left alone in the Valley and was trying to manipulate her nieces into staying with her. Her sister called because she was also afraid and wanted reassurance by sharing her future dreams. Wanda could see it plainly in her aunt and sister, but the method to James's madness still eluded her.

After pouring a cup of steaming coffee, Wanda stepped outside onto her back patio. The early morning air was still fresh and cool. She sat down in an old reclining chair. Her train of thought continued, fueled by the invigorating liquid.

The brilliant, warm sun began to rise, casting its rays in a golden glow against the trees as Wanda continued to think about James. She pictured him, cheerful and optimistic about his future, as he wrote his letter. But, the line about the guards liking him troubled her. She could not quite bring herself to believe that the guards would make an exception for James. Wanda knew all too much about the unwritten code and camaraderie among the guards. His escape had a rippling effect throughout the prison system, making them appear inadequate to their duties. It violated the guards' trust and inadvertently tarnished their honor. Wanda was certain that, like for Quentin being punished for mouthing off, the guards would see to it that James too was punished for escaping.

The Valley songbirds greeted Wanda with their early morning serenade. She smiled, taking comfort in knowing that her sister was listening to the same symphony of nature's melodies: kiskadees, black-bellied whistlers, mockingbirds, and the distant squawks of green parakeets. *Catherine and James—how sad.* Wanda was overcome with an inexplicable, sincere sadness. It enveloped her, like a vine with its tendrils encompassing her heart, neither squeezing nor falling away but holding on tight.

"Wanda, how are you today?" As Wanda answered, she mentally braced herself for another onslaught of Amanda Fields's bemoaning. Throughout the last several months, Wanda had started receiving calls frequently from Albert and Amanda Fields. They had now decided to take a more active role in James's life.

"Oh, I'm fine, how are you doing?" Wanda removed the cake from the oven and placed it on the one available spot on the stove that was already at capacity with pots and pans. She commiserated with her caller, "Must be so frustrating to not get any cooperation from the prison." As Wanda poured icing from one of the pots onto the hot cake, she made sympathizing and attentive comments and exclamations during Mrs. Fields's monologue.

"So, you've been in communication with the prison chaplain, then?" Wanda put the cake back in the oven so the coconut and pecans in the icing could brown for a few minutes. "And, he hasn't been able to get you in to see James?" Wanda expressed her incredulousness at the scenario Mrs. Fields described. "Have you tried talking with his lawyer?"

Mrs. Fields continued to lament. She and her husband, in their view, were to be pitied. They were the dutiful parents, trying to help their child. *You're twenty years too late!* was Wanda's silent response to their efforts to absolve their guilt.

Catherine entered the kitchen, smiling as she sniffed the air. Wanda smiled at her and signaled to her earpiece that she was on the phone. Catherine beamed at the dining table elegantly dressed with beautiful table linens, each setting adorned with polished silver, dainty china, and sparkling crystal, as she walked through to the tiny living room. After several minutes, Wanda was at last able to gracefully end the phone conversation while removing the cake from the oven. She placed it to cool and then joined her sister who was reclining on the sofa.

"Anything serious?" Catherine asked when Wanda collapsed into the living room chair with an exasperated sigh.

Wanda shook her head in exasperation. "Amanda and Albert Fields."

"Them again?" Catherine threw her head back, rolling her eyes. "Why are they all of a sudden interested in him?" Wanda had been keeping Catherine informed about James's plight and the new developments of his case. "Guilty conscience, no doubt," Catherine scoffed.

"Yes, I think they feel some of the blame—"

"As they should! They never cared about him. They just kept trying to pass him off to one hospital and treatment center after another. Probably happy when he ran away so they wouldn't have to deal with him anymore." Catherine's voice and ire rose with every word. She had neither accepted his parents' past actions nor forgiven them for their neglectful abuse.

Wanda acknowledged Catherine's assessment of the Fields. "While they thought he was doing fine in Lexington, they could ignore him and focus on earning money, how good Luke was doing, and their busy lives. They never came to visit James because it cost too much money. They never went to nor planned to go to any of his hearings or trials because of expenses. As long as James's letters were positive— "

"You know he faithfully and cheerfully wrote to them," Catherine chimed in.

Wanda nodded her head in agreement, "They could continue in their denial. I think they do believe that he is innocent. But, I think once James ran away from Lexington, they finally had to acknowledge there were serious problems. It finally sunk in—they realized James's plight." She paused a moment, then added, "It's sad . . . that now, at this stage in his life, they decided to try and include him in the family."

Catherine made no reply at first. Her mind was wrestling with Wanda's description of James's parents. She couldn't grasp what she interpreted as oxymoronic behavior by his parents.

"Do you remember reading the biblical verse, 'the sins of the fathers'?" asked Wanda, continuing her train of thought.

"Sure," Catherine acknowledged. "James is paying the price for his father's actions—and the stepparents', too." Catherine leaned back against the sofa, looking out the French doors at the meticulously maintained, huge mansion across the street that was a reminder of the respectable, stately, bygone days. "Do you think that's what life's all about—paying for sins of the parents?" A depressing cloud settled firmly on Catherine, her mind wandering to disheartening thoughts. "Once life's tainted, it's lost. The end."

Wanda hastily dispelled the gloom. "I think life's an opportunity to make choices. Every person has a choice. As children, each takes these experiences and pulls them through his perceptual screen—for better or for worse. Of course, all of one's childhood experiences, especially how one is treated, influence later behavior—having had an impact on the psyche. But sooner or later, everyone has to make a judgment about his or her responsibility, first to oneself and then to others."

"But, look at what Amanda and Albert did with James. They raised him in such a way that he ended up committing crimes. That's evil, by your own definition, my dear sister." Catherine leaned forward, gesturing toward Wanda earnestly as she quoted, "'Evil is doing something to *good* people to make them do *bad* things.' Remember?" She shifted her weight forward in her attentive excitement. "Here is a man who wanted to live properly in the world, but he was the one in prison, whereas his 'parents' walked freely about, living their lives according to their needs and desires. He is paying the price for his parents' sins. You said yourself that sin is missing the mark—and that they did. They abused and neglected James on the physical, mental, and emotional levels throughout his developing years." Catherine ticked off each on her fingers for emphasis.

Wanda nodded in acknowledgement. The sisters sat in silence, both deep in thought.

Catherine broke the silence, "Have you heard from James recently?" Is he still in solitary?"

"He's been removed from isolation and is in a cell—"

"Wonderful! That's good for him to be out of there." Catherine interrupted, ready to grasp on to an improvement in conditions.

"With an inmate serving a life sentence for murder," Wanda finished.

"Oh," Catherine replied quietly, her earlier enthusiasm gone.

"James's letters indicated he wished to be alone rather than be vigilant twenty-four seven. His *celle* taunts him, using profanity. He's challenging James's good nature."

Catherine quickly recovered and assessed, "You're right. The guards aren't going to let him get away again with running away. They want atonement—blood atonement."

Knocking at the door interrupted their sobering contemplation. Aunt Denise had arrived, and it was time to start the night's festivities. Wanda brought out glasses of plum wine to toast Catherine, the guest of honor. She was celebrating a new life. Her oncologist had given her a very positive report.

The family of three enjoyed the evening, talking and sharing stories, their laughter and merriment fueled by the wonderful family-inspired dishes. During the course of the festive affair, Wanda watched her sister. A deep sadness grasped Wanda's heart, chilling her. She tried to quiet the voice that softly, resolutely whispered fearful concerns about Catherine's future.

"Ms. Cook," the nurse announced as she opened the door to the modest but neat waiting room, "the doctor will see you now."

Catherine got up, reluctantly, to follow the nurse. She unceremoniously put away the magazine she was browsing—more as a nervous distraction than any sincere interest in the contents. Gracefully, she stood and calmly made her way to the door. Catherine, despite the tiredness and fraying that showed just slightly around her eyes, looked beautiful. She was elegantly dressed in a freshly pressed linen pant ensemble. Her jewelry had a south-of-the-border flair. More than one pair of eyes looked at her like someone admiring a masterpiece. However, Catherine's face was drawn tight in resignation and dread. She was not pleased to be there in the office of her oncologist. She had been pushed by Wanda to call this meeting with her doctor. Wanda followed her sister to the examination room, equally elegantly dressed, expressing a similar countenance and likewise unaware of the admiring glances.

"I don't know why we are here," Catherine finally recoiled once the nurse left the sisters alone to await the physician's entrance. She could no longer hold back the fearful frustration. The thickness in the air that clung to her and her sister since the appointment was scheduled hinted at a graver reason for this call than just a friendly check-in.

"I think it's important to talk about the future and make sure we are all on the same page." Yet, Wanda's calm and concise response only added to the heaviness pressing upon them. Wanda did not add that she had confronted the doctor earlier the week before. The concern, which increasingly and violently seized her, refused to be quieted or ignored. Wanda was left with only one choice: to appease it. She had picked up the phone and with polite audacity confronted Catherine's oncologist. Dr. Radcliff was unable to broker Wanda's genteel tenacity and acquiesced to meeting with Catherine about her future. Both anticipated the doctor's message; like the roar of crashing waves in the distance, a great fall was coming. It was just a matter of time.

"Good morning, Mrs. Cook . . . You look great!" Dr. Radcliff jovially greeted Catherine, extending his hand and taking hers and shaking it affably. He likewise greeted Wanda and similarly complimented her.

Dr. Radcliff was a well-respected oncologist. The full waiting room was a testimony to his reputation for treating cancer patients. He took pleasure and pride in offering life to patients while other physicians assigned death. Those diagnosed with cancer clamored to engage him as their doctor. Revering him as a saint, patients thought that to engage him as their physician was, in itself, an effective cancer treatment. Yes, this doctor was one of the best in the area, well-trained and sincerely concerned for his patients' well-being. He reveled in snatching people from the jaws of death, but ignorance was bliss to this specialist—the stark truth sometimes was too unkind.

Catherine smiled at him, wishing for the opposite of what she dreaded. Wanda steadily gazed at him, expectantly waiting for him to carry out his responsibility. Dr. Radcliff shifted his eyes between the two sisters. His shoulders drooped, he averted his eyes to the medical record in his hand.

"We've tried five different chemotherapies," the doctor admitted in resignation. "The newest treatments . . . these were the most up-to-date treatment guidelines." The doctor buckled under the weight of his most dreaded task. He continued to sadly explain the reality of Catherine's sickness.

When the sisters had entered the doctor's office, the younger defiantly led the way. Now, the elder gently guided the younger out of the office. Her spirit broken, Catherine appeared battered. She clung to her sister's arm with one hand, as if trying to keep her head above water. The other arm was dragged down by the weight of a small paper thrust upon her by Dr. Radcliff just before leaving. It was a prescription for hospice.

"How's James?" Catherine, wearing a colorful turban to disguise her lack of hair, was ready for a change of subject having nothing to do with her health. "Would you like a cup of coffee?" she asked as she got up. "I'm going to have one."

Wanda accepted it as she sunk into an armchair across from Catherine. Wanda didn't want her sister, painfully and visibly ill, to exert herself. However, Wanda knew that Catherine needed to hold on to her sense of independence and normalcy.

"Yes, I just got a letter from him today."

"Oh, what's happening? Any progress with his new case?" Catherine's voice rose above the clinking of cups and saucers. "Will they dismiss the charges? That guy told James numerous times he was a dead man. It was self-defense . . . He even tried to change cellmates without any success. This guy was trouble . . . Anyone could see that," Catherine argued vehemently.

After James completed his six months of restriction upon his transfer to the big prison in McAlester, Oklahoma, Wanda had been in a steady correspondence with James. Then a few months went by until she had an unexpected letter from him. She remembered her shock when she saw his handwriting. Instead of James's neat, carefully formed cursive, it was frantically scratched print. His greeting to

Wanda was an earnest declaration that he needed to tell her something. He went on to describe how his *celle* relentlessly continued to harass him. One night, the cellmate tried to get James to fight with him, but James refused. Wanda reread, several times, a portion of the letter James sent to her:

> *Before I realized what was happening, my celle came at me. He had a shank. I was able to dodge his arm, and I twisted the man's arm and jabbed it into him. He fell limp. I called the guards for help. They came in and checked him. He was dead. I knew it was my life or his.*

Catherine and Wanda agreed that it was self-defense, and everyone knew it. However, because of James's escape record, he was placed back in solitary confinement.

"He was appointed a public defender," Wanda informed Catherine as she presented a fresh cup of hot coffee to her. "He called me about James's case. He said he'd met with him and that he likes James."

"So when is the hearing? Are you going to testify?" Catherine eagerly inquired.

"I'm not sure. The attorney said it would be a long time before any hearing would occur. James's case would be placed as the last order of business in the justice system. So, I don't even know when they'll start to work on his case."

Catherine whistled and shook her head disapprovingly, "Swift justice at work, again." Catherine took a sip of her coffee. "Are his spirits any better? Last few letters seemed to me like he was really starting to get depressed and had a feeling of despair."

"No, he's not doing well. No, not at all." Wanda paused to take a sip.

"I don't think he's really, truly grasped the situation he's been in since Lexington. He's been preoccupied with fantasies of picking up where he left off before his escape and Stella—"

"Oh, that vixen!" Catherine spat out. "Does she really understand what she cost him?" Catherine's anger rose at the mention of James's half-sister. "I wish I knew what she said to James. She was the last one to see him before his escape from Lexington, and she left two hundred dollars on the books for him." Catherine had to put her cup and saucer down in her anger.

"I think James was so desperate for a family that he fell in love with Stella." Wanda paused to note Catherine's leery expression. "The idea of having a family, a new one where he could start fresh, must have been thrilling to him. It must have meant so much to him that a family member wanted to know him, even though he was in prison. I think he made an instantaneous but pseudo attachment to her. His intellectual side often gave way to his emotional needs . . . Even if he couldn't articulate them." Catherine nodded in agreement, contemplating James's life.

Wanda disturbed the silence by adding a thought, "It's interesting . . . James is in solitary confinement, which they call 'the hole' . . . What a metaphor for his life . . . He lived a pitiful hole of a life." Again, silence descended upon the two sisters.

"He should write his story," Catherine broke through. "Writing might be very helpful and therapeutic for him. Look how it helped John Carlyle."

"I tried to urge him to write his story . . . His grammar and writing skills are better than mine, and he didn't even have a high school education. But, he said he couldn't write. He was too depressed. He even asked me to contact his Uncle Roy. He said he just couldn't do it himself."

Catherine leaned back, deflated. "It's like he realized he's on a sinking ship, but now there are no more lifeboats—except what he can have in his fantasies." Wanda looked at her sister, impressed again with her insight. *She understands having to end a fantasy and face the stark reality,* Wanda thought.

"Who's Uncle Roy again?" asked Catherine.

"That's Matlilda's brother." Wanda then added, "Sandy's brother-in-law." Though Catherine was too young to attend school with Sandy, she knew of him and met him a few times.

"Wow!" Catherine said smiling. "I forgot about that connection—what a small world!" She smacked her forehead much like her sister did nearly eighteen years earlier. "Do you ever regret that part of your life . . . a missed connection or disconnection?"

"Well, I don't consider it a disconnection because we are still very connected as friends. We have, I think, a special relationship."

"But, think of what you missed out on!" Catherine blurted out. Her mind was caught up in the past. "That lie ruined what could have been a fairy-tale life!"

"No, I disagree." Wanda said firmly. "At that time, Sandy and I had a wonderful relationship. I had a wonderful experience that helped guide my perspective for future relationships—connections, friendships, and acquaintanceships." Wanda shifted a little in her chair, as if arranging her thoughts. "If I would have stayed with Sandy, I would have been a farmer's wife—something at the time I wanted to be—but I would not have done all I have and would not have been able to do what I do now." Wanda paused. She mentally surveyed her life. "I believe that we have a choice—to take the good experiences and use them to help us appreciate life even more. I have been married three times, and I have been divorced three times. But, I do not regret my marriages, and I most certainly do not regret my divorces . . . There were problems that needed to be taken care of. However, I learned a lot from each marriage . . . about myself, other people, and the world." Wanda took a sip from her now-cold cup, more to moisten her mouth than to enjoy it. "Relationships are beautifully complex . . . They're dynamic, not stagnant. At this stage in my life, Sandy and I have a wonderful friendship that we both enjoy. I am very grateful for all my life's experiences."

Catherine neither responded in agreement nor disagreement to her sister's speech. On one level, she understood her sister's sentiment about the undulations of life. Many experiences surprised and amazed her, drastically altering her own life. Yet, there was an element in Wanda's philosophy of life that Catherine could not quite grasp. There was a hurdle in her way, and she wasn't ready to conquer it—not just yet. Instead, she offered, "How about I reheat your coffee? I know you don't like cold coffee any more than I."

Déjà vu, Wanda thought as she found herself awake late at night reading James's latest letter, only to be interrupted by a phone call from Catherine.

"I need some comfort food!"

"All right. I'll have a surprise for you in about an hour."

Wanda hung up, threw on her clothes, and went to the cottage kitchen. It didn't take her long to mix the pie dough, roll it out, and cut strips that she then twisted and placed on the baking sheet. Making this family-favorite delicacy always brought back pleasant memories from their childhood. Their mother often made this treat with scraps of bread and pie dough. Catherine, a great student of their mother, enjoyed cooking, but nonetheless took pleasure in Wanda making the treasured treats.

While the "micky twists" were baking, Wanda thought she would finish reading James's latest letter. She had hoped for some good news to relate to Catherine. Yet, Wanda was disappointed and grieved at his letter, which followed the same pattern as his previous ones. After expressing his appreciation for Wanda's continued support, he thanked her for helping his Uncle Roy work on the process to mail him the family Bible that Matilda wanted him to have. Wanda had thought that this last act of love for James by his grandmother would revive James's spirits. It did on one level, but it didn't dispel the hopelessness that seemed to slowly consume him, like a cancer. James continued in the letter to say:

> *I haven't heard from my lawyer for a long time now. I'm not sure if anyone remembers that I'm here.*
>
> *I'm sorry to say this Wanda, but I can't read the Bible anymore. I try, but I just can't concentrate. I can't even exercise. I just don't have the energy. I miss the outside the most. I remember that even with my old celle I could at least go outside. The courtyard is enclosed with high, thick concrete walls, but I could feel the sun on my face for one hour. I wish they would let me out for just ten minutes—long enough for the sun to warm my limbs. Praying is becoming harder and harder. But, I keep praying each day that I will fall asleep.*

Wanda's interpretation of James's life was one of torture. *He survives day-to-day, only to face the same torment—day after day for 365 days a year,* Wanda mentally quoted Aleksandr Solzhenitsyn. She was alarmed by the depths of James's despair. After nearly two decades of working with James, Wanda was keenly aware of the tones and inflections between the lines of his letters. She was alarmed by the undercurrent of desperation. *Oh, James, I hope you don't do anything rash,* she silently begged.

Wanda's thought was interrupted by the ding of the oven timer. The little pastries were ready. As Wanda took them out of the oven, the sweet aroma swept away the gloom.

Catherine had the door open before Wanda made it to the front step. She hugged her sister, taking the basket of goodies and ushering her to the table. Catherine had brewed a pot of decaffeinated coffee and set the table for a midnight tea party. Like two children again, the sisters laughed and giggled as they enjoyed their hot treats long into the night.

"Catherine, what would you like for breakfast?" Wanda called down the hall of her sister's house. Wanda had just gotten out of the shower and was finishing getting dressed. She had been staying with Catherine the last couple of weeks. "To be closer, in case you need anything," she had told her sister. But Wanda secretly didn't want to leave her alone. Wanda was afraid to leave her sister. As long as they were together, their family remained intact.

The two continued to work on Wanda's cases. Catherine continued to meticulously review documents, making very astute notes. Wanda had already started updating James's LifePath in anticipation of going to court. In the course of a few days, they had established a comfortable routine at Catherine's house that was less taxing on her low level of energy. When not working on the cases, Catherine watched Wanda work in the garden and offered opinions to her sister's inquiries about plant placement.

"How does fried cream sound?" she called out as she slipped her shoes on and made her way to the kitchen.

"Catherine?" Wanda asked as she entered the living room. She took a step back, an unexplainable feeling of loneliness hit like a wave of fire. "Catherine?" Wanda whispered, her voice suddenly giving out on her.

"She's so beautiful," the mortician exclaimed to Wanda. "Oh, she must've been a heartbreaker." He and his assistant were removing Catherine's body to the funeral home. Wanda only nodded, smiling weakly. The tears were still fresh in her eyes. They had stopped only long enough for her to make the call to the funeral home and then to open the door for him and to sign the necessary documents for a legal death. As soon as the door closed, the tears spilled past her clenched eyes. "My precious Catherine . . . my baby sister," escaped her throat. She collapsed to the floor, sobbing. *I knew she would wait until she was alone to breathe her last.*

Wanda was inconsolable. She awoke in the middle of the night, her pillow drenched with tears. She grieved and longed for her sister. She was painfully aware of the wrongness that she, the eldest, would outlive the youngest. Ghosts of memories surrounded her. She dreaded going into her garden, the one place that had always been her refuge. But, now she had no one to share the excitement of a new bud and no one to rejoice over the uniqueness of a blossom with her. A thick fog of realization enveloped Wanda. It overwhelmed her, constricting her lungs. It squelched her every breath.

The darkness flooded into the studio from the skylight. She stood, gazing out at the patio through the windows. Clouds had blotted out the moon. They were too thick for the moon's beams to penetrate. Wanda was awakened by a forgotten nightmare that faded quickly into her subconscious. The only trace of it was the trail of tears down her cheeks and her pillow. Wanda was torn within herself; she was restless with grief but exhausted with sadness. In one swift move, she thrust open the doors and walked boldly out into the darkness. She defied the stillness, daring it.

A breeze gently caressed her still-wet cheek. It made Wanda shiver and turn her cheek away. But then she caught the perfume of the roses. She turned her head back into the breeze. She breathed in the fragrance. It soothed and calmed her. She took her first deep breath in a long time, closing her eyes. When she opened them, the moon had broken through the heavy vapors. It illuminated the plants, every leaf and petal gleamed with ecstasy. The wind swirled through the garden. The stems, stalks, and branches swayed, gently sighing. Wanda was surrounded by beauty, a peace like the whispers of angels enveloping her. In the middle of the backyard in the dead of night, Wanda was not alone.

The sun brightly shined in the cloudless, afternoon sky. It was still too young in its summer-hood to generate the heat expected across the Hill Country. Wanda was back on Comet Trail and working in her rose garden at her newly constructed home. Although her new garden consisted only of a few rose bushes she had thus far transplanted from her recently sold, ranch-style home, Wanda already knew where the path would need to turn and twist to accommodate the blossoms and growth of the bushes. Her rose-filled reverie was interrupted by a ringing in her ear.

"Hello?" Wanda answered with a touch on her earpiece. "Hi, Ted! How in the world are you?"

"Fine. How are you doing?" Attorney Holtz sincerely inquired.

"Good," Wanda replied cheerfully. "It's a beautiful day. My roses are wond—"

"Have you heard?" he cut her off. "About James?"

"No. What?" Wanda asked, picking up on his very serious tone. The usual gaiety was gone from his voice. "Are we finally going to trial? I hope you're going to defend him." Wanda's mind was already reeling. She felt that her mind was traveling 550,000 miles per hour—the rate the solar system travels around the galaxy. *At last, we'll be going to trial with James's case.* Her thoughts continued to go at galactic speeds. *They're asking Ted to take the case and me to testify. Finally, I'll be able to put together over two decades of research showing James's broken attachment and, consequently, his broken life.*

"Sorry, my friend," Ted's voice finally broke through her thoughts. "James is dead . . . He hung himself."

Wanda was dumbstruck, paralyzed. It took her several swallows before she could ask, "Can you . . . um . . . can you . . . tell me . . . how it happened?"

"According to the information from the warden, James . . . he was found hanging from the ceiling of his cell. Evidently, he'd tied sheets together. That's all I know."

Wanda's thoughts suddenly returned to James and his plight. She remembered the cheerful, polite young man. He had a childlike innocence that never matured. *Did he really hang himself?* Wanda was incredulous at James's apparent suicide. Her thoughts inadvertently returned to Lexington and his escape. *Was that his way of surrendering?* Wanda asked herself another question in response to the question of why James called her after he escaped. She remembered the first time he escaped the dental van. He had tried to find her at the health science center. Again, he offered no resistance. Yet, again, he ran from Vinita, climbing the fence, only to be caught a few feet away. As the pattern continued, he never protested being returned to confinement. In each of these instances, his only rationale was the need to feel free. Another thought struck Wanda: *What did James do in those few days he spent in Bryan? Did he feel a tugging desire to go to his Grandmother Matilda, find her grave, and pay his last respects?* Wanda pictured him asleep on his grandmother's back doorstep or kneeling before her headstone and then, settling atop a university building. The unanswered questions spinning around in her mind had translated into silence over the phone line.

"Wanda, you there?"

"Yes," she replied, coming back to the present. She parted her lips to speak but couldn't. Finally, she mustered the strength to say, "This is hard . . . surreal . . . it feels . . . so . . . unfinished," Wanda swallowed hard. "Guess I'll call . . . check on the Fields. Let's keep in touch. Thanks, Ted . . . thanks for letting me know. And thanks for your help with James over the years."

He needed to connect with someone with whom he had formed a semblance of a bond, at least a bond of confidence, Wanda's thoughts continued as she clicked her earpiece off. Like the sun creeping through the trees, casting warm rays, Wanda felt the warmth of this realization radiate through her body. *James craved a connection—the beginning of one was stunted when his parents divorced. What was left was starved by Albert's behavior and his mother's lack of coping skills. Finally, it died along with his mother when he was just a young child.* Wanda saw James as a young man who cherished the idea of family more than his own well-being.

Wanda never sheds tears over court cases. But, with James's lifetime of losses, she picked up the garden shears and cut a bouquet of roses—with teardrops glistening on every petal.

Epilogue

S o could you say that people can become broken . . . like the defendants?"
Wanda nodded, affirming she was following Mr. Ladero's question. "Then,
do we as a society just need to view their behavior as broken . . . like a
meaningless machine to be discarded?"

Wanda shook her head. "All behavior has a purpose . . . and each of these
defendants who committed a crime is ultimately responsible for his actions
because there is never an excuse . . . There is, however, an explanation." Wanda
paused a moment, considering her next thought. "Behavior is a complex pattern,
like cobblestones and pavers, connected and held together by mortar . . . and
how these pieces are put together forms the pathway or direction to a given site.
Likewise, life circumstances and personal connections form the developmental
pathway that leads to a person's destiny."

"Please explain the mortar metaphor," he requested, fascinated.

"Life's mortar is the bonding between parent and child. When the bond
is weak or broken, the pathway loses its strength and tenacity and the traveler
stumbles along a rocky road that often gets off track, only to wind down to a
dead-end constraint."

"How does all this look in these defendants' lives or in our lives?" Ladero asked rapidly, engrossed in the conversation. The audience was forgotten momentarily. He was interested in understating mankind at a little deeper level.

"The cobblestones and pavers," Wanda smiled at her use of this analogy, "represent key developmental milestones. We all live in continual interaction with our surroundings and our human environment . . . from the time we are confronted with anxieties and irrational attitudes until we die." Wanda shifted in her seat, scanning the audience. "Each of these defendants, in the four cases I have chosen to share, represented a unique set of circumstances. The paths their lives took were vastly different. Yet, each one was charged with a capital crime. Let's consider these men.

"James was not a criminal . . . He grew up having lost both parents by the time he was a preschooler. He never felt accepted by his stepparents. After being placed in psychiatric hospitals, he finally ran away—Why? Was it because he believed his stepparents didn't love him or because he felt he would never measure up to their expectations? James was a troubled child, but was he a killer? He was appreciative of help from others: truck drivers, Molly and her family, his stepparents, and even the man who rescued him and took him in on a cold, wintry night. Was he a killer or a troubled man who ended his life needlessly?

"Joseph was a criminal . . . a rejected child who never bonded with either parent. He was catapulted into fears of betrayal trauma and abandonment. He saw his family disintegrate, leaving him ill-equipped to face the world as a lonely survivor, plagued by his use of drugs and psychotic episodes. Joseph became a criminal. Was he simply born bad, or was he a product of circumstances that made his path too rocky to navigate?

"Jackson was a criminal . . . a misplaced child from birth throughout his lifetime. Disorganized and dissociative attachment disorder was his rod and staff that led him down the path of drunkenness, yearning for intimacy but without any models or guidance of how to achieve it. Yes, he raped and killed a little girl, but was it with malicious intent, premeditated to destroy a life? Or was he acting out of a childhood background of emotional and sexual abuse, alcohol abuse, criminal birth parents, and betrayal trauma, all of which propelled him into a drunken stupor motivated by pain so deep he lost all control of a rational mind?

"Quentin was a criminal . . . a compulsive thief but not a killer. He had none of the characteristics of a rapist . . . no sexual or physical abuse, no alcohol or drug abuse, no violence in his home life, and he had a loving relationship with his mother. He had a foul mouth, but does that make him a killer?" Wanda stopped. She took a moment to recollect her thoughts after this passionate analysis.

"Yet, where there is humanity, there is potential. Potential for contentment and for conflict—both emerging from either complementary or conflicting values, socially transmitted through family and the larger world."

"But how does this impact development in our everyday lives?"

Wanda shifted forward in genuine interest. "For example, when a toddler starts to explore the world, there is a natural inclination—a sense of wonder— to go beyond the moment to discover herself through interaction with the environment. If this toddler has not made a secure attachment—has not bonded—with the parent, she is off to a limited way of learning. If she is not encouraged or given the freedom and trust to reach out, she may develop a fear of the world beyond mother. She may inadvertently believe the world is not to be experienced . . . It begins to feel like a fearful world. If the attachment is ambivalent or disorganized, the child grows into adulthood with a fear-based orientation."

"Are you saying childhood is key to adulthood?"

"Exactly. The first ten years of a child's life will likely be born out in adulthood. It's like the old saying, 'What goes around comes around.' Children with a good start in their first years of life will be on their way to facing their challenges and opportunities with assurance and self-confidence."

"Could you tie development and behavior with personality?"

"Yes, we can think of it as what people choose to do in relation to others. The pathways of one's unfolding maturation—socially, psychologically, intellectually, and physically—vary in style and dynamics with each person and, thereby, impact development to form unique patterns of behaving. These patterns are the result of pulling life experiences through one's perceptual screen, by which reality is viewed. Remember, perception is one's reality. And the power of relationships forms the lenses for how a person sees himself and interacts with the world he lives in. A person's life revolves around intimate connections with others. When these connections are corrupted by default or design, one's lenses may become cracked or shattered—unless there can be a new prescription for clearer vision. Broken people wear broken lenses."

Dr. Ladero paused thoughtfully, "Ultimately, how do you explain broken people?"

"Even these people, as pathological and broken as they may appear, have a wholeness about them they have yet to discover within themselves," Wanda continued.

"But how is this possible—with people who have committed such heinous crimes that they will live in prison for life or die by the death penalty?"

"We often forget the spiritual dimension of personality, which sometimes remains dormant until the human psyche awakens it through a tragedy or crises that may take a lifetime to heal."

"Would you expand on the spiritual?"

"Residues of one's past can be reexamined and brought into present consideration. Or, one can begin now, leaving the past behind. What's important—and critical to healing—is how one handles and deals with present anxieties; feelings of guilt and self-forgiveness have rational implications. Also important is one's willingness to look at one's own potential now and for the future. One must also form new attachments—man is not an island unto himself."

"So, what is attachment? What is its purpose?"

"Attachment is the unfolding or maturation of relationships between the self and the world—through minute connections first with the mother at birth and then with the world beyond mother. Attachment is the foundation for discovering how one connects with the world. At birth, the umbilical cord separates the newborn from the mother—the source of safety and possibility. The child's challenge is to reconnect with the source." Wanda reflected a moment. "The human spirit drives man to reach back into his own history to reconnect, to make that ultimate connection with the Universe . . . exemplified by the baby's initial attachment to the parent. Man will go to any length to expel his unexpressed power that propels him toward that connection . . . even willingness to kill and to shed the blood of another human to grasp the essence of being connected . . . however pathological and insane it may be. Conversely, the human spirit also drives man to connect with the Ultimate through love and all that love empowers one to be."

Ladero glanced at his watch. "I'm sorry; time is running short. This has been absolutely fascinating. But, before we conclude, I have two more questions: How can we as parents, as society, avoid creating more Allens, Fields, Mathews, and Dells? How do we create healthy attachments, positive ones?"

The audience and Ladero were very anxious for the answer. After hearing these cases, Wanda knew that they felt a little disheartened and at a loss for how to encourage and create success stories, not tragedies.

Wanda smiled, recognizing their concern. She gestured again in storytelling fashion. "As I said moments ago, the first ten years of life serve as a powerful force that will ultimately shape a person's adult behavior. A child does not suddenly, at the age of eighteen years, become competent to make judgments and choices in the best interest of oneself and others. Spiritual strength comes in many forms: acts of love toward others, prayer, contemplation, honoring life, and having reverence for others and ourselves. She reflected a moment. "I would like to close with a short story."

The wind howled through the cracks in the old house called Box Place. The baby lay still in a coma in her mother's arms. Mother and child were wrapped in a World War I tattered army blanket, rocking in the old family rocking chair. Early 1935 was one of the worst winters and fell on a depressed economy. The baby's parents had lost everything in the Depression and were just trying to survive an unusually cold winter. The house was hardly more than a shack on a farm owned by a man who took pity on the couple, who had a two-year-old son and a newborn daughter. The father worked the farm for the owner in lieu of rent. There was no heat in the house, and the baby contracted pneumonia. The doctor told the parents to give her up because she was in a coma and would not survive. "Let her go. You have a son. You are young, and you can have other children." He turned quietly and left.

The parents had no money, and their possessions were meager. The father had traded a trailer-load of green peppers for one pound of hamburger meat. His wife stretched the meat with a few vegetables from their garden to make stew that would sustain them for a week. Thankfully, they had a cow, and milk was one of their staples. They made butter and ate fried cream. The soured milk was used to make clabber, which they ate with cheap syrup.

The baby girl's father told his wife they had to keep the baby alive until he could get some heat in the house. They refused to give up their baby daughter.

So, the father walked three miles to town to find a stove to get heat in the house. He went to the bank to see the bank president, whom everyone knew in that small town of only five hundred people. The banker told the father of the sick little baby that he could not loan him any money. "You don't have any collateral," he explained to the young man trying to save his child. But the father continued to beg and beg him for seven dollars to get a stove because his baby was dying.

At last, the banker finally gave him the seven dollars from his own pocket. The grateful father purchased the stove and dragged the 175-pound iron, pot-bellied stove home in a toe sack. He stoked up the fire with some old wood from the citrus orchard and fallen fence posts.

Then the mother and father took turns holding their baby close and rocking her in front of the stove. For seventy-two hours, the baby girl was held and cuddled, never being put down. Her parents rocked and rocked her, holding her close to keep her warm. Tears streamed down their faces while silent prayers poured out for their baby to survive.

Finally, the little infant began to move her head. Her ears began to drain. The father, elated, walked back to town to find the doctor. When he found him, he said, "You have to come. Our baby is coming out of the coma." The doctor replied, "No, you are imagining your wishes. She cannot survive, but you have a son, and you're young. Like I told you, you can have other children. You need to forget about this baby."

"But," the father pleaded. He pressed on until the doctor gave in, and they climbed in his horse-drawn buggy. They trudged down the old dirt road along the canal bank until they reached Box Place.

When the doctor saw the baby, he could only say, "It's a miracle! She will be all right. Keep her warm and keep breastfeeding her. You have saved her." The doctor did not charge them because he knew they had no money. As he mounted his buggy, he just shook his head. "I don't understand it . . . She was almost gone the last time I was here. I thought she would not live through the night."

Silence covered the audience. Wanda spoke, her voice full of emotion. "And, yes, I did live through the night. I stand here today as WITNESS to the miracle of bonding through seventy-two hours of parental love and devotion."

About the Authors

Wanda Draper, Ph.D., brings over three decades of insightful experience and an action-packed lifestyle to this text. She has worked as expert witness in over a hundred capital murder cases. As professor emeritus of human development, she has taught behavioral science for twenty years at the Oklahoma University College of Medicine to physicians in their psychiatry residency programs. Her writing and consulting abroad is balanced by Texas Hill Country living and gardening with her pet kittens by her side. Her website is www.educationfuturesinternational.com, and the book's website is www.wandadraper.com.

Collin Stutz, a Vassar College and American Film Institute graduate, has coauthored three editions of the officially authorized *James Bond Encyclopedia*. He has worked as a film development executive, has had one of his screenplays optioned, and is a recognized film historian. He is a Writers Guild of America, West member.